CHILDREN IN THE
URBAN ENVIRONMENT

Second Edition

CHILDREN IN THE URBAN ENVIRONMENT

Linking Social Policy and Clinical Practice

Edited by

NORMA KOLKO PHILLIPS, D.S.W.

Professor and Director
Social Work Program
Lehman College
City University of New York
New York, New York

and

SHULAMITH LALA ASHENBERG STRAUSSNER, D.S.W.

Professor and Director
Post-Master's Certificate Program in the
Clinical Approaches to Addictions
Editor, Journal of Social Work Practice
in the Addictions
New York University School of Social Work
New York, New York

CHARLES C THOMAS • PUBLISHER, LTD.
Springfield • Illinois • U.S.A.

Published and Distributed Throughout the World by

CHARLES C THOMAS • PUBLISHER, LTD.
2600 South First Street
Springfield, Illinois 62704

©2006 by CHARLES C THOMAS • PUBLISHER, LTD.

ISBN 0-398-07669-3 (hard)
ISBN 0-398-07670-7 (paper)

Library of Congress Catalog Card Number: 2006044476

With THOMAS BOOKS *careful attention is given to all details of man-
ufacturing and design. It is the Publisher's desire to present books that are satisfactory as to their physical qualities and artistic possibilities and appropriate for their particular use.* THOMAS BOOKS *will be true to those laws
of quality that assure a good name and good will.*

Printed in the United States of America
CR-R-3

Library of Congress Cataloging-in-Publication Data

Phillips, Norma Kolko.
    Chilren in the urban environment : linking social policy and
clinical practice / by Norma Kolko Phillips and Schulamith Lala
Ashenberg Straussner.--2nd ed.
        p. cm.
    Includes bibliographical references and index.
    ISBN 0-398-07669-3 -- ISBN 0-398-07670-7 (pbk.)
    1. City children--United States. 2. Children with social disabilities
--United States. 3. Social work with children--United States. I.
Straussner, Schulamith Lala Ashenberg. II. Title.

HT206.C445 2006
362.70973--dc22

                                                      2006044476

CONTRIBUTORS

GREGORY ACEVEDO, PH.D.
Assistant Professor
Fordham University Graduate School of Social Service

STEPHEN BURGHARDT, PH.D.
Professor
Hunter College School of Social Work
City University of New York

GRACIELA M. CASTEX, ED.D.
Associate Professor
Social Work Program
Lehman College
City University of New York

JOHNNIE HAMILTON-MASON, PH.D.
Associate Professor and Director of Doctoral Program
Simmons College School of Social Work

GLADYS GONZALEZ-RAMOS, PH.D.
Associate Professor
New York University School of Social Work

RICHARD HOLODY, D.S.W.
Assistant Professor
Social Work Program
Lehman College
City University of New York

SALLY HILL JONES, PH.D.
Assistant Professor
School of Social Work
Texas State University-San Marcos

CHRISHANA M. LLOYD, PH.D.
Research Associate/Policy Analyst
MDRC

CARL MAZZA, D.S.W.
Assistant Professor
Social Work Program
Lehman College
City University of New York

DIANE M. MIRABITO, D.S.W.
Clinical Assistant Professor
New York University School of Social Work

MERYL NADEL, D.S.W.
Associate Professor and Chair
Social Work Department
Iona College

DORINDA N. NOBLE, PH.D.
Professor and Director
School of Social Work
Texas State University-San Marcos

NORMA KOLKO PHILLIPS, D.S.W.
Professor and Director
Social Work Program
Lehman College
City University of New York

DANIEL POLLACK, M.S.W., J.D.
Professor
Wurzweiler School of Social Work, Yeshiva University
Senior Fellow, Center for Adoption Research
University of Massachusetts Medical School
Worcester, Massachuttes

HILDA P. RIVERA, PH.D.
Assistant Professor
Hunter College School of Social Work
City University of New York

MARTHA G. RODITTI, PH.D.
Assistant Professor and Field Coordinator
School of Social Work
New Mexico State University at Las Cruces

SHULAMITH LALA ASHENBERG STRAUSSNER, D.S.W.
Professor and Director
Post-Master's Certificate Program in the Clinical Approaches to Addictions
Editor, Journal of Social Work Practice in the Addictions
New York University School of Social Work

ADELE WEINER, PH.D.
Professor
Metropolitan College of New York
Audrey Cohen College of Human Services and Education

PREFACE

Since the first edition of this book was published ten years ago, the cities have been revitalized and enriched by the absorption of increasingly diverse immigrant groups from around the world. Urban communities continue to be the intellectual and artistic centers of this country, with an ever-increasing diversity of music, foods, and crafts representing their new populations. As in the past, the cities become home to those seeking new opportunities in life, while also harboring those suffering economic deprivation.

Yet, much has changed. Urban communities in the U.S. have witnessed great disasters, both man-made and natural, including the terror attacks of September 11, 2001 and the devastation of New Orleans by Hurricane Katrina in August 2005. The globalization of the marketplace has had serious impact on the job market, and critical resources have been diverted to various war efforts during the past decade. Further, 1996 brought with it welfare reform—new welfare policies that transformed how this country views public welfare and responds to the needs of its people. The gap between the "haves" and "have-nots" has grown wider than in many previous generations.

It is these changes that led us to do a second edition of this book. The 12 chapters in this edition address some of the current key social and economic factors impacting on urban children today, including poverty, immigration, health and mental health issues, and youth gangs. The book also focuses on familial factors affecting urban children, including: children in out-of-home placement, those in substance-abusing families, as well as children with incarcerated parents, urban teen parents, and urban street children, most of whom arrive in the cities in search of a better, or at least a different life. This second edition ends with an epilogue that discusses the critical role of the community in addressing the many issues confronting children in today's urban environments.

We wish to thank the chapter authors for their hard work in bridging the links between social policies and clinical practices with children and families. We also would like to thank our own children, Adam, David, Sarina, and Allie, for helping us in our understanding of the many and diverse needs of children and youth. We are grateful to our publisher, Mr. Michael Payne Thomas, for seeing the value of an updated edition of this book and waiting for it patiently. Finally, we are grateful for the friendship, support, and the intellectual stimulation that resulted from this endeavor.

Norma Kolko Phillips

S. Lala Ashenberg Straussner

CONTENTS

Page

Preface ix

Chapter

SECTION I: INTRODUCTION

1. GROWING UP IN THE URBAN ENVIRONMENT:
OPPORTUNITIES AND OBSTACLES FOR
CHILDREN 5
   Norma Kolko Phillips

SECTION II: SOCIAL AND ECONOMIC FACTORS
IMPACTING ON URBAN CHILDREN

2. URBAN CHILDREN LIVING IN POVERTY 29
   Johnnie Hamilton-Mason and Gladys Gonzalez-Ramos

3. IMMIGRANT CHILDREN IN THE UNITED STATES . 50
   Graciela M. Castex

4. HEALTH ISSUES AFFECTING URBAN CHILDREN . . 75
   Diane Mirabito and Chrishana Lloyd

5. MENTAL HEALTH ISSUES AFFECTING URBAN
CHILDREN 97
   Dorinda N. Noble and Sally Hill Jones

6. URBAN YOUTH GANGS 122
   Gregory Acevedo

**SECTION III: FAMILIAL FACTORS IMPACTING ON
URBAN CHILDREN**

7. CHILDREN IN OUT-OF-HOME PLACEMENTS 145
   Richard Holody

8. CHILDREN IN SUBSTANCE-ABUSING FAMILIES . . 169
   Meryl Nadel and Shulamith L.A. Straussner

9. CHILDREN OF INCARCERATED PARENTS 191
   Carl Mazza

10. URBAN TEEN PARENTS 216
    Martha G. Roditti

11. URBAN STREET YOUTH: SEX, DRUGS AND HIV . . 244
    Adele Weiner and Daniel Pollack

EPILOGUE: THE ROLE OF THE COMMUNITY

12. IT TAKES A VILLAGE: MOBILIZING URBAN
    COMMUNITIES FOR IMPROVED CHILD WELFARE
    SERVICES 269
    Hilda Rivera and Stephen Burghardt

Index 281

CHILDREN IN THE
URBAN ENVIRONMENT

Section I

INTRODUCTION

Chapter 1

GROWING UP IN THE URBAN ENVIRONMENT–OPPORTUNITIES AND OBSTACLES FOR CHILDREN

Norma Kolko Phillips

Social problems exist in every setting, whether urban, suburban, exurban, rural, or small towns, and present profound obstacles for children and youth as they attempt to cope with developmental tasks of childhood and adolescence. Yet, because of the population density and the pervasiveness of social problems in urban areas, particularly in the inner-cities, the consequences of these problems are most visible there, as is their negative impact on children and youth. It is not surprising then, that organized responses to social problems developed in the cities.

Some social problems, such as homelessness, family poverty, unemployment, crime, drug abuse, language barriers, and discrimination may be coincidental to the urban environment. Other social problems, such as violence in schools and on the streets, gang activity, noise in public spaces, and overcrowding in schools and housing may be exacerbated by population density. Whether the problems were coincidental to, or were a product of the cities, their high visibility and the frequency of social disruptions evoked responses from community and political groups, and from the helping professions. These responses took the form of direct services to individuals, families, groups, and communities, as well as political actions aimed at the creation of policies that would increase opportunities for children and youth to fulfill their potential. These approaches also served to protect the social order.

The opportunities and obstacles confronted by children and youth in urban areas in the United States can be understood within the context of processes such as migration, immigration, urbanization, discrimination, education, and employment. This chapter will briefly examine the plight of urban children and youth through these windows. It will focus on historical periods that produced significant social change, on practice approaches that were developed in response to social change, and on social policies affecting families and children, particularly in urban areas.

OPPORTUNITIES FOR URBAN CHILDREN

In spite of the many social problems, the cities present opportunities, rich beyond comparison in areas such as ethno-cultural diversity, and intellectual, educational, medical, recreational, and socio- cultural resources. The "park bench" phenomenon, a socialization opportunity for young children and their caregivers, is a unique benefit of urban life. Whether this gathering together takes place on a tenement stoop on a summer night, or in a private park, noone needs to raise children in isolation in the city, as frequently happens in suburban, exurban, or rural areas. An informal gathering of preschoolers not only offers them play and peer socialization experiences, but no less important, it offers opportunities for peer support for the parents or caregivers. Community parks may also provide relatively sophisticated playgrounds, and in some cases, state-of-the-art equipment, compared to the small playgrounds or the backyard swingset of an exurban or rural family. Stimulating programs for preschoolers are found, free in libraries, museums, and parks, and costly in theaters and private gyms. Street fairs and block parties, parades, and festivals in the parks can enrich the early experiences of young city children. In such settings, all families, including single parents and same-sex parents, are more likely to find social supports, both for themselves and their children.

The availability and accessibility of quality day care in the cities, even for infants, make it possible for parents to work and take advantage of job opportunities and advancement possibilities while raising a family. Parents can select from a variety of programs, ranging from expensive private care at one extreme, to means-tested, publicly subsidized day care centers at the other.

As children grow, recreation in the cities takes on a vastly different character than in other areas. The constant supervision required for young children outside of the home keeps play for the urban child a more constricted experience than it is for their counterparts in the country. Exploration of nature and spontaneous outdoor adventures that are daily experiences for country children are lacking for children in the cities. Yet, organized teams, after-school programs, settlement house and "Y" programs, private sports programs, and summer day camps in both the public and private sectors provide many options for families with children. For the young adolescent seeking independence, the cities make it possible to move around using public transportation while their suburban, exurban, and rural counterparts remain dependent on transportation by family or friends beyond bicycling distance.

Although the problems in urban public schools, both educational and social, drive many families out of the cities, families with children who have particular needs, whether for greater academic challenge or additional supportive services, have far greater opportunities in the cities. Alternative school programs, programs for gifted and talented children, and services for academically and physically challenged can be sought out in the public system. For those with the means and inclination, private schools offering the full spectrum of programs, including specialized services, are in abundance.

UNDERSTANDING THE URBAN ENVIRONMENT

While there have been many approaches to understanding the environment of the cities, it is particularly useful to focus on those that can help understand the range of experiences of children as they grow up. While many young people find the sensory stimuli of the cities, such as their varied sights and sounds, to be interesting and challenging, some experience them as what Stanley Milgrim (1970) described as "psychic overload." Such a reaction might lead to both physical and emotional stresses that can threaten one's health (Fischer, 1984).

The size and heterogeneous nature of urban environments also have been identified as critical factors impacting on people living in the cities. The sociologist Louis Wirth (1938) pointed out that size, density, and heterogeneity can lead to both stress and social alienation for people living in the cities. Neighborhoods develop that are defined by the values and lifestyles of their inhabitants. These, in turn, attract other people of similar lifestyle and values. Consequently, each neighborhood assumes its own characteristics.

The lives of most people, however, are not restricted to one neighborhood. For example, young people living in a particular neighborhood may go to school and to other activities in different neighborhoods, thereby confronting different values and norms. For some, this may be an enriching experience, but for others, it presents conflict and a sense of not belonging to any one community. According to Wirth (1938), this may lead not only to isolation, but also to a failure to conform to particular social norms. Consequently, antisocial behaviors may be seen. In an effort to control these behaviors, there may be an increase in laws and policies, including rules, bureaucratic procedures, and police interventions. Such procedures tend to value the norms, interests, and priorities of some groups above others (Fisher, 1984; Wirth, 1938).

Other sociologists have viewed the cities as a "mosaic of social worlds," built on "intimate social circles based on kinship, ethnicity, neighborhood, occupation, lifestyle, or similar social attributes" (Fisher, 1984, p. 32). The composition of each neighborhood is related to its function, such as employment opportunities or educational resources. The range of cultures contributes to the formation of urban "enclaves" (Abrahamson, 1996), which provide cohesiveness, protection, and a sense of security for their members. Therefore, while children living in segregated communities may experience exclusion and estrangement from a larger society, they also experience the security that may be offered by their particular urban enclave.

It is also important to remember that urban neighborhoods and urban enclaves may form not only because their members choose to live amongst a familiar cultural or religious group, but also because the society limits the choice of their members by denying them access to other options. Factors such as discrimination and other manifestations of institutional oppression, as well as economic oppression, have led groups to live in defined urban enclaves (Turner & Herbig, 2005). These factors have been with us since the earliest days of urbanization.

CHILDREN IN THE CITIES DURING THE
NINETEENTH CENTURY

The shift from an agrarian nation to industrial capitalism that took place in the United States between 1865 and 1900 resulted in "a spectacular expansion of productive facilities and output that was without parallel in the history of the world" (Trattner, 1999, p. 81). This shift resulted in the growth of urban communities and also served as a catalyst for other processes, such as migration from rural areas to the cities and immigration from other countries. Along with urbanization came an exclusive dependence on employment and wages; opportunities for the self-sufficiency typically found in an agrarian economy were lost (Leiby, 1978).

Between 1860 and 1920, the proportion of the population of the United States living in the cities increased from one-sixth to one-half (Trattner, 1999). In addition to farm workers migrating from rural areas to the cities, 23 million European immigrants arrived in the United States between 1860 and 1910 (Trattner, 1999). Many were poor and without knowledge of the country, its culture, or its language. They settled in the cities where they worked as laborers in factories, construction, and transportation. During this period, the population of cities such as New York, Philadelphia, and Boston increased 300 to 400 percent, while Midwestern cities such as Chicago, St. Louis, Cleveland, and Detroit grew even more dramatically (Trattner, 1999). Tenement districts developed in order to house the growing urban population. Added to this was the depression of the 1870s, which left three million workers unemployed, contributing to the poverty of masses of people living in urban areas.

By 1890, more that 1,200,000 people, or three-quarters of the population of New York City, were living in tenements. The wretched living conditions of children in the tenements of New York City's lower east side were vividly described by Jacob Riis. Writing in 1890 about financial exploitation of poor immigrants and the problems they confronted, Riis described the overcrowded rooms, and the lack of consideration for light, ventilation, sanitation, or safety. According to Riis (1890), "Where two families had lived ten moved in. . . . Thousands were living in cellars. . . . Young vagabonds, the natural offspring of such 'home' conditions, overran the streets. Juvenile crime increased fearfully by the year" (pp. 6, 11). Unable to care for their children and lacking social supports, some mothers abandoned their infants, leaving them in gutters to be picked up by the police, or, during the winters, in hallways of buildings, where as many as three or four might be found in one night. Some babies were left outside the homes of the wealthy, and were turned over to the police. Ninety percent of such abandoned babies died (Riis, 1890).

AWAKENING TO THE NEEDS OF URBAN CHILDREN: THE FORMATION OF SOCIAL AGENCIES

Such appalling conditions stimulated the development of various strategies aimed at helping urban children living in poverty. During the latter part of the nineteenth century, approaches based on moral reform of the individual gave way to the recognition of the social and economic bases of the problems of the urban poor. Work programs for poor women, institutions for homeless children, medical care, nurseries for children of working women, and facilities for feeding and housing the poor were established (Leiby, 1978).

During the latter part of the nineteenth century, voluntary agencies were formed to address a variety of social problems affecting urban children and youth, supplementing the minimal local public relief services that were available. For example, the Salvation Army, which took hold in this country in 1880, provided summer programs for urban children living in poverty, as well as nursing and medical care, and homes for prostitutes and their children (Leiby, 1978). By 1890, the Children's Aid Society, which "came into existence as an emphatic protest against the tenement corruption of the young" (Riis, 1890, p. 140), had served 300,000 children, and the Society for the Prevention of Cruelty to Children had provided services to more than 25,000 children (Riis, 1890). While the voluntary agencies assisted individuals and groups in need, they also served the function of imposing social control. For example, while removing vagrant boys from the streets of New York and sending them to foster homes in rural areas, the Children's Aid Society aimed both to improve opportunities for its clients and to protect the city from what it termed "the dangerous classes" (Brace, 1872).

THE SETTLEMENT MOVEMENT: LINKING SOCIAL POLICY AND URBAN SOCIAL PROBLEMS

A different approach to helping urban children emerged through the Settlement House movement, which began with the founding of Hull House in the slums of Chicago during the late nineteenth century. In addition to identifying the multiple problems impacting on poor immigrant children and families and providing direct services to them, the settlement movement made a unique contribution through the identification of the linkages between social policies and social problems. Settlement leaders demonstrated that in order to improve the lives of the urban poor, social change must be sought through political activity (Commager, 1961).

The Settlement House movement joined efforts with national organizations and succeeded in influencing social policies aimed at increasing opportunities for a better quality of life for immigrant families and their children (Bremmer, 1956). For example, settlement workers' observations of the behavior of employed children led them to join in efforts to gain legislation prohibiting child labor. Conditions for working children as young as five years of age were vividly described by John Spargo (1906): "(They) worked sixteen hours at stretch, by day and by night. They slept by turns and relays in beds that were never allowed to cool, one set being sent to bed as soon as the others had gone to their toil" (p. 133). In her writing about the early efforts of the settlement workers to influence social policies, Jane Addams (1961) identified the importance of working together with the National Child Labor Committee, noting that "local measures can sometimes be urged most effectively when joined to the efforts of a national body" (p. 214).

In addition to efforts to establish child labor laws, the Settlement Movement became a dominant force in advocating for legislation aimed at improving the lives of urban children in a variety of areas, including housing and sanitation, improvements in children's health services, the establishment of juvenile courts, and educational reforms (Commager, 1961). Settlement leaders were active in realizing the creation in 1912 of the United States Children's Bureau, which assumed an important role in establishing norms for child rearing and education (Cremin, 1988).

As a consequence of the work of settlement leaders, the focus of social welfare shifted: "By 1912 the nineteenth-century concern about paupers, criminals, and institutions for their relief or correction was somewhat eclipsed by a bold new notion of 'social welfare' that addressed itself to impersonal causes of poverty and injustice and looked towards a more equal and just society. So philanthropy and social policy were brought closer together" (Leiby, 1978, p. 144).

RESPONSES TO THE NEEDS OF URBAN CHILDREN AND YOUTH DURING THE GREAT DEPRESSION

The crisis of the Great Depression provided the impetus for another surge in social legislation–this time the aim was to increase social and economic security for children and families experiencing financial crises.

Demographic changes during the two decades preceding the Great Depression contributed to the rise in poverty in urban areas. During this period, the black population in both Chicago and New York thrived; the availability of jobs in factories in the northern cities and in the stockyards and packing houses of Chicago had encouraged migration from rural areas, particularly among sharecroppers from the South. Between 1910 and 1930, the black population of Chicago, known as the "Black Metropolis," increased from 44,000 to 234,000 (Lemann, 1991). During the 1920s, Harlem, known as "the Negro Capital of the World"(Takaki, 1993, p. 358), represented a sense of renewal and hope, and a strong sense of community developed as black intellectuals, artists, professionals, and white-collar workers joined together during the Harlem Renaissance (Takaki, 1993; Wilson, 1974). However, discrimination in housing left few housing alternatives, and as migration to New York City continued, Harlem became more congested and ghetto conditions developed.

Two events contributed to the deepening poverty of blacks everywhere during the early 1900s: they were displaced in the workplace as soldiers returned from World War I, and later, when the Great Depression occurred, blacks were most deeply affected by joblessness; "since . . . [blacks] were at the bottom of America's economic structure, Hoover's resistance to federal relief hurt them more that any other group" (Schlesinger, 1960, p. 429). By 1932, more than half of all blacks living in southern cities were unemployed. Faced with the realities of starvation, by 1933, 18 percent of blacks, as well as 10 percent of whites, had turned to local relief agencies (Takaki, 1993).

Voluntary agencies took a more active role in providing assistance during the Depression years. Describing the conditions of families in urban areas in 1931, Smith (1970) stated: "In Chicago, St. Louis and Detroit, it was impossible to walk five blocks without seeing a bread-line operated by a church, hospital, Salvation Army unit, rescue mission, or fraternal or religious order. . . . There was hardly a single block of New York City that each day did not see at least one family numbly sitting on a couch on the sidewalk. Upstairs, their apartment door was bolted up with the eviction notice pasted on the lock. People going by put nickels and dimes in a pot sitting on the family's kitchen table" (p. 66).

While the Great Depression was devastating to many families, "the deepest wounds of the depression were borne by children. Years of poverty, hunger, and disillusionment piled a weight of suffering on shoulders too young to bear it" (Meltzer, 1969, p. 42). Infants and children were undernourished, and education was curtailed as money was unavailable for teachers' salaries. Some schools shortened the school day and the school year, and by the end of 1933, 2,600 schools across the nation had closed down altogether. Once again, as in the previous century, desperate parents sent their children to work in factories or sweatshops. Long hours, low wages, and unsafe conditions became common as child labor laws were openly violated. Unemployed youths who could not find jobs left home so that they would not be a burden to their families. By late 1932, the U.S. Children's Bureau estimated that a quarter of a million youth under 21 years old were roaming the country (Meltzer, 1969).

The policies of the New Deal, introduced during the early year of Franklin D Roosevelt's presidency, addressed many of the problems facing urban families and youth. For example, Harry Hopkins, himself a social worker, encouraged the formation of the Division of Education Projects under the Works Progress Administration (WPA) to develop programs that would provide jobs for teachers who were unemployed; by 1937, almost 1500 nursery schools serving nearly 40,000 preschool children were started across the country, and over 3,200 parent education classes were established, providing parenting skills classes for more than 51,000 parents. Other programs were aimed at assisting youth directly. The National Youth Administration, established in 1935, provided money to fund part-time employment for needy students between 16 and 24 years of age so that they could stay in school, as well as funds for employment and training of youth not in school. Most effective was the Civilian Conservation Corps (CCC), begun in 1933, which provided the sons of families receiving public assistance with work on conservation projects. During nine years, two and a half million youth between 18 and 25 years lived in CCC camps around the country where they worked, earned money, developed skills, and many received an education. By the late 1930s, guidance programs were established in the CCC to assist the young men with personal and vocational planning (Cremin, 1988).

Efforts to address poverty among black families were made during the New Deal years. The prohibition of discriminatory practices based on "race, creed or color," introduced as the policy of the Public Works Administration, opened opportunities for employment for blacks. As a result of this policy change, the Democratic Party gained the support of 75 percent of northern blacks; consequently, this group of voters gained greater power politically (Takaki, 1993; Wilson, 1974).

THE CREATION OF PUBLIC SECTOR SOCIAL WELFARE: BUILDING THE POLICY-PRACTICE RELATIONSHIP

Although programs such as the WPA and CCC were innovative and successful, they were designed as temporary solutions to the poverty of the Great Depression. The creation of a permanent program of federal participation in social welfare did not occur until the Social Security Act of 1935 was enacted and later upheld by the Supreme Court (Freedman, 1967). In spite of the fact that the Social Security Act represented a policy compromise, it succeeded in reshaping the role of the federal government in relation to poor families with children; later amendments to the Act elaborated and strengthened its programs and their provisions for family security. For example, Aid to Dependent Children and its successor program, Aid to Families with Dependent Children, provided financial support and enabled many children and youth to utilize opportunities for social and economic mobility. (This commitment of the federal government to insure family security was interrupted in 1996 with the passage of the Personal

Responsibility and Work Reconciliation Act, as will be discussed later in this chapter and throughout the book.)

With the passage of the Social Security Act of 1935, social workers were employed to implement its various programs, leading to the development of social work as a profession and securing the connections between the public sector of social welfare and the social work profession (Fisher, 1980). Through this partnership of government and social work, the policy-practice relationship as we know it today was established (Phillips, 1985).

URBAN COMMUNITIES DURING THE POST-WAR ERA: SETTING THE STAGE FOR NEW POLICY-PRACTICE APPROACHES

During the postwar years, mechanization in agriculture caused a 45 percent decline in farm employment, and in spite of the fact that urban areas were experiencing a decline in the need for unskilled labor, millions of people migrated to the cities in search of work (Trattner, 1999). Included in the mass migration from farms to cities were black farm workers; while in 1940, 77 percent of blacks in the United States still lived in the South, by 1970, only 50 percent remained, and only 25 percent continued to live in rural areas (Lemann, 1991). Puerto Rican migrants were another group of urban dwellers deeply affected by the lack of jobs during this period. Puerto Rican migration to the mainland had increased from 70,000 by the time of the Great Depression to 650,000 by 1958; until 1965, most settled in New York City (Marden, Meyer, & Engel, 1992; Padilla, 1958). Discriminated against in areas such as employment, housing, and the justice system, most worked in unskilled jobs and lived in segregated communities (Marden et al., 1992).

Geographical splits between racial, economic, and national groups were further stimulated by the rapid development of the suburbs following World War II. In addition to housing, discriminatory practices limited access to jobs and income, education, and social opportunities. Inner-cities grew and became poorer, with devastating effects on children and youth.

In the book *Manchild in the Promised Land* (1965), Claude Brown described life in New York for the children of the former sharecroppers who migrated during the 1940s:

It seems that Cousin Willie, in his lying haste, had neglected to tell the folks down home about one of the most important aspects of the promised land: it was a slum ghetto. . . . There were too many people full of hate and bitterness crowded into a dirty, stinky, uncared-for-closet-size-section of a great city. . . . The children of these disillusioned colored pioneers inherited the total lot of their parents–the disappointments, the anger. To add to their misery, they had little hope of deliverance. For where does one run to when he's already in the promised land? (pp. 7-8)

Drug addiction, particularly heroin addiction, took hold in urban ghettos during the 1950s. Hope and economic and social opportunities were scant. Brown (1965) described its impact on family life:

I remember that around 1952 and 1953, when cats first started getting strung out good, people were saying, "Damn, man, that cat went and robbed his own family. He stole his father's suits, stole his mother's money." . . . It was still something unusual back then. In some cases, the lack of money had already killed most family life . . . since drugs demanded so much money and since drugs had afflicted just about every family with young people in it, this desire for money was wrecking almost all family life. (p. 181)

The unemployment, poverty, discrimination, drugs, and violence that were prevalent in the cities during the 1950s demanded new policy and practice approaches to create opportunities for inner-city youth. For example, the movement towards civil rights, initiated by the Truman Administration's overturning of the separate-but-equal principle, paved the way for the *Brown v. Board of Education* decision in 1954, prohibiting racial segregation in public education. Later in that decade, the civil rights movement gained momentum with the founding of the Southern Christian Leadership Conference (Cremin, 1988), preparing the nation for the transformations in social welfare during the 1960s.

SOCIAL REFORM IN THE 1960S: FEDERAL APPROACHES TO PROGRAMS AFFECTING CHILDREN AND YOUTH

Ten years after the *Brown* decision, the Civil Rights Act was passed, giving power to the attorney general to take legal action to accomplish desegregation in public schools. The Civil Rights Act authorized federal assistance to districts where desegregation was taking place and prohibited federal assistance to programs that continued discriminatory practices. It also established the Equal Opportunity Commission to enforce nondiscriminatory practices. In spite of widespread and intense resistance to school desegregation in the South and the numerous problems and inequalities that persisted, such as *de facto* segregation of poor Mexican-Americans in southwestern cities, by 1972, over 91 percent of black students in the South were attending integrated schools, and over 76 percent of students in the border states, and 89 percent in the North and West were in integrated schools (Cremin, 1988).

The growing recognition of the impact of community on children and youth led to new prevention and intervention approaches during the 1960s; such approaches represented an attempt to transform the infrastructure of power relationships, empowering oppressed racial and ethnic groups that historically had been excluded from opportunities for advancement in educational, social, economic, and political arenas. Programs such as Mobilization for Youth, the delinquency prevention and treatment program first developed in New York City in 1958 and later funded by the federal government and replicated in other cities, were based on the assumption that "juvenile delinquency had to be understood in terms of larger and pervasive community problems, and could be controlled only through programs designed to ameliorate these relevant problems and pathologies" (Clark & Hopkins, 1969, p. 4). Others, such as the Models Cities Program, which was established in 1966, attempted to shift the power structure to achieve improved economic, social, and educational opportunities for residents in poor neighborhoods (Leiby, 1978). The failures of this approach were discussed by Clark and Hopkins (1969): "When some of the poor, particularly the Negro poor and their advocates, took the War on Poverty seriously in a few cities like Syracuse and New York, organizing voters, demanding community control of schools (a prelude to demands for community control of police and civic services), demanding that welfare recipients be treated as human beings, demanding an effective role in urban planning generally, the political forces in the cities deployed for counter-attack. The War on Poverty was a national strategy that never planned for or gained support in most of the large cities where it operated" (pp. vi-vii).

However, some attempts aimed at improving the lives of urban children were more successful, such as Head Start, for preschool children in families living in poverty; Job Corps, which focused on training school dropouts; Upward Bound, which prepared bright children living in the poverty areas for college; and the Neighborhood Youth Corps, which helped unemployed teenagers (Cremin, 1988). In addition, programs such as Medicaid, and in-kind aid to combat hunger, including the federal Food Stamp program (which had been operational from 1939 to 1943, and was brought back in 1961), and school breakfast, lunch, and special milk programs, had lasting positive impacts on the education and health of the urban children living in poverty (Levitan, 1980).

In their evaluation of the War on Poverty, Clark and Hopkins (1969) wrote: "The program was in certain respects successful, not the least in its stated purposes, and in its stimulus to the growth of the Negro middle-class and in arousing Black community leadership to the pitiful conditions of ghetto schools, ghetto housing, and the conditions of life generally" (Clark & Hopkins, 1969, p. ix).

URBAN CHILDREN: 1970s TO 1990s

The 1970s saw a 60 percent increase in the number of people living in concentrated poverty areas; the rate was even higher in large industrial cities. New York City's population living in extreme poverty rose by 269 percent, Detroit and Chicago went up 162 percent, and Indianapolis rose by 150 percent (Garbarino, Dubrow, Kostelny & Pardo, 1992). The 1970s also saw a growth in the number of female-headed households amongst inner-city families–the number doubled between 1960 and 1977. By the 1980s, there had been an exodus of working and middle-class families from the ghettos, leaving areas of concentrated poverty in the inner-cities (areas where 40 percent or more of the population earn less than the poverty level), and by 1984, 73 percent of all female-headed households lived in metropolitan areas (Garbarino et al., 1992).

Data from the U.S. Census Bureau showed that of the over fourteen and a half million children under 18 years who were poor in the nation in 1992, almost half, or six and a half million, lived in central cities (cited in Sherman, 1994). Although the absolute number of children who lived in poverty was greater outside the large metropolitan areas, the density of child poverty in the cities was greater than in suburban or rural areas (Sherman, 1994). A survey of 135 cities in the 50 states showed that about 10 percent of the cities had as many as 40 to 50 percent of their children under the age of 18 living in poverty; the highest of these were Brownsville, Texas, at 54 percent; Camden, New Jersey, at 50 percent; and New Orleans and Detroit at 46 percent (based on U.S. Bureau of the Census, 1990, in Zill & Nord, 1994).

Shifts in population added to poverty in the cities during that period, as immigrants, who were more likely than long-term residents to be poor, came into the metropolitan areas, and long-term residents moved to the suburbs. Wilson (1987) suggested that a contributing factor to the inner-city population becoming poorer was the loss of the stabilizing influence of the middle and working classes. For example, until the end of the 1960s, it was usual for black families of all socioeconomic classes to live in the same communities, using the same schools and community resources. As the black middle class and working class saw greater opportunities deriving from civil rights legislation, they left the inner-cities for other neighborhoods and the suburbs, while those remaining, and particularly the children, lost the stabilizing influence of the middle and working class (Wilson, 1987; see Mazza, this volume). The families who remained in the cities tended to be poorer and experienced less support for schools and other resources important for raising children.

Changing patterns of employment in the cities also contributed to urban poverty, both in the inner-cities and in other urban areas. Higher educational requirements for employment, particularly in the North, diminished employment opportunities for the unskilled (Freeman, 1991; Wilson, 1987). This dynamic was further complicated by the large number of immigrant families who arrived in the cities with teenage children, many of whom also sought entry-level employment (Marden et al., 1992). In addition, corporate cutbacks contributed to a creeping unemployment among all income level groups, and while this was not exclusively an urban phenomenon, it resulted in economic stress and family breakdown for many urban families.

The Impact of Welfare Reform: 1996

Perhaps no other public social welfare policy since the passage of the Social Security Act of 1935 has had as much impact on the quality of life of the urban poor as the welfare reform legislation of 1996, the Personal Responsibility and Work Opportunity Reconciliation Act (PRWORA), the impact of which became clear during the early years of the 2000s. This legislation, which was an effort at deconstructing the public welfare system introduced in the U.S. as part of the Social Security Act of 1935, challenged Roosevelt's commitment to social welfare policies ensuring economic and social security "from the cradle to the grave." Title 1 of the 1996 legislation, Temporary Assistance to Needy Families (TANF), replaced Aid to Families with Dependent Children (AFDC), the Emergency Assistance Program, and the Job Opportunity and Basic Skills Training Program. TANF introduced a federal lifetime maximum limit of five years for receiving public assistance but left the decision about lower time limits for assistance up to each state, and set a two-year limit for assistance if a recipient was not working or in a work-connected activity. The notion of "entitlement" to public welfare was eliminated by this legislation.

While the program was touted as a great success because it lowered the number of people who received public assistance (Welfare Reform Mostly Worked, 2005), during the early years of the 2000s, researchers found that these cuts in welfare spending came at a huge cost, particularly to the children of the poor. A study of female heads of families leaving TANF in 1999, as compared with a comparable group leaving its predecessor program, AFDC, in 1995 (Ozawa & Yoon, 2005), found that "AFDC leavers fared considerably better economically after they left AFDC than did TANF leavers" (p. 246). This study makes recommendations for changes in PRWORA, including giving consideration to family needs such as the health conditions of recipients' children: "For recipients with a larger number of children and who can earn only low wages, it makes sense to help them concentrate on child rearing and becoming good parents, instead of forcing them to join the labor force. . . . Forcing them to join the labor force prematurely is not conducive to maximizing the economic well-being of individual families or of the nation as a whole" (p. 248).

POVERTY AND POLICIES DURING THE 2000s

While some promising efforts were made in several states to improve the quality of life for urban children, such as court-mandated improvement in services to families of abused and neglected children in Alabama (Eckholm, 2005) and supportive living services in the Bronx, New York, for the growing number of grandparent-headed households (Williams, 2005), the situation of urban children remains alarming. In spite of the 1996 legislation, purportedly designed to reduce poverty, the extent of child poverty in the U.S. has risen dramatically. By 2004, the number of children living in poverty in the U.S. topped 13 million, up 12.8 percent from 2000. This increase has affected all racial groups, but its impact has been felt most strongly by the Latino community. During this period, the number of Latino children in poverty increased by 774,000, or 23 percent; black children in poverty increased by 293,000, or 8.4 percent; and white (non-Latino) children increased by more than 322,000, up 7.7 percent. Between 2000 and 2004, there also was a 20 percent rise in the number of children living in "extreme poverty" (annual income for a family of three below $7,610), with 5.6 million children in this category. It is important to note that during 2004, more than seven out of 10 children who lived in poverty had at least one parent employed, but because of the low minimum wage, the family income was not high enough to move out of poverty (Poverty Increases for the Fourth Year in a Row in 2004, August 30, 2005).

Additional research, including research done by journalists during the early years of the 2000s, shed more light on the impact of TANF on the children of the poor. Jason DeParle (2004), in his study of families in Milwaukee who were impacted by the 1996 legislation, described its effect on the children of single mothers who entered the workforce: "While affluent parents endlessly complain of their kids' overscheduled lives, Angie's suffered from the opposite blight, long blocks of empty, unsupervised time, which grew longer the more she worked. Their childhoods passed on a sea of boredom, dotted by landfalls of chaos" (p. 186). Nina Bernstein (2002) also reported consequences of the welfare reform of 1996 for urban children. She noted that more and more children are being raised by what she referred to as "The No-Parent Family," being left with relatives or friends as a result of irregular work hours, low-wages, and loss of benefits of the head of household (p. A1).

Cutbacks in housing programs have also impacted the lives of urban families living in poverty. High rents in private housing and lack of sufficient publicly subsidized housing contribute to problems of homelessness for families. Legislation diminishing the federal Department of Housing and Urban Development's Section 8 subsidized housing program has aggravated this problem, severely narrowing the options for renters, particularly in urban areas where rents are increasing (Gonzalez, 2005; Steinhauer, 2005).

The severely deficient and unresponsive social welfare system was highlighted for a brief time by media coverage of the shocking living conditions for families and children in New Orleans following Hurricane Katrina in August 2005. New Orleans, which had been identified in the 2000 census as one of the 50 largest cities in the U.S. with the highest rate of child poverty, was second only to Fresno, California, in the clustering of its poorest families: almost 50,000 people lived in neighborhoods that had a poverty rate above 40 percent. In these areas, the average household had less than $20,000 annual income, four out of five children were raised in single-parent families, and 40 percent of adults of working age were neither working nor looking for work (Berube & Katz, 2005). The revelation of these conditions brought widespread criticism of the federal government's policies with regard to the urban poor. Specifically, President George W. Bush was criticized for the gutting of the HOPE VI program, cuts in funding for the Housing Choice voucher program, and proposed cuts to the Earned Income Tax Credit, all of which "erase the advances made in the 1990s" (Bereube & Katz, 2005).

CONCLUSION

Helping professionals in the cities today need to be aware of the impact of problems such as poverty, unemployment, inadequate and costly housing, homelessness, and violence on children and youth. Practitioners and social service agencies have the responsibility to respond not only to the consequences of these problems as they are observed in practice, but also to the social policies that too often have failed to prevent or correct problems, and to the limitations that policies impose on practice. It is only through changes in social welfare policies that the quality of life and of the social environment will improve for all people.

As Marian Wright Edelman (1994) points out, "Child poverty is not an act of God but a reflection of human political and value choices" (p. xv). The chapters that follow in this book discuss the cost in human terms of some of the missing opportunities for urban children and youth, and guide practitioners in their attempts to understand the impact of social policy and social service agencies on clinical practice.

REFERENCES

Abrahamson, M. (1996). *Urban enclaves: Identity and place in America.* New York: St. Martin's Press.

Addams, J. (1961). *Twenty years at Hull-House.* New York: Signet.

Berube, A., & Katz, B. (2005, October). Katrina's window: Confronting concentrated poverty across America. www.brookings.org. Accessed October 23, 2005.

Bernstein, N. (2002, July 29). Side effect of welfare law: The no-parent family. *The New York Times,* p. A1.

Brace, C. L. (1872). *The dangerous classes of New York.* Reprinted: Silver Springs, MD: NASW Classic Series, 1973.

Bremmer, R. H. (1956). From the depths: The discovery of poverty in the United States. New York: New York University Press.

Brown, C. (1965). *Manchild in the promise land.* Toronto: Collier-Macmillan.

Clark, K. B., & Hopkins, J. (1969). *A relevant war against poverty: A study of community action programs and observable social change.* New York: Harper and Row.

Commager, H. S. (1961). Foreword to J. Addams, *Twenty years at Hull-House.* New York: Signet.

Cremin, L. A. (1988). American education: *The metropolitan experience, 1876-1980.* New York: Harper and Row.

DeParle. J. (2004). *American dream: Three women, ten kids, and a nation's drive to end welfare.* New York: Viking.

Eckholm. E. (2005, August 20). Once woeful, Alabama is model in child welfare. *The New York Times,* p. A1.

Edeleman, M. W. (1994). Introduction to A. Sherman, *Wasting America's future: The Children's Defense Fund report on the cost of child poverty.* Boston: Beacon Press.

Fischer, C. S. (1984). *The urban experience* (2nd ed.). San Diego, CA: Harcourt Brace Jovanovich.

Fisher, J. (1980). *The response of social work to the depression.* Cambridge, MA: Schenkman.

Freeman, R. B. (1991). Employment and earnings of disadvantage young men in labor shortage economy. In C. Jencks & P. E. Peterson (Eds.), *The urban underclass* (pp. 103–121). Washington, DC: Brookings Institution.

Freedman, M., annotator. (1967). *Roosevelt and Frankfurter, their correspondence 1928-1945.* Boston: Little, Brown.

Garbarino, J., Dubrow, N., Kostelny, K., & Pardo, C. (1992). *Children in danger: Coping with the consequences of community violence.* San Francisco: Jossey-Bass.

Gonzalez, D. (2005, August 9). For subsidized tenants, hopes and fears collide. *The New York Times.* www.nytimes.com/2005/08/09. Accessed October 23, 2005.

Leiby, S. A. (1978). *A history of social welfare and social work in the United States.* New York: Columbia University Press.

Lemann, N. (1991). *The promised land.* New York: Knopf.

Levitan, S. A. (1980). *Programs in aid of the poor for the late 1980s.* Baltimore: Johns Hopkins University Press.

Mardan, C., Meyer, G., & Engel, M. H. (1992). *Minorities in American society* (6th ed.). New York: HarperCollins.

Meltzer, M. (1969). Brother, can you spare a dime? The great depression, 1929-1933. New York: Knopf.

Milgram, S. (1970). The experience of living in cities. *Science, 167,* 1461–1468.

Ozawa. M. N., & Yoon, H. S. (2005). 'Leavers' from TANF and AFDC: How do they fare economically? *Social Work, 50* (3), 239-249.

Padilla, E. (1958). *Up from Puerto Rico.* New York: Columbia University Press.

Phillips, N. (1985). Ideology and opportunity in social work during the New Deal years. *Journal of Sociology and Social Welfare, 12*(2), 251-273.

Poverty increases for the fourth year in a row in 2004; 1.5 million more children are poor than in 2000. (2005, August 30). Children's Defense Fund press release. www.childrensdefense.org/pressrelease/050830.aspx. Accessed October 22, 2005.

Riis, J. (1890). *How the other half lives.* New York: Scribner's.

Schlesinger, A. M., Jr. (1960). *The age of Roosevelt: The politics of upheaval.* Boston: Houghton Mifflin.

Sherman, A. (1994). *Wasting America's future: The Children's Defense Fund report on the costs of child poverty.* Boston: Beacon Press.

Smith, G. (1970). *The shattered dream: Herbert Hoover and the great depression.* New York: William Morrow.

Spargo, J. (1906). *The bitter cry of the children.* New York: Macmillan.

Steinhauer, J. (2005, August 17). New Yorkers are finding out that much of life costs more. *The New York Times.* www.nyt.com. Accessed October 23, 2005.

Takaki, R. (1993). *A different mirror: A history of multicultural America.* New York: Little, Brown.

Trattner, W. I. (1999). *From poor law to welfare state* (6th ed.). New York: Free Press.

Turner, M. A., & Herbig, C. (2005, September 18). Closing doors on Americans' housing choices. *Tulsa World.* Reported by Urban Institute. www.urban.org. Accessed October 31, 2005.

Welfare reform mostly worked. (2005, July 24). *Orlando Sentinel.* www.urban.org/Template.cfm?NavMenueID=24&template-/TaggedContent/ViewPub. Accessed August 17, 2005.

Williams, T. (2005, May 21). A place for grandparents who are parents again. *The New York Times*. www.nytimes.com/2005/0521nyregion/21grandparents.html. Accessed June 10, 2005.

Wilson, W. J. (1974). *Coming of age: Urban America, 1915-1945*. New York: Wiley.

Wilson, W. J. (1987). *The truly disadvantaged: The inner city, the underclass, and public policy*. Chicago: University of Chicago Press.

Wirth, L. (1928). Urbanism as a way of life. *American Journal of Sociology, 44*, 3-24.

Zill, N., & Nord, C. W. (1994). *Running in place: How American families are faring in a changing economy and an individualistic society*. Washington, DC: Child Trends, Inc.

Section II

SOCIAL AND ECONOMIC FACTORS IMPACTING ON URBAN CHILDREN

Chapter 2

URBAN CHILDREN LIVING IN POVERTY

JOHNNIE HAMILTON-MASON AND GLADYS GONZALEZ-RAMOS

Poverty remains a pervasive and pernicious social problem in urban environments today. Despite a recent drop in child poverty, approximately one in five children in the United States is poor (Children's Defense Fund, 2004). During 2003, the poverty rate was 10 percent for all families: it was lowest for married-couple families, at 5.4 percent, and dramatically higher among female-headed households, at 28 percent (The Green Book, 2004; The Urban Institute, 2004). The poverty rate is particularly high in central cities, at 17.5 percent, almost twice the 9.1 percent rate found in the suburbs (Children's Defense Fund, 2004).

The consequences of poverty, which are highly visible in urban areas, are inextricably linked to other problems, such as high rates of crime, substance abuse, dropping out of high school, teenage pregnancy, unemployment, and underemployment (Phillips & Straussner, 2002). Children living in poverty face a higher risk of developing a variety of socio-emotional problems than children in families with greater financial resources. For example, studies indicate that family poverty contributes to higher incidences of impairment in children's social, behavioral, and academic functioning (Bronfenbrenner, 1995; Duncan, Brooks-Gunn & Klebanov, 1994; Eamon, 2001; Garmezy, 1993; Webb, 2003).

The economic and social conditions of poor, urban youth–largely made up of people of color–have deteriorated in spite of civil rights legislation, and in spite of targeted social policies and services. Economic, social, and political factors contribute to the perpetuation of poverty and to the ongoing social and economic problems of the urban poor. These systemic factors are often ignored when considering the causes of poverty, with an overemphasis placed on individual attributes (Newman, 1999, 2004; Schorr & Schorr, 1988, 1997; Wilson, 1987).

In order to address both the psychological and social issues impacting on poor, urban children, interventions require broad-based efforts that focus on both political and economic remedies, as well as essential clinical interventions. This chapter discusses policy and practice issues that impact children living in impoverished urban environments. Cases are used to illustrate both assessment and intervention issues.

THE SOCIAL WORK PROFESSION AND CONCERN
FOR THE POOR

Concerns for the poor and the alleviation of poverty have always been central to the social work profession: "The original twin missions of social work were those of relieving the misery of the most desperate among us and building a more just and humane social order" (Simon, 1994, p. 23). Social workers remain as committed to this statement today as when the profession was established. For example, the preamble of the National Association of Social Workers' *Code of Ethics* states that "the primary mission of the social work profession is to enhance human well-being and help meet the basic human needs of all people, with particular attention to the needs and empowerment of people who are vulnerable, oppressed, and living in poverty. . . . Fundamental to social work is attention to the environmental forces that create, contribute to, and address problems in living" (NASW, 2004). The need for social workers to support communities is also identified by the National Association of Black Social Workers (NABSW) as critical for the profession. The NABSW states in its mission: "If a sense of community awareness is a precondition to humanitarian acts, then we must use our knowledge of the Black community, our commitment to its self-determination, and our helping skills for the benefit of Black people as we marshal our expertise to improve the quality of life of Black people" (NABSW, 1968). Both NASW's and

NABSW's *Code of Ethics* exemplify the fundamental values of the profession, which derive from the concern and commitment that early social workers had, and continue to have for vulnerable populations, particularly children and the poor (Hamilton-Mason, 2004).

POVERTY IN THE UNITED STATES

Conventional definitions of poverty are based on the federal poverty level, which compares pretax cash income with the poverty threshold. This figure is adjusted for the annual cost of living and varies according to family size. The official poverty level for a family of four in 2003 was $18,500. The usefulness of this figure, however, is limited because it is not adjusted by geographic locations with different costs of living. Moreover, such figures miss those families who live in urban regions where housing costs are so high that, despite incomes above the poverty line, they cannot afford the most basic necessities, such as health insurance, day care, and clothing. Further, due to the low minimum wage, employment does not guarantee that a family will not live in poverty. As pointed out by Newman (1999), during 1996, 58 percent out of the 7.4 million Americans living in households with annual incomes below the official poverty line were employed full time.

The rates of poverty in the United States have changed throughout the twentieth century. The late 1950s marked the highest rate of poverty since the Great Depression (which began 30 years earlier), with 39.5 million people, or 22 percent of the population living in poverty (Ginsberg, 1994). Due to changes in social and economic conditions during the 1960s, including the War on Poverty, this high rate declined dramatically between 1959 and 1969, to 12.1 percent. After 1978, however, the poverty rate rose steadily, reaching 15.2 percent in 1983. While twenty years later, in 2003, the rate of poverty among the general population decreased to 12.5 percent, *the poverty rate for children had increased to 16.7 percent* (The Green Book, 2004).

SOCIAL WELFARE POLICY AND ITS IMPACT ON CHILDREN

Policy and practice are inextricably linked. Following the passage of the Social Security Act in 1935 during the Great Depression, public social welfare policies addressed the needs of children living in poverty. All children in families that met state income eligibility criteria were entitled to assistance under the Aid to Dependent Children (ADC) program, later changed to Aid to Families with Dependent Children (AFDC). With President Lyndon Johnson's declaration of the War on Poverty in the 1960s, a family's AFDC receipt assured ready access to other benefits, such as Medicaid and Food Stamps. Families who participated in AFDC-related work programs were also eligible for childcare assistance, although these programs were often underfunded and involved only a fraction of eligible families (Phillips & Straussner, 2002).

Program structures, priorities, and funding streams all changed dramatically with passage of the 1996 Welfare Reform law, entitled the Personal Responsibility and Work Opportunity Reconciliation Act. This Act brought many changes to the broad array of programs serving low-income children and their families. The federal AFDC program was replaced with a new program, Temporary Assistance for Needy Families (TANF), which was funded by block grants to states. This legislation eliminated the tradition established with the Social Security Act of 1935 of lifelong "entitlement" to public financial assistance, since each state was now free to establish its own standards for eligibility, amounts of assistance, and the length of time a person could receive assistance, which was capped by federal legislation at five years throughout one's lifetime. The intention of this legislation was to encourage people to work rather than receive assistance, with the underlying premise that children would benefit from seeing their parents leave welfare and go to work (Longres, 2000; The Urban Institute, 2004).

Welfare reform, although trumpeted as an unmitigated success (the welfare roles diminished and poverty rates decreased slightly), has been a disaster for many poor children and their families. Those requiring assistance may no longer be eligible for it, employment tends to be sporadic and does not ensure a living wage, and in many instances, people have lost eligibility status for additional benefits, such as Medicaid, housing subsidies, and Food Stamps. In addition, parents working for minimum wage cannot afford to hire baby-sitters to supervise their children after school (DeParle, 2004).

Since the passage of welfare reform, the national debate on poverty has slowed down. However, both poverty and the problems resulting

from it persist. Many conservative observers explain poverty by looking at culture and behavior—bad parenting, high out-of-wedlock birth
rates, teenagers who don't know the value of work (Herrnstein &
Murray, 1996). On the other hand, many liberals feel the real problems are economic, a combination of underfinanced public schools
and a dearth of well-paying semiskilled jobs, which make it impossible
for families to pull themselves out of poverty (Newman, 1999; Tough,
2004).

CHILDREN LIVING IN POVERTY

The United States now has the greatest income disparity between
rich and poor families of any modern democratic nation, and propor-
tionally more children live in poverty in the U.S. than in any other
industrialized nation. In 2002, approximately 16 percent of American
children—more than 11 million—lived in families with incomes at or
below the poverty level. An additional 37 percent, more than 26 million, lived in low-income families, meaning that their parents earn up
to double what is considered the poverty level (Children's Defense
Fund, 2004). These families faced material hardships and financial
pressures similar to those of families who are officially counted as
poor.

Younger children are most likely to live in low-income families.
Almost five million infants and toddlers live in low-income families,
with 2.2 million of them meeting the official definition of poverty.
Among kindergarten-age children, 40 percent, or 1.5 million children,
live in low-income families, and more than half-a million meet the federal criteria for poverty. Among school-age children, 38 percent, 10.5
million, are regarded as low income, of whom 4.6 million are officially considered as living in poverty. The percentage continues to
decrease among older children, with 32 percent of adolescents, 6.2
million, living in low-income families, with 2.4 million meeting the
official poverty criteria (National Center for Children in Poverty,
2004). One possible explanation for this decrease in the number of
older children in poverty may be the greater employment of mothers
as their children get older.

In many instances, poverty has been racialized—especially in urban
communities (Newman, 1999). While the largest groups of children in

poor families are white, reflecting the general population, black and Latino children (including all Latinos regardless of race) are significantly more likely to live in families with low incomes and account for the largest increase in low-income children in urban settings (Newman, 1999). Although the poverty rate for blacks and Latinos during the 1980s and 1990s was very high at 30 percent, the rate for children in poverty in these population groups during that period was even higher. According to The Children's Defense Fund (2004), 31.5 percent of black children and 28.6 percent of Hispanic children are poor. These children tend to grow up in geographic isolation in their urban communities (Schorr & Schorr, 1988; Wilson, 1987). As pointed out by Ogletree (2004), "there was a buffer zone just a few blocks north of the tracks that encompassed downtown, where whites and blacks shopped, indifferent to one another. . . . The wealthiest white families lived in a middle-class community. . . . The vast majority of black citizens lived on the south side of the railroad tracks" (p. 23). hooks (2000) also elaborates about the isolation experienced by urban poor, stating that "More and more our nation is becoming class segregated, especially in urban inner city environments. The poor live among the poor. . ." (p. 3).

THE IMPACT OF POOR QUALITY EDUCATION

One factor contributing to the perpetuation of poverty among urban children is the poor quality of their education (Richman & Bowen, 1997). Schools in urban communities are often both racially and economically segregated. As Derrick Bell pointed out in a *Boston Globe* article:

> There is good reason to celebrate the 50th anniversary of the Supreme Court's landmark decision in Brown v. Board of Education, but school desegregation is not one of them. Surely the process has been beneficial to many children; but the grim statistics of continuing racial segregation in the public schools, the inferior resources available in the mostly black and Hispanic background schools, even the tracking and other devices that isolate students by race in nominally desegregated schools tells the real story. (Bell, 2004, p. 11)

According to the United States Department of Education, there is a positive correlation between poverty and poor school performance, high stakes test failure in school, and substantially separate and completely separate special education classes (Bali, & Alverez, 2003; Eamon, 2001; Garbarino, 2000; National Center for Education Statistics, 2004). Children growing up in poor households also face greater odds of dropping out of school. Census Bureau data of 2004 indicate that among teenagers between 16 and 17 years of age, dropping out of school is almost two times as prevalent in the cities as in other communities.

The consequences of dropping out of school are not just confined to the economic arena. Dropouts are more likely than high school graduates to be arrested, to have substance abuse problems, and to be unwed parents (Schorr & Schorr, 1988). Therefore, it is not surprising that dropouts are twice as likely as high school graduates to be unemployed and to live in poverty. The disparity in income between graduates and dropouts increases over the individual's lifetime and reinforces the cultural and social context of poverty. Compounding the problem of school failure is the absence of constructive role models in many inner city neighborhoods (Longres, 2000; Wilson, 1987).

THE IMPACT OF POVERTY ON CHILD DEVELOPMENT

Individuals of all ages are affected by poverty; however, the impact is more detrimental if exposure is persistently experienced throughout childhood. Theorists suggest that few children living in poverty escape developmental risk completely, and it is the accumulation of such risk that jeopardizes development, particularly when there are no compensatory forces at work (Davies, 1999; Eamon, 2001; Garbarino, 2000; Webb, 2003).

Poverty has an especially profound impact during the early development of children. Brain development has been found to occur earlier and more rapidly than previously believed, and the impact of daily life experiences on brain development has been found to be critical. Research elaborating on the physiology and the biochemistry of the brain has established that the first three years are the most crucial to the development of human capacities (Perry, 2000). Studies of early development indicate that human emotions, behaviors, and thoughts are responses to ongoing interactions between the specific neurobiology of the individual and his or her psychosocial and cultural environments. Normal development involves an unfolding sense of self-consolidation and the emerging capacity to regulate internal demands (Davies, 1999). A child's ability to mediate early exposure to poverty is determined not only by internal capabilities, but also consistent nurturing care by adults (Saleeby, 2001). Therefore, most manifestations of psychological functioning are related to ongoing interactions between the child and the immediate environment. These interactions are recursive—going on continuously, back and forth; the child's biology affects the environment, and the environment affects the biology of the child (Davies, 1999).

Many children growing up in extreme poverty conditions may lack the responsive care and nurturing that is required for optimal development (Davies, 1999; Eamon, 2001). Nonetheless, as pointed out by Bernard (1991), while many high-risk children develop various problems, most of them become healthy, competent adults. Similarly, Rutter's research on children growing up in poverty revealed that half of the children living under conditions of disadvantage are resilient and do not have difficulties in their adult life (Rutter, 1989).

Research carried out by the Annie E. Casey Foundation (2004) assesses the quality of life of children by examining educational, social, economic, and physical well-being indicators. The findings show that children living in large cities are more likely to have more difficulties in these areas than children living in the nation as a whole. Although there are many factors that put urban children at risk for social, emotional, and behavioral difficulties such as depression, violence, unplanned pregnancies, substance abuse, HIV/AIDS, and homelessness, nothing predicts negative outcomes more powerfully than growing up poor (Annie E. Casey Foundation, 2004).

Kotlowitz (1992) portrayed the devastating impact of growing up in the inner city in his powerful book, *There Are No Children Here*. Kotlowitz spent time with two boys in one of Chicago's most devastated public housing projects. The children's story illustrates the overwhelming magnitude of poverty, which, as alluded to by the title of the book, results in the eradication of childhood. The boys' narrative deconstructs the causes of poverty as being culturally constructed, rather than due to biological or innate differences.

Unequal distribution of wealth, power, and opportunities must be taken into account when addressing the problems confronting poor, urban children (Hamilton-Mason, 2004). Race and ethnicity are also crucial factors to consider. West (1993) argues that race and ethnicity matter because structural factors in society obstruct the motivation of members of subordinated groups. He asks us, therefore, to critically evaluate both external and internal constraints that may place subordinate groups at risk.

ASSESSMENT OF URBAN CHILDREN LIVING IN POVERTY

Clinical assessments of children reared in urban poverty need to be guided by an appreciation of the particular biological and psychological dynamics of the child within the context of his/her environment. The impact of factors, such as the family's race, ethnicity, and culture, must be understood in order to plan helpful and culturally-sensitive interventions.

Using a biopsychosocial framework and an ecological perspective, a clinician needs to assess the following:

Child System

- genetic factors, such as temperament and genetic susceptibility to physical and emotional disorders;
- biological factors, such as nutrition, immunizations, and general health;
- capacity for resiliency;
- age/stage appropriate achievement of developmental tasks;
- psychological factors, such as ego functioning, coping skills, adaptation, and adequacy of self-esteem;
- social factors, such as peer relationships;
- intellectual and academic functioning;
- special stressors, such as chronic illnesses or disabilities;
- areas of strength, mastery, and competence;
- for immigrant children: cultural factors, such as level of acculturation, acculturative stressors, and language skills development;
- perception and meaning of poverty for the child, such as how poverty is experienced by the child on a day-to-day basis;
- perceptions and experiences of racism and discrimination.

Family System

- family systems dynamics, such as roles, cultural norms and values, boundaries, parent-child and sibling relationships, communication patterns;
- general physical living/housing conditions of family unit;
- special stressors, such as substance abuse problems and/or physical illnesses and disabilities;
- available supports from extended family, neighbors, friends, religious and social organizations;
- current and previous income level and entitlements received by family members;
- family coping styles and areas of parental strength and competence;
- previous experiences and outcomes with helping systems, such as TANF, and social service and health care agencies;
- for immigrant families: migration history and any attendant trauma, level of acculturation, and language skills development of parents/caregivers;
- perceptions and experiences of racism and discrimination.

Environmental System

- general condition of neighborhood, such as availability of illegal drugs, presence of gangs and violence, employment and housing opportunities, schools, parks and other recreational facilities, and transportation;
- available resources, such as religious, social, educational, and self-help organizations, and availability and accessibility of a network of nearby social services and health agencies.

Such comprehensive assessment may require a number of contacts with the child and family. However, even during short-term crisis intervention, it is important that the practitioner recognize that both assessment and treatment processes occur simultaneously and are ongoing.

THE CASE OF KEISHA–ASSESSMENT FROM
AN ECOLOGICAL PERSPECTIVE

The following case illustrates some of the sources of stress that families living in poverty may endure as they try to adapt to life transitions.

Keisha, a seven-year-old of Panamanian and African-American descent, was referred to a community mental health center by her school social worker because of oppositional behaviors, including biting, scratching, and kicking. Keisha has been in kinship foster care with her 60-year-old maternal grandmother, Mrs. Alonzo, since the age of six months because of her mother's chronic substance abuse and affective disorder. Keisha's mother has infrequent contact with the family, and her father has never been involved in her life. Mrs. Alonzo, an immigrant from Panama, has been living in Boston for over 25 years. Mrs. Alonzo resented the referral, having been previously involved with child protective services following a court-mandated intervention based on Keisha's allegation of sexual abuse by Mrs. Alonzo's long-term partner. Mrs. Alonzo, however, was pleased to have a black social worker assigned to work with her and Keisha at the center.

Keisha's family includes her mother Julia, age 26, who is the youngest of two children. Julia's 39-year-old sister lives on the West Coast. Mrs. Alonzo was abandoned by her husband 22 years ago, shortly after the family immigrated to Boston. She subsequently had a nineteen-year relationship with a partner, referred to by Keisha as "Papi." Mrs. Alonzo described him as an alcoholic. They separated almost two years ago following Keisha's allegation that Papi molested her. Mrs. Alonzo felt that Keisha's allegations were responsible for Papi leaving (Keisha has since recanted). After Papi left, Mrs. Alonzo was unable to maintain their apartment, and she and Keisha lived in homeless shelters until three months prior to this referral. They are now living in a subsidized apartment.

Keisha is a precocious, bicultural child who presents with symptoms of oppositional, aggressive, as well as provocative and sexualized behavior. Mrs. Alonzo is an attractive woman who is always stylishly dressed and appears younger than her stated age. Prior to assuming custody of Keisha, Mrs. Alonzo worked as a chef in a small restaurant. She then received public assistance, and since Keisha started school, she has been working part-time as a bus monitor and a "lunch mother" at Keisha's school. She is worried about lack of income during the summer school vacation when she will not be working, and is concerned that if she reapplies for public assistance she will exhaust her lifetime eligibility for benefits under TANF.

Mrs. Alonzo presents as somewhat demanding and emotionally labile, with high expectations of Keisha. She feels overwhelmed with Keisha's behavior and emotional neediness and her own economic situation.

Discussion: Assessing Risk and Protective Factors within an Ecological Framework

The interrelationships between Keisha, her family, and the various systems within their environment can be understood from an ecological perspective. An assessment based on such a perspective assumes interactive processes and inter-relationships between and among the child, family, and environmental systems.

Both risk and protective factors may be present in all systems. Risk and protective factors are attributes of the child, family, or environmental systems that may influence positive or negative outcomes (Brofenbrenner, 1994; Eamon, 2001; Greene, 2002). The balance between risk and protective factors may shift based on genetics, the child's age, capacity for resilience, and changes in familial and environmental supports.

Child System

Keisha was assessed as engaging, precocious, affectionate, and likeable. At the same time, she is biologically vulnerable based on her mother's history of substance abuse and affective disorder. No information was yet available about Keisha's biological father. As a child living in poverty who had the experience of living in homeless shelters, and with a possible history of sexual abuse, she is also dependent on a primary caregiver who is overwhelmed with her own life stressors and is holding Keisha responsible for their plight. In addition,

Keisha has difficulties relating to her peers, making it hard to participate in school-based and community activities for children her age.

Family System

This is a family that has limited and unstable income. Mrs. Alonzo feels that at her age she does not have enough energy to work full-time and also care for Keisha. However, she has been resourceful in finding part-time work that also enables her to be available as a caregiver for her granddaughter. Neither of Keisha's biological parents has had a positive involvement in her life.

Environmental Systems

The *education system* has been an important resource. Although the teachers in Keisha's school were unable to help with her lack of appropriate socialization skills and Keisha resorted to acting-out behaviors, they did recognize her need for help and the social worker made the needed referral. The local school also became a source of financial support for the family when Mrs. Alonzo began working there; however, the work was seasonal and represented underemployment considering her past work history.

There was a lack of resources that might have made it possible for Mrs. Alonzo to maintain her apartment, and consequently she turned to the *housing system*. The only available housing option for her and Keisha was to live in a homeless shelter until moving into a publicly subsidized apartment.

The family has been involved with the *child welfare system* since Keisha was six months old, when Mrs. Alonzo became a kinship foster parent for her. There was also involvement with child protective services, and despite Mrs. Alonzo's negative views of this system, they did attempt to assume a protective role with Keisha.

Mrs. Alonzo's response to her involvement with the *mental health system* was relatively positive, as she felt that the community mental health center could be responsive to her needs because she was able to connect with the black social worker there.

THE CASE OF DAISY–APPLYING SKILLS OF INTERVENTION

Techniques of interventions with children and their families living in poverty not only grow out of good assessment skills, but also may need to expand on traditional treatment principles. Since living in poverty produces multipronged problems, treatment interventions, as well as public policies, also need to be multipronged. The practitioner needs to be cognizant of the child's family system and his/her environment, and make creative interventions encompassing individual, familial, and environmental systems: This can be seen in the case of Daisy:

Daisy, a 10-year-old Caucasian child, was referred to the local mental health clinic by her school social worker because of her decreasing school performance and her withdrawn behavior during the past few months. Daisy and her recovering alcoholic mother had been burned out from their low-income residence six months ago. Unable to afford other housing, were living in a small homeless shelter for families run by the local church while they were put on a waiting list for subsidized permanent housing.

Daisy was not eager to come for help. She would miss sessions or come in up to a half-hour late. Rather than giving up and labeling Daisy as resistant and unmotivated, the worker was creative in searching for ways to be helpful to her. While visiting Daisy's school and speaking to her teachers, the worker discovered that Daisy excelled in arts and crafts. She encouraged the mother to enroll Daisy in a free after-school arts and crafts program and then advocated with the program coordinator to allow Daisy to become the art teacher's "assistant," helping other children with their projects. This helped Daisy feel more competent, raised her self-esteem, and at the same time helped her feel more at ease with other children.

The worker tried to drop by the center for a few minutes every week to see how Daisy was coming along. After a few months, Daisy was able to return to the mental health clinic where, through both talking and play therapy, she was able to work on some of the emotional issues that were getting in the way of her school performance. The worker also involved the mother in a weekly mothers' group held at the clinic to help her with her feelings of isolation.

Discussion: Maximizing Resilience During Intervention

Resilience is a dynamic process that is a function of the individual's unique strengths, capacities, vulnerabilities, and "goodness-of-fit" with the demands and opportunities of the environment. The goodness-of-fit depends on the quality of the match between an individual's personal characteristics and the qualities of a person's environment (Greene, 2002).

The worker needs to be able to delineate the personal, family, and environmental factors that promote resilience and present opportunities for adaptive functioning (Nash & Fraser, 1998). In this case, the worker was able to recognize Daisy's strengths and the strengths in the environment, thereby maximizing her resilience. Daisy's role as a "teacher's assistant" in the after-school program was a critical part of the intervention. It empowered her by building on her innate skills and also served as a "psychological bridge" to more formal treatment.

Principles and Techniques for Working with Children and their Families

Practitioner's Attitudes and Use of Self

While not negating the importance of linking clients to entitlement programs and other concrete services, help will be severely limited without a relationship between the practitioner and a child and his/her family. The most needed referrals, whether to after-school programs or for concrete services, may not be used or followed up by the client unless practitioners establish at least a minimally "good enough" relationship.

While at times social workers are quick to label clients living in poverty as "resistant" or "unmotivated" to get help, workers need first to be sure that they are not the ones who are resistant, unmotivated, or rigid in their thinking or in their approaches. At the same time, social workers need to be prepared that children and families living in poverty may be reluctant to trust or feel comfortable with them. It is essential to remember that through the various manifestations of institutional oppression, many individuals living in poor families feel that they are not highly valued by society. As discussed previously, the poor are typically ignored by society; they are provided substandard housing, limited access to health care, and poor quality education. Is it any wonder, then, that poor families may not be so ready and willing to quickly trust a worker who they may see as representing the larger society?

Since the practitioner and client may come from different socioeconomic and cultural backgrounds, practitioners need to be aware of feelings they may have about clients who are different from themselves. It is difficult for practitioners who see themselves as openminded and liberal to acknowledge feelings of prejudice towards people living in poverty. Yet, the socialization process in most cultures instills biases of which one may not even be aware. It is essential that social workers have opportunities to examine such feelings and attitudes honestly, to discuss them in a safe environment, such as supervision, peer groups, and seminars, and to work these through, recognizing that gaining self-awareness is an ongoing and difficult process. Left unattended, such biases will prevent practitioners from developing a trusting and respectful relationship with clients, and will interfere with effective work.

As part of the close examination of personal attitudes toward differences, workers need to become aware of their assumptions or stereotypes about poverty. While some practitioners may themselves have grown up in poor families, one can never assume the unique meaning and impact of poverty on a particular child and family. If one does not inquire about the specific perceptions, ideas, and feelings the child holds about him/herself, family members, and his/her environment, but assumes to know how poverty and its stressors are experienced by that child, then the clinician will continuously miss the opportunity to connect with and empathically respond to that child's unique experience of his/her situation (Garbarino et al., 1992; Webb, 2003).

Practitioners need to be aware of their own feelings of wanting to rescue children whose lives are bounded by poverty and who often experience much loss and trauma. They need to be flexible and creative in their interventions and not be led by simplistic notions about life in poverty.

Linking Families to Services and Benefits

It is often not sufficient just to refer a parent to an office to apply for financial assistance or other help. A worker may have to make some initial calls to get appropriate information, and help the client fill out forms and get necessary documentation together. At times, role-playing with a client as to what they want to say or need to ask for may be helpful. Clients may feel humiliated, ashamed of needing help, or anxious about being turned down. Any of these feelings can cause them to be less effective in advocating for themselves. The use of "rehearsing" techniques, such as role-playing, can help clients learn to advocate for themselves, and by anticipating consequences, makes them feel more empowered. Rehearsing can also be used as a clinical tool, enabling the practitioner to observe how the client handles difficult situations. Because clients living in poverty may not have a phone, the practitioner may need to make or help them make calls to a variety of agencies from the office. At times practitioners may need to accompany clients when they are applying to agencies in order to facilitate access to services and to model advocacy techniques.

Since few agencies can begin to provide for the multitude of needs of families in poverty, workers have to be knowledgeable about a host of formal and informal community services, such as a church-sponsored clothing distribution program, a community group that helps children with homework and tutoring, or a parenting group offered by a social service agency. Workers need to serve as coordinators of services or case managers, and frequently may find it useful to visit agencies and establish a working relationship with the coordinators of the programs. Such networking relationships become crucial when a family is in a crisis and needs immediate services.

Working with Strengths, Building Competency, and Empowerment

It is easy to overpathologize families living in poverty and overlook the fact that to live in poverty conditions and survive from day to day takes considerable strength. One of the basic tenets of treatment needs to be the empowerment of families. The work must lead to a greater sense of competence, greater sense of control over their lives, and a general feeling of hopefulness. Clients need to build their sense of personal power in order to bring about changes in their lives. The worker does not present him or herself as knowing all the answers to a client's problems, but rather establishes a collaborative partnership that helps the client develop insights, skills, and a greater capacity to resolve his or her own difficulties (Saleebey, 2001).

As one assesses the family's situation, it is important to look for and reflect back to the client's areas of strength, such as coping capacity; ability to reach out and follow through; availability of support from extended family, neighbors, and friends; and a family's capacity to parent. Many children living in poverty and facing multiple stressors have areas of strength, are eager to receive help, have the ability to use resources in their environment, and have talents and areas of interests that can be supported and developed.

BALANCING BETWEEN CLIENTS' INTERNAL DYNAMICS AND ENVIRONMENTAL STRESSORS

Clinicians must be careful not to be oversimplistic in their understanding of a client's life in poverty. There can be a tendency to understand clients' various problems only in terms of their poverty conditions, overlooking their internal psychic life, conflicts, fantasies, and dreams. Finding the right balance between meeting a client's inner needs through talking, gaining insight into problems, ego building techniques, and environmental change is a critical task as these needs are interrelated, and one set of needs cannot be ignored for the other. The necessary balance must be dictated by an objective and thorough assessment; it cannot be guided by a practitioner's countertransferential blocks, prejudices, or stereotypes.

In cases of families living in poverty with an array of complex personal and socio-economic problems, it is common for a clinician to experience parallel or similar feelings to those of the family, such as being overwhelmed by multiple and complicated needs. Practitioners need to avoid becoming reductionistic in their approach as a way of dealing with the complexity of a case. It is essential for practitioners to realize that they need to help clients to partialize and prioritize problems, and develop realistic long and short-term goals.

The environmental conditions in poor neighborhoods, such as living in chronic fear of violence or crime, loss of friends or relatives through sudden violence, and pressures of substance abuse, often include daily assaults on the ego, which can create high levels of anxiety and distress and can leave a child vulnerable to ego deficits (Garbarino et al., 1992).

Children with ego deficits often have an inability to fully verbalize their feelings and thoughts, and can show impaired impulse control. Since coping capacities and defensive functioning may not be operating at optimal levels, their sublimated play activities in treatment can break down and become more direct enactments of the violence, anxiety, and stress which they may be experiencing. Given poor ego functioning, particularly in the area of the regulation of drives and affects, they can become flooded by their internal feelings and act in a frenzied manner in the treatment room. This "wild activity" is often a defense against frightening feelings of which they are unable to speak. Their body movements convey physically what they are not able to sublimate in play or say in words. In such situations, the worker often needs to assume the role of the auxiliary ego, becoming an active and stable force in their lives, and slowly help such children to internalize the self-soothing and ego-regulatory capacities that they lack.

Determining whether anxious or disorganized behaviors are the result of an ego deficit, a regressive pull precipitated by sudden, overwhelming trauma, or the result of situational crises stemming from lack of money or other factors in the environment is an important aspect of assessment, which will lead to appropriate clinical and/or environmental interventions.

CONCLUSION

It is clearly unjust that in the United States, one of the wealthiest countries in the world, so many children are growing up in debilitating and detrimental social and economic conditions. There are far too many children who grow up in poverty and it poses tremendous risk factors for them. It is important for social workers to fulfill the role of the policy practitioner and advocate for policies that reflect social justice for the poor, thereby working to change existing structural economic and social deficits, such as lack of access to quality day care and health care for children.

Social work, as a profession with historical commitments to addressing the needs of the poor, needs to assume two roles with regard to children living in poverty: responding clinically to their multiple and complex needs and the needs of their families, and serving as advocates of public policies aimed at prevention and amelioration of poverty.

REFERENCES

Bali, V., & Alverez, M. (2003). Schools and educational outcomes: What causes the "race gap" in student test scores? *Social Science Quarterly, 84* (3), 485–498.

Bernard, B. (1991). *Fostering resiliency in kids: Protective factors in the family, school and community.* Portland, OR: Northwest Educational Lab.

Bell, D. (2004). 50 years after Brown v. Board of Education: The failed legacy of Boston school desegregation. *The Boston Globe.* p. E11.

Bronfenbrenner, U. (1995). Developmental ecology through space and time: A future perspective. In P. Moen, G.H. Elder, Jr., & K. Luscher (Eds.), *Examining lives in context: Perspectives on the ecology of human development* (pp. 619–647). Washington, DC: APA Books.

Bronfenbrenner, U., & Ceci, S. J. (1994). Nature-nurture reconceptualized: A bio-ecological model. *Psychological Review, 101*(4), 568-586.

Children's Defense Fund. (2004). Key facts about American children. In *The state of America's children.* http://www.childrensdefense.org/data/keyfacts.asp. Accessed June 20, 2004.

Davies, D. (1999). *Child development: A practitioner's guide.* New York: Guilford Press.

DeParle, J. (2004). *American dream: Three women, ten kids, and a nation's drive to end welfare.* New York: Viking Books.

Duncan, G. J., Brooks-Gunn, J., & Klebanov, P. K. (1994). Economic deprivation and early childhood development. *Child Development, 65,* 296–318.

Eamon, M. (2001). The effects of poverty on children's socioemotional development: An ecological systems analysis. *Social Work, 46* (3), 256–266.

Garbarino, J. (2000). *Lost boys.* New York: Anchor Books.

Garmezy, N. (1993). Children in poverty: Resiliency despite risk. *Psychiatry, 56:* 127-36.

Ginsberg, L. (1994). *Understanding social problems, policies, and programs.* Columbia, SC: University of South Carolina Press.

Greene, R. (2002). Human behavior: A resilience orientation. In R. Greene (Ed.), *Resiliency: An integrated approach to practice, policy, and research* (pp. 1–29). Washington, DC: NASW Press.

Hamilton-Mason, J. (2004). Psychodynamic perspectives: Responding to the assessment needs of people of color. *Smith College Studies in Social Work 74,* 2, 315–332.

Herrnstein, R. J., & Murray, C. (1994). *The bell curve.* New York: Free Press.

hooks, b. (2000). *Where we stand: Class matters.* New York: Routledge.

Kotlowitz, A. (1992). *There are no children here: The story of two boys growing up in the other America.* New York: Anchor Books

Longres, J. F. (2000). *Human behavior in the social environment.* Belmont, CA: Brooks Cole.

Megan, D. (2004, May 17). Unfinished business. *The Boston Globe,* p. 7.

Nash, J., & Fraser, M. (1998). After-school care for children: A resilience-based approach. *Families in Society, 79,* 370–382.

National Association of Black Social Workers. (1968). *Code of Ethics.* Washington, DC: Author.

National Association of Social Workers. (1996). *Code of Ethics.* Washington, DC: Author.

National Center for Education Statistics. (2001). *The condition of education 2001.* Report 2001072. Washington, DC: Author.

National Center for Children in Poverty. (2004). *Annual Report.* Columbia University. www.nccp.org/pub-cpfo4.html. Accessed May 11, 2004.

Newman, K. (1999). *No shame in my game: The working poor in the inner city.* New York: Alfred Knopf and Russell Sage Foundation.

Newman, K. (2004). *The wages of fear.* www.thenation.com/journals/315. Accessed November 30, 2004.

Ogletree, C. (2004). *All deliberate speed.* New York: W. W. Norton.

Perry, B. D. (2000). The neurodevelopmental impact of violence in childhood. In D. Schetky & E. Benedek (Eds.), *Textbook of child and adolescent forensic psychiatry.* Washington, DC: American Psychiatric Press.

Phillips. N. K., & Straussner, S. L. A. (2002). *Urban social work: An introduction to policy and practice in the cities.* Boston: Allyn & Bacon.

Richman, J., & Bowen, G. (1997). School failure: An ecological-interactional-developmental approach. In M. Fraser (Ed.), *Risk and resilience in childhood* (pp. 95–116). Washington, DC: NASW Press.

Rutter, M. (1989). Pathways from childhood to adult life. *Journal of Psychology and Psychiatry, 22,* 323-356.

Saleeby, D. (2001). *Human behavior and social environments: A biopsycho-social approach.* New York: Columbia University Press.

Schorr, L., & Schorr, D. (1988). *Within our reach: Breaking the cycle of disadvantage.* New York: Doubleday.

Simon, B. (1994). *The empowerment tradition in American social work.* New York: Columbia University Press.

The Green Book. (2004, March). *Background material and data on programs within the jurisdiction of the Committee on Ways and Means.* Washington, DC: U.S. House of Representatives.

The Urban Institute (2004). *Poverty gap between whites, blacks, Hispanics narrows between 1996-2001.* Washington, DC: Author.

The Annie E. Casey Foundation. (2003). *Kid count data book.* www.aecf.org/kidscount/databook/summary.htm. Accessed May 13, 2004.

Tough, P. (2004, June 20). The Harlem Project. *The New York Times Magazine,* p. 44.

United States Census Bureau (2002). *Poverty in the United States.* Washington, DC: US. Department of Commerce (Economics and Statistics Administration).

Webb, N. B. (2003). *Social work practice with children.* New York: Guilford Press.

West, C. (1993). *Race matters.* Boston: Beacon Press.

Wilson, W. J. (1987). *The truly disadvantaged: The inner city, the underclass and public policy.* Chicago: University of Chicago Press.

Chapter 3

IMMIGRANT CHILDREN IN THE UNITED STATES

GRACIELA M. CASTEX

Working with immigrant children and their families may provide great rewards to the clinician, yet it also offers daunting challenges. One of the great challenges for both policy makers and practitioners is understanding the diversity among immigrants: They come from all over the world; they arrive in multigenerational family units or alone; and they may have refugee, residence, citizen, temporary, or no recognized status of documentation. Furthermore, today's immigrants represent a very wide range of racial, linguistic, religious, and socioeconomic statuses.

In the last decade, and particularly since the turn of the twenty-first century, intensification of two societal trends have profoundly affected both immigration to the United States and the lives of all immigrants residing here. The first trend is the result of the globalization of world society, and the second is due to the political and social climate that resulted in policies hostile to immigrants following the attacks of September 11, 2001. This has been exacerbated by—at this writing—two wars, neither of which is resolved, and subsequent terrorist attacks in Madrid and London. Multiple terrorist attacks and a climate of apprehension towards immigrants have come to dominate policy considerations at the highest levels; immigration regulations and their administration and enforcement has been reorganized and tightened. These changes have reinforced a sense of uncertainty that pervades many interactions and interventions with immigrant families and their children. These two trends notwithstanding, social workers still need to

50

attend to a central experience universal among immigrants–they have all gone through a well-defined immigration process.

This chapter includes a discussion of immigration processes in general in order to better understand family dynamics and the effects of immigration on children. Drachman's (1992) stage model of the immigration experience is central to this analysis. Each of the components of this model–premigration and departure, transit, and resettlement stages–may have ongoing effects long after immigration to the host country. Thus an analysis of the impact of the immigration experience at both the individual and the societal level is important to understanding the situation and experiences of immigrant children living in urban environments, and in providing services to them.

THE IMPACT OF GLOBAL TRENDS ON IMMIGRATION

While the individual reasons for immigration are as varied as the immigrants themselves, decisions to immigrate are not formed in a social vacuum. Societal factors operating at both national and international levels create both "push" and "pull" effects that promote or impede both emigration from a homeland and immigration into the United States (Potocky-Tripodi, 2002). At the human level, factors that push an individual to emigrate from their homeland might include unemployment, poverty, natural disaster, war, fear of political or religious oppression, and the lack of social, creative, or educational opportunities. Pull factors into another country might include employment and business opportunities, a desire for personal freedom, unification of families, access to educational opportunities, and better health care. These push and pull factors are affected, and often directly determined by larger world social trends and policies.

The growing interconnectedness of the world's peoples through the integration of the world's economic, communications, and transportation systems–"globalization"–has had a profound impact on immigration to the United States. Internet access, overnight delivery systems, and cell phone and fax technologies reinforce social networks and economic relations between people and businesses in the U.S. and such distant locations as rural Mexico or Pakistan or Russia. Information about one's activities, successes, employment availability, and even methods of immigration is communicated more readily and in greater detail than ever before.

Decreasing transportation costs–inexpensive airline tickets, dropping freight costs–and elimination of trade barriers and taxes have resulted in massive economic shifts, with the dislocation of farmers and workers, and transfers of resources among economic sectors in almost every country throughout the world. Factories owned by U.S. companies operating in Mexico, for example, moved to the Dominican Republic in search of cheaper labor and are now operating out of China, leaving thousands of workers without jobs as companies move from country to country. Cheap food imports have destroyed the livelihood of traditional farmers in many countries. Europe offers another example of the world's growing interconnectedness. With a common currency, the Euro, economic integration is leading towards political integration, with common trading and employment regulations, as well as immigration laws affecting more than 400 million persons.

The integration of national economies into a world economy is likewise fueled by an integration of world capital markets. Literally trillions of dollars a day are transferred electronically across borders (the "same" dollar may participate in thousands of such transactions) greatly easing the concentration of large sums of money to finance projects in virtually any place on Earth. Likewise, the loss of confidence of these electronic capital markets in a currency may bankrupt a national economy in minutes, as was the case during the East Asian financial crisis of the 1997-1998.

Globalization, the product of both technological progress and policy decisions, underlines the importance for the social work profession to continue to attend to, and when possible influence, national and international policies and to develop appropriate services.

Impact on Immigrants of the September 11, 2001 Terrorist Attacks

The terrorist attacks on New York City and Washington, D.C., and the tragic plane crash in Pennsylvania, with their thousands of fatalities, have had profound, long-lasting effects on U.S. society. Among these effects are the Patriot Act reinforcing police powers, the restruc-

turing of the administration of U.S. immigration laws, and the fostering of a growing anti-immigrant/immigration sentiment. The effects
for immigrants and on immigration were immediate and are ongoing.

Regulating Immigration and the Immigrants

Following September 11, 2001, the administration of immigration
policies was moved from the old Immigration and Naturalization
Service (INS) of the Department of Justice to the U.S. Citizenship and
Immigration Services (USCIS, or more commonly, CIS) of the new
Department of Homeland Security. All new arrivals must negotiate the
laws and regulations governing immigration statuses administered and
implemented by the CIS, as do all noncitizen residents of the United
States. Pressured by the perceived need to secure borders under the
threat of international terrorism, having one's paperwork processed by
the CIS has become increasingly arduous, expensive, and marked by
ever greater delays. For travelers to the U.S., it has become more difficult to get visas, and complaints about refusals have grown.

The fear of arbitrary deportation haunts the consciousness of immigrants regardless of their immigration status, be they residents, asylees,
refugees, visitors, or students. Obviously, those most vulnerable to
deportation are the seven million (according to INS estimates) or
more persons in the U.S. who lack the proper documentation (INS,
2000). Many immigrants–even those who are now U.S. citizens–may
find themselves looked upon with suspicion. Even some with resident
status ("green cards") are fearful that their continued presence in the
U.S. is contingent upon the whims of anonymous bureaucrats or other
officials. Furthermore, regulations are in flux; social work practitioners
have reported to the author that they must check the USCIS web site
daily–where new regulations are first published–so that they can accurately assist clients. The risk of misinformation in such circumstances
is high, although the CIS is making attempts to distribute information
helpful to new immigrants (U.S. Department of Homeland Security,
2005). Other guides available for social workers may not always be
up-to-date.

Legislation is also in flux. On May 11, 2005, for example, the REAL
ID Act–passed as an amendment to a disaster relief bill–was signed
into law by President Bush. It imposes new federally mandated stan-

dards for state issued driver's licenses and IDs, replacing rules enacted in 2004. When fully implemented in 2008, federal agencies will be barred from accepting as an ID those licenses that do not include eight elements of identifying information that can be read by a computer. An applicant for a driver's license or state ID card must also present extensive proof of his or her identity, address, and legal right to be in the U.S. If a state does not comply, its residents will not, as a minimum, be able to enter federal buildings and courthouses, or board airplanes (and perhaps trains and buses). As a practical matter, it will be advisable to possess such an ID whenever one is asked for it by an official or by the police, even if one doesn't drive: This legislation effectively converts a driver's license into a national ID card (McCullagh, 2005; Sanchez, 2005). The REAL ID Act also limits the rights to judicial review of the actions of immigration judges and the CIS, which can include indefinite imprisonment (McCullagh, 2005). The ramifications of this act are yet to be assessed; nor is it clear at what age children will have to obtain IDs.

The exacerbation of already existing anti-immigrant and pro-nativist sentiments following September 11, 2001, may be seen in other government actions that have resulted in reductions in health care, emergency services, educational support, and other benefits for immigrants.

Anti-Immigrant Sentiment

While young children may not be aware of changes in immigration regulations, many experience the direct verbal and physical manifestations of xenophobia. Hostility may be expressed through painful comments about their clothing, language usage, food preferences, and even handwriting. Growing anti-immigration feelings among the general population can also have enormous effects on the physical security and psychological health of a child and his or her family. For example, after September 11th, Muslim children and their families were a frequent target of media attacks as well as community harassment. The targets of this type of hostility may also extend to other immigrants, and in extreme cases, include murder. An arsonist in Columbus, Ohio, for example, set fire to an apartment building housing mostly immigrants; ten people died, including a couple and their three young children (Cienfuegos, 2004).

Anti-immigration hysteria has also led to self-appointed border patrols (some people call them vigilantes) such as the Minuteman Project which started patrolling the Arizona/New Mexico border with Mexico in the Spring of 2005. Following national publicity, 40 additional such private groups popped up across the country by mid-July 2005 (Mansfield, 2005). These patrols may have indirectly contributed to at least 12 deaths in one week, including a pregnant woman and two teenagers, as immigrants from Mexico were forced to use dangerous desert routes near Yuma, Arizona (Madigan, 2005). Expressions of feelings against immigrants or "foreigners," are not new; stereotyping and scapegoating can be traced to the European colonization of North America, although the stereotypes and groups have changed over time (Delgado, Jones, & Rohani, 2005).

DEMOGRAPHICS OF RECENT IMMIGRANTS

Arriving they are, though in numbers that cannot be well counted. That the Bureau of the Census undercounts, that there are large numbers of undocumented immigrants, and that there are gaps in the records of the INS, all are universally acknowledged. A March, 2003 U.S. Census Report enumerated 33.5 million "foreign born" persons in the United States–11.7 percent of the total population–of whom 2.99 million (8.9 percent) were children under the age of 18 (U.S. Bureau of the Census, 2004a). In comparison, the 1990 Census counted 19.8 million foreign born residents, of whom 2.2 million were children (U.S. Bureau of the Census, 2004a). Thus, net immigration into the 50 United States from 1990 until 2003 exceeded 14 million persons, and may in fact have been much higher.

The above data exclude U.S.-born children of foreign born parents and persons born abroad to United States citizens. Moreover, these figures exclude immigrants and immigrant children arriving from Puerto Rico, Guam, and the U.S. Virgin Islands because they are U.S. citizens and not counted as foreign born, but are often treated like "foreigners" in U.S. society. The 2000 Census counted 3.4 million persons in the 50 United States with Puerto Rican origins, for example, but it is unclear how many of them were first generation immigrants (U.S. Bureau of the Census, 2001).

Thus, even allowing for deaths among migrants and the return of some migrants to their homelands, conservative government estimates place the total net migration to the United States in the 1990 to 2004 period to be at about 15 million persons (5 percent of the U.S. population) of whom at least 3 million were, in 2004, under the age of 18. In 2004, the Census Bureau estimated an annual net immigration of about 1.4 million persons, with at least 20 percent, or 300,000 being children (U.S. Bureau of the Census, 2004a). Given that many immigrants are undocumented and that census undercounts of immigrant communities are assumed to be larger than that for the population as a whole, the number of arriving immigrant children is probably significantly higher.

These children are quite likely to be living in urbanized environments; 44.4 percent of foreign-born U.S. residents currently live in central cities, with another 50.3 percent living in suburban areas of metropolitan regions. Thus, more than nine-tenths of the foreign born population–and therefore, presumably, of immigrant children–live in or around urban areas (U.S. Bureau of the Census, 2004a).

SOCIAL PROFILE OF IMMIGRANTS

While it is impossible to precisely characterize the immigrant population on the basis of statistical indices, some crude indications of the demographic and social profiles of the major immigrant groups can be ascertained. Such factors as geographic origins, family composition at the time of arrival, gender ratios, age composition, education, employment and role changes, income, language, and race are likely to affect the adaptive strategies of families and their children now living in the U.S.

Geographical Origins

An immigrant child may arrive from any country on earth, but more than 60 percent of them originate from the Americas, which roughly reflects the immigration flows into the U.S. since the late 1980s. In 2003, for example, 53.3 percent of the 33.5 million foreign-born residents of the 50 states (which excludes Puerto Rico and other

U.S. dependencies), and 61.5 percent (1.84 million) of the 2.99 million foreign-born children were from Latin America and the Caribbean.

Overall, the foreign-born population of the United States derived from the following world regions (the first figure is the total number of immigrants, the second is the number of persons under 18 years of age):

- *Central America* (12.35 million; 1,365,000): This includes immigrants from Mexico (the great majority), Guatemala, El Salvador, Belize, Nicaragua, Costa Rica, and Panama.
- *Asia* (8.38 million; 656,000): The largest numbers of immigrants are from the Philippines, China, Korea, and India.
- *Europe* (4.59 million; 275,000): Includes large numbers of recent immigrants/refugees from the former Soviet Union and refugees from Balkan conflicts in addition to such traditional sources of immigration as the United Kingdom, Poland, and Germany.
- *The Caribbean* (3.48 million; 250,000): Leading Caribbean countries of origin include the Dominican Republic, Jamaica, Cuba, and Haiti, but excludes immigrants from Puerto Rico.
- *South America* (2.31 million; 224,000): Led by Colombia, Ecuador, Peru, and Guyana.
- *Other Areas* (2.68 million; 214,000): This catch-all category includes Canada, the African continent and Oceania (Australia, New Zealand, and the Pacific islands). The largest large numbers of immigrants derive from Canada, Nigeria, Ethiopia, and Egypt (U.S. Bureau of the Census, 2004a, p. 1; Table 3.1; Table 4.1).

Age and Gender

The median age at entry for INS-documented immigrants during the 2000-2003 period was 27.2 years, and many, if not most, adult immigrants were of child-bearing age. Thus it is not uncommon for immigrant households to have both U.S. and "foreign-born" children. In this period, more males migrated (2.38 million; 52.4 percent of all immigrants) than females (2.16 million; 47.6 percent), possibly reflecting an immigration strategy in which the males pioneered and established themselves and then either brought their families over, or continued to support them from the United States (U.S. Bureau of the

Census, 2004a). This is an especially common strategy among Asian and African immigrants as well as some Dominican, Ecuadorian, and Mexican immigrants. On the other hand, a demand for domestic servants and health-care workers has sometimes encouraged a bias towards female pioneers among some groups.

This common immigration strategy, which involves splitting the family for a time period, may obviously have profound affects on family dynamics and interrelationships both before and after immigration.

Education

Immigrants run the gamut in educational attainment. Some arrive with doctorates, some come to study and receive degrees in the U.S., and yet others may be virtually illiterate in their native languages. After arrival, some immigrants, including adults, may receive further education in English even while remaining illiterate in their native languages. The formal education of most immigrants falls in the spectrum in between the extremes. In 2003, for example, 87 percent of "native" born U.S. adults had high school diplomas; a figure that is roughly equaled by immigrants from Asia, Europe, and "Other Regions" (including immigrants from the African continent). The high school graduation rate for South Americans, at 79.3 percent, is also high. Central Americans, however (which, for statistical purposes includes Mexico), have only a 38 percent high school graduation rate. Native- and foreign-born U.S. residents are equal in the percentage of adults who have college, graduate, or professional degrees: 27 percent (U.S. Bureau of the Census, 2004a, p. 5).

Special note should be taken of the effects of disjunctions between educational systems on immigrant children, particularly those in their teens, and the effect of these differences on the life choices available to their parents. A good example is offered by the apparent low number of high school graduates among Central Americans, the large majority of whom are Mexicans. To some extent this statistic is an artifact of the differences between the systems of public education in the two countries. While it is true that in many cases a low number high school graduates reflects a lack of formal education among the arriving immigrants—they may truly have attended school for only a few years—low "high school" graduation rates also reflect differences between the educational systems of Mexico (which was modeled after the French system of the early twentieth century) and that of the United States.

In Mexico (and in this, it is not unique), one leaves "secondary school" (*escuela secondaria*) after 10 years of schooling, at about the age of 15 or 16. One has a bit more education at this point than one would receive in the United States after middle school, and it is the common termination point of formal education unless one is bound for the university or a technical/trade school. Such a diploma is not the educational equivalent to a high school diploma in the United States, however, nor does it prepare the Mexican student for entry into a University. University study requires one to attend a *preparatorio* ("college prep"), often operated by a university, until about the age of 19 or 20. A *preparatorio* diploma (confusingly, for us, called a bachelor's degree; *bachillerato*) would be roughly equivalent to a junior college diploma in the United States or the French *bac*.

This structural difference between the two systems explains a significant, if undetermined, proportion of the low numbers of "high school" graduates among Central Americans immigrants. Many of them had achieved the social, if not educational, equivalent of a high school diploma in their homelands, which may have been all that was available. The lack of high school diploma may, however, make it difficult for some immigrants to continue schooling in the United States without, for example, getting a GED; it may also affect employment or other opportunities in this country. There are no doubt similar situations that may affect immigrants from other countries whose educational systems differ from that of the U.S. As a first order point of evaluation, however, a clinician interviewing a 16-year-old *escuela secondaria* graduate should realize that the client is not likely, in any sense, to consider him- or herself the social equivalent of a high school dropout in the United States.

The clinician cannot make assumptions about either the level of educational attainment or attitude of parents towards education for their children based on the parents' current occupational status. Many immigrants with advanced degrees may be working in nonprofessional positions. A Nigerian street merchant in Philadelphia may have a master's degree, or the Bosnian woman cleaning an office in Chicago may have once taught economics in Sarajevo. Likewise, one must guard against preconceptions regarding a child's attitudes concerning schooling based on parental educational attainment. Parental perception that schooling offers the surest road to advancement for their children in the United States is a key factor in the success of many immigrant children, even though the parents themselves may have lacked such training.

It is not unusual for immigrants to come to the United States to offer their children educational opportunities unobtainable in their homelands. This may be especially true for children of some Asian immigrants and those from the nations that comprised the former Soviet Union. For example, historically, during the 1970s, many persons of the Sikh faith from India immigrated to the Central Valley of California, where they worked in agriculture. Although these immigrants commonly had limited schooling by U.S. standards, a significantly higher percentage of their children finished high school and graduated college than did those of local white "Anglo" families (Gibson, 1988).

Employment Opportunities and Role Changes

There has long been a clear tendency for most immigrants to settle in urban areas. This appears to be largely due to the availability of employment and the relative ease of transportation, perhaps reinforced by information networks developed to the country of origin once urban ethnic enclaves are established. Exceptions to this are those immigrants working in agriculture—which has a tradition of also utilizing child labor—and in rural food processing plants.

The wide range of occupations of recently arrived workers may challenge the preconceptions of some. In 2003, 23 percent of immigrants worked in the service industries, 18 percent in production or transportation, 12 percent in construction and maintenance or material moving, and 1.6 percent in agriculture. It is important to note, however, that 27 percent overall, and 29.5 percent of the women, worked in management and professional specialties (U.S. Bureau of the Census, 2004b).

As indicated previously, a worker's occupational status in the United States might not reflect his or her status in the country of origin. This is particularly noteworthy of some professionals, especially attorneys and physicians who may have difficulty recertifying to practice in the United States.

In general, women may initially find it easier to obtain employment than men. Some of the admittedly low-paying jobs offered immigrants, such as house cleaning or child care, usually are only offered to women. At more skilled levels, women may be able to take lower status jobs than men with less loss of self-esteem. In many instances, the woman's income relative to her husband's may have risen, or the woman may now be working outside the home for the first time. In both cases, roles and power relationships may change within the marriage, and the changing roles of parents may have both positive and negative psychological effects on children.

Nah (1993) reports high rates of marital and family problems among Korean immigrants, citing the changing roles of wives and the threat to patriarchal authority as factors. Conflict between older arrivals who sponsored newly arrived relatives was also reported, with the new arrivals sometimes disappointed by the limited support offered by established relatives, while the old hands expressed impatience with the slowness of the newcomer's acquisition of cultural skills.

The fact that many migrants may have suffered a loss of occupational status, or may be undergoing a difficult period of retraining and recertification, may place psychological and economic stresses on all members of the family.

Income

All children live in a household though not all households have children. The median income of households headed by a foreign born individual was $37,499 in 2002; those headed by a native born householder averaged $44,347 that year. But these figures need to be disaggregated. Those headed by naturalized citizens, for example, had income of $46,049 that year, which exceeded native households, whereas those headed by a non-citizen averaged $32,806. Noncitizen householders are likely to have been in the United States for a shorter period of time and be younger than naturalized householders, and younger persons with a shorter period of U.S. residence are likely to earn less. And by definition, foreign born children could not have arrived in the United States more than 17 years before the data was collected (Bureau of the Census, 2004b, p. 4). While households with immigrant children may be much poorer, over time, they tend to experience significant increases in income. Overall, there is little indication of a "culture of poverty" seen among immigrant families to the United States, whether or not there is in any other group. Thus the urban environment offers the immigrant child in the United States many models, often within the family, for at least modest financial success.

Taken as a group, therefore, immigrants may be wealthy, middle income, or poor, but those with foreign born children are likely to have less money than the population of immigrants as a whole. Incomes also vary radically by region of birth, which in turn, as discussed above, correlates highly with the amount of formal education of immigrant adults. The median income of Asian households in 2002 was $61,792; of European, $53,184; "Other Areas" $50,009; and Latin America and the Caribbean $34,798. In 1999, the almost 3 million households headed by a Mexican-born person averaged $31,503 in income. But again, it is important to guard against easy, stereotyping assumptions; in 1999, 24,070 of households headed by a Mexican immigrant (about one in 120) had incomes exceeding $200,000 annually (Bureau of the Census, 2003).

Clearly all are not doing so well, of course. In 2002, the overall poverty rate for immigrant children was 28.5 percent compared with about 15 percent each in all immigrant age groups 18 years of age and older. The poverty rate for all children in 2003 was only 17.6 percent, about 7.5 percent of that number were foreign born (U.S. Bureau of the Census, 2004a, p. 7; 2004b, p. 10).

If undocumented immigrants were adequately represented in the data, mean incomes would most likely be lower and the poverty rate higher. Undocumented status renders family members especially vulnerable to exploitation in the workplace and closes off many avenues for economic and professional advancement. Many undocumented persons are hired as nannies, gardeners, cooks, and other forms of nonprofessional jobs at low salaries and without benefits, increasing the stresses on their dependent children.

Language

Many immigrants, especially those arriving from the English-speaking Caribbean, Canada, Great Britain, Ireland, the Philippines and

India, speak English upon arrival. The vast majority of immigrants, however, do not speak English as their native language. According to the 2000 census, 83 percent of foreign born persons over the age of four spoke a language other than English, and 62 percent of them (15.7 million persons) reported that they did not speak English "very well." The situation for immigrant children is harder to ascertain–for one thing, children, particularly young children, tend to learn a language quickly and easily (U.S. Bureau of the Census, 2003).

The Census Bureau sometimes utilizes a related concept–the "linguistically isolated household"–in which no person over the age of 14 speaks English "very well." Not all such households are composed of immigrants, of course; included would be speakers of Native American languages, Spanish in old Spanish communities in New Mexico, creole French speakers in Louisiana, and so forth. But it would be fair to assume that the vast majority of these linguistically isolated households are primarily comprised of immigrant families. The 2000 Census identified 4.4 million such households, encompassing 11.9 million persons. Of those persons aged between five and 17, 9.8 million speak another language (18.4 percent), of whom 6.3 million speak English "very well" and 3.5 million speak English "less than very well." Of those last, 1.3 million speak English "not well" or "not at all." The census counted 2.7 million children living in linguistically isolated households (Bureau of the Census, 2003, p. 10; Table 2).

Limited English proficiency affects not only employment opportunities, but also the power relations among adults and children within families. For example, if the only persons with proficiency in English are preteenaged children–and it is common for younger children to acquire English proficiency before their parents or older siblings, these young children sometimes assume the role of mediators with, and spokespersons to, the social world for the family (Gibson, 1989).

Race

One of the most powerful factors affecting the opportunity structures of immigrants to the United States is the system of racial ascription. While the social effects of racial ascription are quite complex, practitioners should bear in mind a key impact on many immigrants: the system of ascription in their native land most likely differed in important respects from that in the United States. As Hoetink (1985) points out, a man ascribed as being "white" in his native Dominican Republic might travel to Puerto Rico and find himself categorized a "trigueno" (mixed or "wheat colored"), and then, after stepping off of a connecting flight in Atlanta be considered "black" or African American, with all the social disabilities that implies in the United States.

The practitioner should be aware that the immigrant may regard him or herself as having a different racial status than that commonly ascribed in the United States and therefore may be experiencing a dramatic adjustment to this new status.

Strategies of Migration

Migration networks tend to develop over time. Commonly, a few "pioneers" initially establish themselves in the United States. In time, information about opportunities filters back to relatives and friends in the homeland. Others decide to make the journey, perhaps helped by the "pioneer" with advice and/or financing. They in turn help/encourage others to immigrate, creating what is called a "chain" migration, which may involve kin networks, information flows, the development of ethnic enclaves, and the flow of goods and services (Potocky-Tripodi, 2002; Takaki, 1993).

Chain strategies are strongly influenced by both economic opportunities and the laws and regulations governing the issuance of residency documents. Current United States law favors immigration of family members of citizens and residents. Once an individual obtains permission to live and work in the United States, one's relatives may apply to immigrate based on a position on a preference list. Children and parents rank high on such a list, brothers and sisters somewhat lower. For example, one middle-class Colombian woman who obtained work, briefly, as a maid in Miami served as the eventual immigration vehicle for a prosperous extended family of more than twenty persons. First she brought over her older daughter and then her temporarily disabled husband, followed by her youngest child. A variety of brothers, sisters, and cousins followed.

In some cases, how the immigrant gets to the U.S. may have profound consequences for the functioning of families. For some immigrant flows, immigration as a family unit may be the norm. Regulations that governed immigration from the former Soviet Union almost uniquely favored families immigrating as a unit. Often these families were multigenerational and included grandparents (Castex, 1992). Other migratory streams have been characterized by very different patterns. An individual, perhaps a nursing school graduate from the Philippines or Jamaica, might lead the way. These persons may establish families in the United States or, if married, send for their families only after a modicum of financial security has been attained. In some cases years pass before the family is fully reunified, and often school-age children and grandparents are the last to arrive because both parents are working. And, of course, some of the emigrants may abandon or divorce their spouses at home and form new families in the United States.

Attention should also be paid to the difficulties of getting travel documents and to the actual experiences of the journey. Sometimes immigrants have been living for months or years in a state of almost suspended animation awaiting approval to immigrate. Since the future lay abroad, long-term planning was avoided. Many entrants have left their countries under the most trying circumstances. For example, many refugees have escaped under harrowing conditions and sometimes spent months in refugee camps before arriving in the United States. Sometimes young children are not accompanied by any adult family member and must be placed in foster care in the United States. For some political refugees, immigration is seen as a one-time event with no possibility of returning even for a visit; others regard their stay in the United States as temporary while they await political changes in their homeland.

The journey to the United States is particularly harrowing for the undocumented, especially if border controls must be avoided. Anecdotal accounts abound of people who have walked and hitch-hiked to the United States from Central America, prey to every sort of economic and physical abuse; as exemplified below:

The R family—husband, wife, and three children—attempted to walk to the United States from Ecuador, passing around the jungles of Panama and through the Panama Canal by hiding under a false bottom in a banana boat with the fruit loaded on top of them. As they were smuggled off the boat, the family noticed that the oldest daughter had been bitten in the thigh by a spider. Her leg was beginning to swell, and by the time the family finally reached the Mexican border, the daughter's leg had to be amputated due to infection. The mother and two daughters remained in Mexico while the father and son continued on to the United States. The trip lasted three and a half months.

The father made his way to New York City, where he survived by selling flowers at street corners, sending spare funds to his family in Mexico. The family came to the attention of a social welfare agency when the 10-year-old son was referred by the school for truancy and depression.

Immigration regulations often structure the family unit so that the children may be the last to arrive in the United States. Consequently, the child may harbor mixed feelings: joy at the reunion, anger at a sense of abandonment, grief for lost friends and caretakers, a sense of excitement about new possibilities being offered, and/or a sense of disappointment that the new country may not be living up to its advance billing as the place in which all problems will be resolved.

Family composition may also change dramatically. One study of 136 immigrant families in Los Angeles found that 97 (71 percent) did not contain the child's birth parents (Benjamin & Morgan, 1989). Some marriages break up under the stress of migration: parents and siblings may die or are lost; and remarriage results in a reconfiguration of the family.

On the other hand, the cultural norms of a homeland may continue to regulate family life even after migration. Such cultural dynamics must be recognized by practitioners working with immigrant groups (McInniss, 1991). A striking example may be seen among the 100,000 Hmong refugees from Laos, whose traditional social structure, based on a clan system, continues to function in the U.S. The existence of a "super family" led by a clan leader must be understood and acknowledged by practitioners seeking to mobilize economic, community, and emotional support for clients.

Immigration Status

Immigration status is a key issue for all new arrivals. Legal immigration permits, among other things, residency, educational support, and employment, allowing the immigrant to build a more "normal" life in this country. As previously indicated, an undocumented person lives in perpetual fear of deportation, may have to accept employment at substandard wages, and may find it difficult to make long-term plans. In addition, eligibility for many government benefits depends on the applicant's immigration status.

Since eligibility for public benefits varies greatly from state to state and changes over time reflecting the political environment, the worker must be familiar with federal and state regulations. Although certain benefits, most notably the right to emergency medical treatment and the right to a public education, have been available to everyone, regardless of the immigration status, immigrant rights to public services has recently have been challenged in a number of states and in federal law. Currently, some proponents of limitations on services are advocating for the exclusion of non-U.S. citizens, including legal immigrants, from many elements of the existing social safety net.

CONSIDERATIONS FOR TREATMENT

A "stressful event" was defined by Janis and Laventhal (1968) as "any change in the environment which typically . . . induces a high degree of emotional tension and interferes with normal patterns of response" (p. 1043). Even when the move to this country offers new and exciting opportunities for the child and family, by its nature, stress is inevitable. A child often focuses on the most practical details to ensure the stability of his or her world: Where will I go to school? Who will take me there? Who will pick me up? Who will play with me? Can I go outside and play? What will there be to eat? Immigrant parents may not be able to offer the security of having answers to these questions.

Adjusting to new living situations, different food, often learning a new language, learning how to get around, making new friends, and all the other details of daily life in a new country create stress for both parents and children. Unfortunately, stress may interfere with the availability of parental help for children at a time when the children have lost all their other support systems. Further, it may be difficult for children to separate the fact that they barely speak English from their strengths. They may have a low self-concept because they speak English with an accent, feeling dumb, shy, and isolated when to an adult they may seem bright, charming, and doing quite well.

Of course many other issues can affect self-esteem. A middle school boy from Ghana, fluent in English, has been asked by his (racially and ethnically diverse) classmates "Why are you so dark?" The child has no answer. On another occasion, a girl comments to him: "No-one will go out with you. You will make real dark babies." He begins to feel that he will never fit in and will always be looked upon as weird.

The events that people regard as stressful may differ at different stages of the life cycle. A stressful event for a child differs from that perceived by an adult. For example, an immigrant child accustomed to receiving top grades in school may now be struggling just to keep up, and the parent's statement that "the only thing we expect is that you do the best you can" does not help the child incorporate an understanding of the difficulties in the adjustment process nor does it address the underlying emotional issues that the child may be experiencing.

Age of the Child

The age of the child at the date of arrival is an important factor in adjustment (Castex, 1992). Learning English, for example, without a "foreign" accent may not be an issue for a child who migrated as a preteen, yet an older sibling who will speak with an accent for the rest of his or her life may always feel like a "foreigner" and perhaps be stigmatized by his or her peers. Likewise, a teenager entering the United States may experience delays in the mastery of age-appropriate developmental tasks while adjusting to the new environment.

Changing Roles

With a potential reconfiguration of the family and a novel social setting, the roles of all family members will likely be renegotiated. The authority of the parents and the confidence with which they exercise their authority may be challenged by role shifts in the family. Sometimes the role of the school-aged child is enhanced, especially, as is often the case, if the child develops English language proficiency more quickly and at a higher level than the parents.

Children become responsible for negotiating with landlords, serving as translators in school settings, medical facilities, financial institutions, and negotiating purchases. Such power in the hands of children creates stress because children may not always understand the implications of what they are translating and may feel that the burden of the family's relations with the world are upon their shoulders. For example, a young child may accompany a parent to the hospital and serve as the interpreter, even though the child may be unfamiliar with medical terms in English and may be worried about the condition of the parent. The child may also be placed in a particularly difficult position if he or she is the subject of the conversation that is taking place. Therefore, as much as possible, the clinician should use a trained interpreter when providing services to immigrant families who do not speak the language of the worker, rather than utilize services of a child. In addition, if a child's education and the opportunities available in the United States are stated reasons for immigrating, such expectations may place the burden of the whole family's sacrifices on the child, compounding the burden of identifying and achieving his or her own goals and ambitions.

The maturation process of any child calls for continuing renegotiation of appropriate roles into adulthood. But for immigrants there is the additional conflict created by the child's immersion into the host society. Concepts of appropriate behavior may be examined from two differing sets of values: those of the homeland at the time of emigration and those of the United States at the current time. For many adolescents, common conflicts include such issues as dating, financial support of the family, or forms of address to elders. The assumption of responsibilities for dealing with the social world may paradoxically inhibit adolescents from assuming a more independent stance in relation to their parents. For example, they may feel too guilty about leaving their parents to go away to college. They may also feel too psychologically insecure in the new country to begin their own lives.

Loss, Grief, and Trauma

Children as well as parents experience the loss of a homeland with all of its traditions and associations, friends, speech forms, and climate; even the look and smell of the homeland can be experienced as a loss. Every member of an immigrant family may be grieving his or her losses; however, it is important to realize that their individual perception of those losses might be quite different. A child may be missing family and friends, native climate, surroundings, and other familiar things, even the type of bread or his or her favorite pillow. Sometimes the child's homeland, such as Yugoslavia, may no longer exist–some people literally can't go home again. Given the magnitude of their losses, and the stresses they have endured, there may be a need for a long period of mourning.

On occasion, however, these losses become entangled with the gains that the child experiences as a result of immigration such as more food, a more sophisticated technological life style, new friends, and the excitement of a new physical environment. Therefore, the child may have difficulty sorting through his or her mixed emotions.

Many immigrant children also will be dealing with trauma: the trauma of abuse, of death, of violence, of hunger. One study found a 60 percent rate of posttraumatic stress disorder among refugee children from El Salvador who had witnessed political violence (including massacre, death squads, and torture) and had been separated for a period of time from their primary caregiver (Oakes & Lucas, 2001). A trauma for a child–unlike for an adult–interrupts a growth process and interferes with the acquisition of new skills. It is not enough for these children to return to old levels of functioning; they must make up for lost time (Steele, 2004).

INTERVENTIONS

The broad diversity among immigrants underlines the impossibility of devising uniform protocols for the delivery of services to immigrant children. Clinicians must recognize the diversity among members of each group and of the constantly changing composition of immigrant streams, even those deriving from the same country. Moreover, patterns of migration may differ within families. Cookie cutter or programmed models of practice that tend to stereotype people are largely ineffective for any client; the fact that immigrant populations are by their nature diverse merely underlines the need for individualized interventions as the basis of effective practice.

Intervention approaches need to take into account such individual factors as country of origin, time of arrival, age, race, religion, and eco-

nomic status, to name a few. A comprehensive asses
way for the clinician to address issues arising from th
current situation. Clinicians need to select the most a
ment model, such as play therapy, "talk" therapy wi
bibliotherapy, group work, or family therapy. Clini
be become familiar with community resources availaɒic ɪu ɔ
These include medical/dental, educational, housing, nutrition, recreational resources, keeping in mind that the legal status of the immigrant child may limit the services available to them.

Several well known assessment and treatment perspectives are particularly helpful when providing direct services to immigrant children. They include the "Stage-of-Migration" framework developed by Drachman (1992), which identifies three phases in the migration process. In exploring the first phase, the *premigration and departure* phase–the clinician has the opportunity to learn about the social, political and economic factors that affected the child back home. It also addresses reasons for departure, losses and other pertinent issues. The second phase, *transit,* alerts the clinician to the experiences during the journey to the United States, such as residing in refugee camps relocations, mode of transportation, perils encountered. Information about the final phase, *resettlement,* fosters an understanding of the client's life after arrival in the host country as well as the concerns and issues for referral (Drachman, 1992).

The Life Cycle model (Hutchinson, 2003; Zastrow & Kirst-Ashman, 2004) offers useful insights based on the developmental tasks of individuals as they move through the life cycle. This model takes into account not only the age and stage of the child from pre-school to adolescence, but also the stages and challenges facing the various family members. The Ecological Systems perspective (Germain, 1973) looks at the child's interactions and the "fit" between the child and his or her physical and social environment. Both of these models may be particularly useful when working with immigrant children who are facing developmental tasks while simultaneously attempting to master a new, "foreign" environment.

In order to effectively help immigrant children with their numerous challenges, such as new cultural norms and language, making new friends, and dealing with stresses at home, the practitioner will need to utilize a variety of clinical strategies. Among those particularly useful when working with immigrant children are the following:

- **Generalization:** Given the isolation common to many new immigrants, it important that children's experiences be normalized. With young children, it may be helpful to read stories about immigrant children and about the feelings that accompany this life change, thereby helping children to understand that their experiences are not unusual.
- **Expression of Feelings:** Activities such as drawing, play, and interacting with other immigrant children may be utilized to help children express feelings about their life changes. Putting together a child's life-book, which includes stories, photos, maps, and other available momentos, as well as souvenirs documenting the immigration experience—their arrival and adjustment—can be a powerful healing technique as a child incorporates his or her history.
- **Peer Support:** With adolescents, peer support groups comprised of immigrant children may help to normalize their feelings as well as provide practical advice regarding social survival. Adolescents can talk about the situations and emotions that they are experiencing. Books, films, field trips to different neighborhoods, cooking classes using favorite family recipes, and the encouragement of writing poetry and journals may also be effective techniques for helping adolescents work through their emotions and concerns as they try to bridge their past lives with the present.

In addition to these direct interventions, practitioners need to become involved with policy practice, particularly as social welfare policies affect immigrant children and their families.

CONCLUSION

For most immigrants, the United States offers opportunities unavailable to them in their homelands. In helping immigrant families benefit from these opportunities, interventions need to address both concrete resettlement issues, such as finding housing, employment, healthcare, appropriate school placement, and acquisition of language skills. In addition, clinical issues that focus on the social and emotional adjustment to a new society must be addressed. The practitioner must have a knowledge base of available resources as well as an awareness of the various issues and dynamics impacting immigrant parents and children.

While life in the United States may have been presented unrealistically to the child, as a sort of utopia, for example, a realistic sense of hope can be defined, leading him or her in the direction of realizing some of these opportunities and the enjoyment of a full life. Regardless of the legal and policy changes, vigilante border patrols, or other means that may be developed to discourage people from coming to the United States, people will come. Furthermore, there is a need for their labor, energy, and creativity.

Helping immigrant children access new opportunities for growth and development and adjust to the best of their capacities, and working on a policy level to improve their lives, can be a most rewarding and satisfying experience for social workers.

REFERENCES

Benjamin, M. P., & Morgan, P. C. (1989). *Refugee children traumatized by war and violence: The challenge offered the service delivery system.* Washington, DC: CASSP Technical Assistance Center, Georgetown University Child Development Center.

Castex, G. (1992). Soviet refugee children: The dynamic of migration and school practice. *Social Work in Education, 14,* 141–152.

Cienfuegos, E. (2004, September 14). Heinous hate murders of undocumented Mexican immigrants on the rise. *La Voz de Aztlan.* http://www.aztlan.net/murder_mexican_immigrants_rise.htm. Accessed June 25, 2005.

Delgado, M., Jones, K., & Rohani, M. (2005). *Social work practice with refugee and immigrant youth in the United States.* Boston: Pearson Education.

Drachman, D. (1992). A stage-of-migration framework for service to immigrant populations. *Social Work, 37,* 67–72.

Germain, C. B. (1973). An ecological perspective on social work practice. *Social Casework, 54*(6), 323–330.

Gibson, M. A. (1988). *Accommodation without assimilation: Sikh immigrant children in an American high school.* Ithaca, NY: Cornell University Press.

Hoetink, H. (1985). "Race" and color in the Caribbean. In S. W. Mintz & S. Price (Eds.), *Caribbean contours.* Baltimore: The Johns Hopkins University Press.

Hutchison, E. D. (2003). *Dimensions of human behavior: The changing life course* (2nd ed.). Thousand Oaks, CA: Sage.

Janis, I. L., & Laventhal, H. (1968). Human reactions to stress. In E. F. Borgatta & W. W. Lambert (Eds.), *Handbook of personality theory and research.* Chicago: Rand McNally.

Madigan, N. (2005, May 26). Early heat wave kills 12 illegal immigrants in the Arizona desert. *The New York Times.* A18.

Mansfield, D. (2005, July 18). Volunteer group fighting illegal immigration spreads far from the Mexican Border. *Seattle Times.* http://www.seattletimes.nwssource. com (The Associated Press). Accessed July 19, 2005.

McCullagh, D. (2005, February 14). National ID cards on the way? http://news.com.com/National=ID=cards=on=the=way/2100-1028_3-5573414.html Accessed July 19, 2005.

McInniss, K. (1991). Ethnic sensitive work with Hmong refugee children. *Child Welfare, 70,* 571–580.

Oakes, M. G., & Lucas, F. (2001). How war affects daily life: Adjustments in Salvadoran social networks. *Journal of Social Work Research and Evaluation, 2*(2), 143–155.

Nah, Kyung-Hee. (1993). Perceived problems and service delivery for Korean immigrants. *Social Work, 38,* 289–296.

Potocky-Tripodi, M. (2002). *Best practices for social work with refugees.* New York: Columbia University Press.

Sanchez, M. (June 15, 2005). Steer clear of national ID card. www.fortwayne.com/ mld/newssentinel/news/editorial/118995. Accessed July 19, 2005.

Steele, W. (2004). Helping traumatized children. In S. L. A. Straussner & N. K. Phillips (Eds.), *Understanding mass violence: A social work perspective* (pp.41-56). Boston: Allyn & Bacon.

Takaki, R. S. (1993). *A different mirror: A history of multicultural America.* Boston: Little, Brown & Company.

U.S. Bureau of the Census. (2004a). *The foreign-born population in the United States: 2003.* Current Population Reports, P20-551. Washington, DC: Author.

_____. (2004b). *Income, poverty, and health insurance coverage in the United States: 2003.* Current Population Reports, P60-226. Washington, DC: Author. (With supplementary tables at www.census.gov.)

_____. (2003). *Language use and English-speaking ability: 2000.* Census 2000 Briefs Series, C2KBR-29. Washington, DC: Author. (www.census.gov.).

_____. (2001). *The Hispanic population: 2000.* Census 2000 Briefs Series, C2KBR/01-3. Washington, DC: Author. (www.census.gov.).

_____. (1993a). Profiles of the foreign-born population: Selected characteristics by place of birth. CPH-L-148. Washington, DC: Author.

_____. (1993b). *Statistical Abstract of the United States, 1993.* Washington, DC: Author.

U.S. Citizenship and Immigration Services website: http://www.uscis.gov.

U.S. Department of Homeland Security, U.S. Citizenship and Immigration Services, Office of Citizenship Services. (2005). *Welcome to the United States: A guide for immigrants.* Washington DC: Author.

Zastrow, & Kirst-Ashman. (2004). *Understanding human behavior and the social environment.* (6th ed.). Belmont, CA: Brooks/Cole.

Chapter 4

HEALTH ISSUES AFFECTING URBAN CHILDREN

DIANE MIRABITO AND CHRISHANA LLOYD

Children living in urban communities experience a range of particular health risks. This chapter will provide an overview of common health concerns and discuss health care policies and service delivery issues affecting urban youth and families. The health issues addressed include asthma, lead poisoning, sickle cell disease, obesity, and adolescent health. In addition, a description of the multifaceted role of social workers in a range of health care settings, including inpatient and outpatient services, and community-based health clinics is explored.

RISK FACTORS IN HEALTH CARE

The impact of poverty, environmental pollutants, and limited access to health care all contribute to increased risks for poor health among children and adolescents and their families living in urban communities (Schneider & Northridge, 1999).

Poverty as a Risk Factor

Research studies show that children living below the poverty level are less likely than children in higher income families to be described as being in "very good" or "excellent" health (Federal Interagency Forum on Child and Family Statistics, 2004). They have also been found to be at greater risk of dying earlier than their peers. For example, according to Schneider and Northridge (1999), as a result of health risks, only one out of three boys and two out of three girls, age 15, who are growing up in Harlem in New York City, are expected to live to age 65. It is also clear that many of these health problems are preventable (Epstein, 2003).

Homeless children and their families, especially those in urban communities, are at particularly high risk for health problems. They experience an increased incidence of health and mental health problems related to poor nutrition, lack of medical and dental care, environmental stresses, and life stresses. They are more likely to suffer from cold symptoms, diarrhea, and are at a greater risk for infections, chronic respiratory difficulties, and behavioral problems. In addition, homelessness is associated with increased risk of burns, accidents, injuries, and exposure to lead (Nabors, Weist, Shugarman, Woeste, Mullet, & Rosner, 2004).

Environmental Risk Factors

Poor air quality, substandard housing, lack of safe outdoor space for exercise and play, and community violence, place urban children at high risk for a variety of health problems, such as asthma, lead poisoning, and obesity. In 2002, 34 percent of children under age 18 lived in areas that did not meet one or more of the Primary National Ambient Air Quality Standards, a significant increase from 19 percent reported in 2001 (Federal Interagency Forum on Child and Family Statistics, 2004). Children are uniquely vulnerable to environmental pollutants due to their rapid growth rate and less-developed metabolism. As a result, there are greater possibilities of latent effects of asthma and lead poisoning in exposed children as compared to adults.

Environmental pollutants also affect infant mortality, which increased during 2002 for the first time in decades. In addition, research has shown that prenatal exposure to environmental pollutants adversely affects fetal development (Perera et al., 2003). While low birth weight (under 5.5 lbs) averaged at 7.8 percent nationally, the rate for African-American infants was 13.4 percent. This was the highest rate reported among all racial and ethnic groups (Federal Interagency Forum on Child and Family Statistics, 2004).

Lack of Access to Health Care

More children in the United States have been immunized against diphtheria, influenza, hepatitis B, measles, mumps, pertussis, rubella, tetanus, and chicken pox than any time in the past; however, large numbers of urban children, particularly recent immigrants, remain under-immunized. This is primarily due to exclusion from federal assistance programs, language and cultural barriers, and high levels of mobility and relocation (Schneider & Northridge, 1999).

While impoverished urban children and families require additional services to improve their health outcomes, they experience numerous barriers to obtaining medical care, including transportation difficulties, language and cultural obstacles, and a lack of health insurance. As a result, urban children and families receive less optimal medical care and tend to use emergency care services more frequently than other children (Redmond, 2001).

Urban adolescents have special health care needs, but due to lack of medical insurance, they are not always able to access needed health care. The largest health care expenses for adolescents are for injury, mental health, substance abuse, and pregnancy, in contrast to younger children for whom health care focuses on congenital and respiratory conditions (Millstein & Litt, 1990; Newacheck, Wong, Galbraith, & Hung, 2003).

HEALTH CARE POLICIES AND THEIR IMPACT ON URBAN CHILDREN

The United States is the only industrialized country in the world that has not established universal health coverage. Many children lack health insurance, including children in poor families who currently do not receive Medicaid, and the working poor and middle class families who do not receive health insurance through their employment and are unable to afford to pay for health insurance themselves. In 2003, 8.4 million, or 11.4 percent of all children in the U.S., were without health insurance. Children of color who were living in poverty had the highest uninsured rate. This was particularly true for Hispanic children; in 2003, 21 percent were without health insurance, as compared to 14.5 percent African-American children, 12.4 percent Asian children, and 7.4 percent white children (Kenney, Haley, & Tebay, 2003). Adolescents are more likely to be uninsured than younger children. Approximately one out of every six teenagers ages 15 to 18 lacks health coverage (Newacheck et al., 2003). In 2003, 12.7 percent of children 12 to 17 years old were uninsured, compared to 10.6 percent of younger children (Kenney et al., 2003).

The introduction of the new welfare legislation, Temporary Assistance to Needy Families (TANF) in 1996, resulted in rapidly declining welfare rolls; however, it left many families previously covered by Medicaid without any health insurance. Prior to the introduction of this legislation, people receiving public assistance automatically received health insurance through the Medicaid program. The new legislation "de-linked" TANF and Medicaid, providing for separate administration of these two programs, with separate eligibility requirements for each. Despite their eligibility, many people did not enroll in the Medicaid program, resulting in their loss of health insurance (Lloyd, 2002; Wood et al., 2002). In a study by Polit, London, and Martinez (2001), it was found that 30 percent of women who left welfare had children who were eligible for Medicaid, but had not been insured during the previous month, as compared with 7 percent of women who remained on welfare. In addition, many families who were determined to be ineligible for TANF were also improperly terminated from Medicaid (Schott, 2000).

Another health insurance program that was developed especially for children in families transitioning from welfare to work, as well as in other low-income working families, is the State Children's Health Insurance Program (CHIP), which was mandated by the federal government in 1997. By placing greater responsibility for public health insurance programs with the individual states, CHIP represented the most profound change in federally sponsored, state implemented health insurance since the introduction of the Medicaid program in 1965. CHIP provided states with $40 billion in federal block grants over a ten-year period to further expand publicly provided health insurance for children. Each state determines eligibility criteria for the Children's Health Insurance Program, resulting in a wide variation in how it is implemented (Shore-Sheppard, 2003). Since its inception, CHIP has been highly underutilized due to lack of public information about its availability (Phillips & Straussner, 2002).

HEALTH ISSUES AFFECTING CHILDREN AND ADOLESCENTS IN URBAN AREAS

While there are many health conditions that are commonly seen in children and adolescents living in the cities, and a wide variety of environmental issues contributing to their existence, this section will focus on some of the most common urban health problems, including asthma, lead poisoning, childhood obesity, sickle cell disease, and health conditions affecting adolescents. Such chronic health conditions increase daily stresses for the caregivers caring for these children, and they are more likely to experience high levels of anxiety and depression due to frustrations often connected to emergency room visits and the higher likelihood that their children will be hospitalized (Wood, Smith, Romero, Bradshaw, Wise, & Chavkin, 2002).

Further, exposure to urban violence has a particularly destructive impact on families caring for a child with a chronic illness. Families exposed to violence are more likely to view their world and their lives as being out of their control, to suffer more harmful effects from stress, and to face greater challenges managing a chronic illness, such as following up with medical care and exercise programs. Children who are kept indoors as protection from potential violence in neighborhoods tend to develop a sedentary lifestyle, placing them at even greater risk for continued health problems, particularly asthma and obesity (Wright et al., 2004).

Asthma

Asthma, a chronic respiratory illness, is the most prevalent chronic childhood disease in the United States, and over the past thirty years, there have been substantial increases in its prevalence, morbidity, and mortality (Wood et al., 2002). Asthma rates have increased by 42 percent over the last decade, affecting approximately 7 percent of children under age 18 (Federal Interagency Forum on Child and Family Statistics, 2004). The incidence and mortality rates from asthma are increasing considerably more rapidly among urban children from low socioeconomic backgrounds (Mitchell & Murdock, 2002). The prevalence and mortality rates associated with asthma in poor urban communities are disproportionately higher than national rates (Graham,

2004; Schneider & Northridge, 1999). While the national prevalence of asthma in children under 18 years of age is estimated at 7 percent, prevalence rates in urban African-American and Hispanic-American populations are reported to be 20 to 25 percent (Graham, 2004).

The rapid increase in the incidence of asthma in poor urban communities is linked to the prevalence of risk factors within these environments, including air pollutants, environmental and in utero tobacco smoke, viral infections, and indoor allergens, such as cockroach allergen, which are often found in substandard housing (Schneider & Northridge, 1999). In addition to these environmental risk factors, there is increasing evidence that exposure to violence, high levels of stress, and unpredictable daily life experiences, common elements of life in the inner city, all place children at substantially higher risk for asthma (Wright et al., 2004).

Like many chronic illnesses, asthma is particularly difficult to manage because it generally cannot be cured and its path is unpredictable. While the majority of children do not grow out of asthma, the severity tends to decrease with age. With proper treatment and attention to environmental details, asthma can be managed fairly effectively. Unfortunately, contextual and environmental stressors often make it difficult to successfully manage asthma in low-income urban children and adolescents.

Youth who are diagnosed with moderate and severe asthma may experience a multitude of psychosocial issues that merit social work attention. Children and adolescents often need to take medications during school hours, requiring that social workers collaborate with school medical staff to help facilitate this process. Moreover, children may need to limit their participation in physical education classes and extracurricular sports activities, creating an increased risk of obesity and an increase in social isolation. They also may miss school frequently due to unpredictable asthma attacks, resulting in poor academic progress and limited social relationships. In addition, caregivers of children with asthma often experience higher levels of stress because they need to be available to accompany their children to multiple medical visits. Working, low income caregivers are often penalized financially and face potential job loss resulting from the time taken from work to care for their children (Lloyd, 2002).

The incidence of asthma has been found to be more than six times the national rate in a study of a random sample of homeless children in New York City. In addition to experiencing more severe symptoms, homeless children with asthma also tend to lack consistent medical treatment and have more frequent emergency room visits (McLean et al., 2004).

Lead Poisoning

Lead poisoning is one of the most serious environmental health hazards threatening children. After repeated exposure, lead is absorbed by the body and may cause learning disabilities, neurological problems, attention difficulties, developmental delays, behavior problems, kidney damage, and at very high levels, seizures and death. As of 2004, almost 900,000 children had elevated blood lead levels and it is estimated that one out of every 20 children in the United States has some lead poisoning without visible signs or symptoms. However, severe lead poisoning requiring the attention of a physician occurs in only a small percentage of children, primarily those who are medically underserved (Federal Interagency Forum on Child and Family Statistics, 2004).

While all children are at potential risk of lead exposure, the risk is significantly higher for children of color whose families live in older housing in urban communities. Minority children are at five times greater risk of exposure to lead poisoning than white children. Good nutrition can offset the effects of exposure to lead. However, children with poor diets lack the opportunity to reduce the toxic effects of exposure (Children's Defense Fund, 2004).

Since lead poisoning is an environmental problem that is entirely preventable, it is essential to educate families and health care providers about both strategies to prevent its occurrence, and the importance of screening children who are at risk while they are young. The American Academy of Pediatrics recommends that all children considered at risk of lead poisoning receive a blood lead test from a health care provider. If blood testing shows a high level of lead, it then becomes essential to eliminate the sources of lead in the environment and improve nutrition (Children's Defense Fund, 2004).

Cultural Issues

It is important that social workers, particularly those who work with diverse populations in urban environments, are knowledgeable about the role culture may play in the acquisition of lead poisoning. Latino children, particularly those living in Mexican-American families, may be exposed to home remedies for stomach ailments such as "greta" and "azarcon" which are made of almost 100 percent lead (Centers for Disease Control and Prevention, 2002). In addition, certain sweets, particularly those containing tamarind, have high lead content. Further, some pottery and drinking glasses used in Mexican-American families often have high lead content. Children and adolescents in families from the Dominican Republic may be exposed to "litargirio," a peach or yellow colored powder containing lead that has a multitude of uses, including a common use as a deodorant (Washington State Department of Health, 2004).

Asian Indian families may use lead-based folk medicines such as "bala goli," "ghasard," and "kandu" for intestinal problems. Middle Eastern folk remedies include the use of "bint al zahab" for treating colic, and "farouk" for teething babies. Certain preparations used in the Arab and Indian communities may contain "kohl" or "surma," which have high lead content and are generally used for cosmetic and medicinal purposes (Washington State Department of Health, 2004). Since these remedies are native to their particular cultures, caregivers may not think to discuss them with medical staff because they view them as insignificant, or because they might feel that they will be stigmatized by western health providers.

When conducting psychosocial assessments of children and families, social workers must be knowledgeable regarding culturally competent practice. This includes the ability to develop rapport with patients and their families, including nonjudgmental interviewing techniques, to ensure that they feel comfortable sharing information about medical practices native to their countries.

Sickle Cell Disease

Sickle cell disease refers to a group of genetic disorders characterized by chronic anemia causing pain episodes in the back, abdomen, or extremities. Hospitalization may be required, and severe health complications such as organ damage or stroke can result from repeated episodes. As a result of genetic predisposition, sickle cell disease affects African-American and Caribbean children and adolescents at a higher rate than the general population (Lorey, Arnopp & Cunningham, 1996). Approximately one in 400 African- American children is affected by sickle cell disease at birth, a disproportionate number of whom live in the inner city (Burlew, 2002).

Adolescents who grow up with sickle cell disease frequently experience delays in both physical growth and the onset of puberty. Since these children need to rely more on parents and health care providers at a time that they are seeking independence, they often experience feelings of powerlessness, dependence, depression, and low self-esteem. As a result of excessive absences resulting from frequent hospitalizations, adolescents with sickle cell tend to be academically delayed and may need to repeat grades (Telfair & Gardner, 2000).

Individual differences in adjustment to sickle cell are based on psychosocial factors rather than medical severity. Consequently, assessment on a case-by-case basis is particularly important, as there are significant differences in the emotional status of affected children (Burlew, 2002). Interventions may include education, as well as individual, family, and group treatment. Self-help groups may also be useful. Psychosocial treatment often includes cognitive-behavioral interventions for managing pain, nutritional education, and support for developing coping strategies for patients and their families (Kaslow & Brown, 1995).

Support groups can be valuable to youth with this disease as they can help in reducing isolation, fostering a sense of identity, encouraging empowerment, and facilitating giving and receiving support. Adolescents utilize support groups to gain information about sickle cell disease, solve problems, and learn skills and strategies for coping with related life experiences (Telfair & Gardner, 2000). In addition to support groups, social work interventions can empower families by providing them with education about the illness and teaching communication and problem-solving skills to negotiate the medical care system. These interventions enable families to assert themselves with medical professionals in order to ensure that their children receive optimal care (Kaslow & Brown, 1995).

Obesity

Overweight and obesity are both labels for ranges of weight that are greater than what is generally considered healthy for a given height.

Since children's body fatness changes as they grow, the body mass index (BMI), which is used to assess weight appropriateness, is age as well as gender specific (Pietrobelli, Faith, Allison, Gallagher, Chiumello, & Heymsfield, 1998). While only 6 percent of children were overweight in 1980, this proportion rose to 11 percent in 1994, and continued to rise to 16 percent in 2002. Moreover, while the proportion of overweight children in poor urban environments has risen dramatically, so have malnutrition and hunger. In 2002, 18 percent of children nationwide lived in households classified by the United States Department of Agriculture as "food insecure"–lacking nutritionally adequate food sources (Federal Interagency Forum on Child and Family Statistics, 2004).

The prevalence of overweight and obesity in children has increased dramatically in the last 25 years. In 2002, the National Health and Nutrition Examination Survey reported that 16 percent of children and adolescents, ages six to 19, were overweight, and an additional 15 percent of children were considered at risk of becoming overweight. These rates represent a three-fold increase in overweight children and adolescents since 1980 (National Center for Health Statistics, 2003).

Numerous studies have established that there are substantial racial and ethnic disparities in obesity rates. According to the 2003 National Center for Health Statistics, the rate of overweight and obese children, ages two to twelve years, living in predominantly Latino and African-American neighborhoods, ranged from 50 to 68 percent, as compared to the national average of 26 percent. Among the different Latino populations, Mexican-American children, ages six to 11, were more likely to be overweight (22 percent) than black (20 percent) or white children (14 percent). Among adolescents, African-Americans and Mexican-Americans, ages 12 to 19, were almost twice as likely to be overweight (23 percent) when compared to white adolescents (14 percent) (National Center for Health Statistics, 2003).

The increased incidence of obesity among urban children of color is often due to poverty and the prevalence of fast food establishments in low-income neighborhoods (Block, Scribner, & DeSalvo, 2004). Further, sedentary behavior resulting from a reduction in physical education classes in many urban schools and limited opportunities for safe, active outdoor play contribute to the problem. In addition to these factors, the significantly higher rates of pediatric asthma among urban youth curtail children's activity levels, resulting in obesity

(Stagg, 2004). Longer-term physiological effects of obesity include increased risks of medical complications such as diabetes, high blood pressure, heart disease, high cholesterol, and kidney failure (Must, Spadano, & Coakley, 1999).

The psychosocial implications of being overweight are vast. Overweight youth have been shown to be more anxious and have poorer social skills than their normal weight peers. Heavier children are often teased and bullied by their peers, which can lead to feelings of hopelessness and depression (French, Story, & Perry, 1995). While some overweight youth might purposely isolate themselves from interactions with their peers, others engage in self-destructive behaviors that may offer opportunities for peer acceptance, such as smoking, drug use, and other risky activities.

Health Conditions Affecting Adolescents

Millstein and Litt (1990) define adolescent health as, "living up to one's potential; being able to function physically, mentally, and socially and experiencing positive emotional states" (p. 431). Behavioral factors are particularly important in adolescent health because they impact both morbidity and mortality. Moreover, many health-related behaviors developed in adolescence can be linked to the presence of health problems or disease in later life. Adolescent mortality results not only from disease, but also from social, environmental, and behavioral factors that could be preventable (Millstein & Litt, 1990).

The overall health of poor, minority urban adolescents is worse than that of economically advantaged adolescents. Urban adolescents have higher rates of substance use/abuse as well as greater rates of mortality. They also have lower rates of condom use, which places them at greater risk for HIV and other sexually transmitted infections, as well as for pregnancy. Although there has been a 14 percent national decrease in adolescent pregnancy since 1990, pregnancy rates among low-income African-American and Latino youth, while declining, are still considerably higher than the national rates (Battle, 2002).

It is important that clinical interventions address the special needs of adolescents by helping them obtain comprehensive, affordable, and confidential health care (Brindis, Klein, Schlitt, Santelli, Juszcak, & Nystrom, 2003). Social workers need to be knowledgeable about policy issues that determine access to family planning, abortion, and health care services for adolescents, as these vary from state to state. For example, emergency Medicaid is available to pregnant teenagers and, in some states, adolescents may require parental notification or consent for health care services in order to obtain health care services and abortions. In 2000, 43 states required that young women under the age of 18 obtain either parental notification or consent in order to obtain an abortion (Henry J. Kaiser Family Foundation, 2000). In all situations where parents are involved, it is essential to engage and involve parents in a way that balances sharing information about the adolescent's health without violating his/her need for and legal right to confidentiality. When parents have questions about health issues, it is important for them to understand that oftentimes permission from the adolescent is necessary before any information can be provided (Diaz, 1998a; 1998b).

During the assessment and intervention processes, adolescents need to feel free to communicate with health care providers about the wide range of issues related to their health. This includes concerns ranging from acne and weight, to those concerning depression, school, or family problems. A useful tool to guide social work assessment and intervention is the HEADSS Assessment Framework. This tool provides attention to key areas of concern to adolescents, including: *Home, Education* and *Employment, Activities, Drugs, Sexuality,* and *Suicide Risk/Depression Screening* (Cohen, Mackenzie, & Yates, 1991). Utilization of a comprehensive framework that includes exploration of each of these areas can be helpful in obtaining a thorough biopychosocial assessment of both risk and protective factors for adolescents and their families (Diaz, 1998a; 1998c).

THE ROLE OF THE SOCIAL WORKER IN
HEALTH CARE SETTINGS

The health care system in the United States is a vast and complex institution that utilizes the skills and expertise of numerous professionals. Social workers have been part of this system in a formal manner since the early 1900s, when Ida M. Cannon, the nation's first medical social worker, began addressing the psychosocial needs of patients and families who were seen in outpatient medical settings (Bartlett, 1975). Fortunately, social work services are no longer limited to just outpatient settings.

Social work professionals are actively engaged in many aspects of the medical system, including working in emergency rooms, in- and out-patient medical settings, and community-based health care agencies, as well as participating in medical research, and policy development and implementation. A large part of the social work role centers on interdisciplinary collaboration, which is a necessary and valuable part of medical social work. In health-related settings, it is typical for social workers to work with other professionals on interdisciplinary teams, and to communicate with a wide array of professionals such as physicians, nurses, dieticians, occupational, physical and speech therapists, psychiatrists, dentists, child life specialists, teachers, and others.

In addition to interdisciplinary collaboration, social workers working in health care engage in numerous tasks that are distinct to the social work profession. Following is a comprehensive, but certainly not inclusive, discussion of the multiple functions of social workers who practice in urban health care systems with children, adolescents, and their caregivers:

Assessment

Social workers provide input about psychosocial functioning of the child and family to help guide the treatment and intervention process with the identified client (child or adolescent) and often their caretakers (i.e., parents, caregivers, agency staff). Social work assessments should be strengths based and include a comprehensive review of the patient's psychosocial development and history. In addition to eliciting information relevant to the patient, such as biological, psychological, developmental, socioeconomic, and environmental factors, social workers also need to explore sociocultural factors such as race, ethnicity, religion, sexual orientation, culture, and disability, and the ways that these factors may impact the treatment and intervention process.

Treatment/Intervention Planning

Most medical settings require treatment plans, which are written documents that identify and describe all the testing, medical, and psychosocial services planned for a patient. Treatment plans may address the goals related to many areas of functioning, including medical, psychological, and educational goals. Treatment plans also facilitate communication and coordination with medical professionals, parents, teachers, and other professionals who may be involved with the care of the patient outside the medical environment. They are reviewed on a regular basis to assess how well the patient is progressing and are updated and revised as needed.

Discharge Planning

Discharge planning refers to the steps that social workers take to determine the best way to meet the patient's ongoing health care needs following discharge from the hospital or health care facility. Discharge planning involves coordinating and managing services for both the patient and family. Ideally, discharge planning should be an interdisciplinary process that ensures continuity of care and optimal service provision in the home, institution, and/or community.

Counseling

Medical social workers can engage in crisis, brief, or long term counseling. The length of counseling depends on the role of the social worker within the medical setting, as well as on the patients' needs. The counseling process in medical settings generally involves helping children and families maximize the strengths of the child and the family while accommodating to his/her illness. It explores personal and environmental opportunities, as well as the limitations that may interfere with the child's treatment process. In many cases, counseling is an integral component of the child's medical recommendations.

Case Management

In their role as case manager, social workers identify current and potential challenges the child and family may face, and identify and coordinate resources, either in the medical facility or the community, which will contribute to optimal functioning of the child and the family.

Advocacy

In medical settings, social work advocacy includes actively engaging in activities that will assure the best possible services and/or interventions for the child and caregivers. Methods of advocacy include verbal and written communication, and activities that are consistent with supporting, and/or acting on behalf of clients. Advocacy occurs in multiple arenas–ranging from individual client advocacy to policy practice (Phillips & Straussner, 2002).

In addition to performing these roles, social workers engage in other activities in and outside of the medical environment, including: participating in training, supervision, and meetings; making linkages with the community on behalf of the patient; serving on quality assurance panels and ethics committees; and appropriately documenting patient care in accordance with insurance and medical accreditation bodies.

CASE ILLUSTRATION

The multifaceted role of the urban medical social worker is seen in a range of settings where services to children are provided, including community health centers, inpatient and outpatient services, emergency rooms, and school-based health clinics. The roles and skills described above need to be used selectively, based on client need and the role of the social worker within the setting. The following case vignette illustrates the use of many of these roles.

The Case of Victor

Victor Ramirez is a 10-year-old Guatemalan boy living with his biological parents, Miguel and Gina, and a younger sister, Maria, age five, in Washington, D.C. Victor was recently admitted to a well-known children's hospital because of extreme fatigue. After several tests and meetings with medical specialists, it was determined that Victor, who is grossly overweight, was suffering from juvenile diabetes and renal failure. The family was referred to Julia, the unit social worker, by Victor's nurse, who was concerned because the family did not have health insurance. Julia immediately determined that the lack of insurance was only one of many issues that the family would have to contend with in the near future. She was concerned with how the family would be affected by Victor's new diagnoses, and also was concerned about how Victor would experience the transition from the hospital to home and then to outpatient care.

Julia had been assigned to the pediatric inpatient unit because she was noted for having excellent engagement and assessment skills, and, after years of experience, she knew how to develop a rapport with families fairly quickly. Moreover, Julia spoke Spanish, which proved to be very important for this family since the parents had limited English skills.

Her first order of business as the inpatient social worker was to complete a rapid but thorough biopsychosocial assessment, not only of Victor, but the entire family system. During this process, she discovered that Victor's parents were not as knowledgeable about the diagnoses as the medical staff initially thought. Julia also learned that the parents had been referred to the hospital's dietician and had also been given information about a specialist in physical activity management. Neither the dietician nor the activities specialist realized that the Ramirez parents had limited understanding of English. Victor, whose English was much better than his parents, knew that his mother and father did not completely comprehend what was being told to them. However, because of his reluctance to comply with the treatment recommendations, he neglected to clarify important points for his parents. Thus, while the parents appeared open and receptive to suggestions from the staff, Julia's meetings with the family revealed that they had minimal understanding of the severity of Victor's health concerns and that they did not comprehend the specifics of his treatment regimen. Julia raised these issues in the weekly multidisciplinary treatment team conference and arrangements were made for medical interpreters to attend all medical staff meetings with the family.

Julia also recognized that the family would need additional services and follow-up by a social worker once Victor became connected to the outpatient diabetes and renal clinics. She obtained the necessary confidentiality releases so that she would be able to share information with all parties involved with Victor's care. This would ensure that Julia would be able to speak with Victor's school staff regarding his new diagnoses and recent absences. The releases also allowed her to share information with the new social worker who would work with the family once Victor was discharged from the hospital.

In the course of conducting a biopsychosocial assessment, Julia learned that both parents were employed in the service industry; however, they barely made enough to make ends meet and frequently had to work overtime, even though this meant they were out of the house for many hours. In addition, they were unable to afford the additional costs of medical insurance through their employment, and were fearful of applying for government-sponsored insurance such as Medicaid or the Children's Health Insurance Program (CHIP) because they were not U.S. citizens. When Julia learned that they were in the U.S. before August 22, 1996, when TANF legislation was enacted, and that they were legal residents, she informed them that both of their children were eligible for CHIP and that accessing the benefit would not penalize their immigration status.

While making discharge plans with the family, they reviewed Victor's dietary and physical activity needs and discussed next steps for treatment. Julia arranged for the family to briefly meet Christine, the social worker assigned to the outpatient diabetes and renal clinics. During this initial introduction, Christine scheduled a longer meeting with Victor, his parents, Julia, the interpreter, and herself to make the transition from inpatient to outpatient care as smooth as possible. Julia also connected the family to an indigent prescription program to assist with obtaining medications until the CHIP application was processed.

Victor's mother called Christine about a week later stating that Victor was doing well; however, Maria, his younger sister, had started to wet the bed, had been crying a lot, and was having nightmares. Christine responded by normalizing these concerns and stated that siblings are often impacted by illness in ways that families do not anticipate. She suggested that the parents bring Maria with them to their next visit and arranged for Maria to meet with a child life specialist, a professional who is trained to educate and assist children in coping with medical diagnoses, and also to address the fears and concerns of their siblings.

Approximately three months after Victor's initial diagnosis, Christine made a scheduled evening home visit to the family.

Though not the norm, she wanted to meet with the family since Miguel and Gina were unable to attend regular visits at the hospital, and Victor's grandmother often accompanied him instead. While in the home, she observed that although Victor had a close and warm relationship with his mother, his relationship with his father was strained. With the assistance of the interpreter, Miguel was able to share that he was disappointed because he always wanted Victor to play soccer, as he had done. He felt that Victor was "lazy," which led to him being overweight and being sick with diabetes and kidney failure. Christine recognized what research shows–that many fathers have a difficult time adjusting to illness with their children, particularly their sons (Lloyd, 2002).

Christine also made collateral contact with Victor's school social worker, who was able to coordinate a team meeting with the school nurse, guidance counselor, cafeteria manager, physical education teacher, and assistant principal, to ensure that they were all familiar with Victor's medical needs. During this meeting, Christine also advocated for the school to provide a tutor so that Victor's numerous medical appointments would not hinder his ability to keep up with his schoolwork.

Discussion

This case illustrates that the management of pediatric and adolescent illness must recognize not only the role of the family, but also the importance of medical and educational professionals. Further, collaboration with multiple agencies and professionals is essential in order to optimize chances of a successful outcome.

The social workers involved with this family were charged with numerous tasks, including quickly developing rapport with the family members; alleviating initial anxiety and fears regarding multiple diagnoses; and coordinating concrete services such as interpreters, prescription programs, and health insurance. They provided information to the family about immigration issues. In addition, they provided education to the family and school about diabetes and kidney failure; information about treatment options, such as insulin therapy, dialysis, and kidney transplants; and assistance with daily concerns, such as providing insulin injections and selecting an appropriate diet.

All of these steps were crucial in supporting Victor, his family, and the school so that they could comply with the medical regimen. Relationship-building and provision of social work services such as assessment, referral, discharge planning, collateral contacts, psychoeducation, crisis counseling, building community supports, and advocacy are all necessary components of the treatment process that can lead to more successful outcomes with children and adolescents who interface with medical systems.

CONCLUSION: THE INTERFACE OF CLINICAL PRACTICE AND SOCIAL WELFARE POLICY

As discussed throughout this chapter, the multifaceted roles assumed by social workers in urban healthcare settings demonstrate the linkages between social work practice and policy. The strengths and the uniqueness of the social work profession come from its mandate to provide services to individuals, families, and communities, while simultaneously effecting policy changes. In the urban health care environment, this process translates into policy advocacy on several fronts, including, but not limited to, equal access to health care and insurance, amelioration of environmental problems that cause health disparities in populations and communities that are disadvantaged, negotiation of managed care (Redmond, 2001), and access to culturally and linguistically appropriate services. As advocates for the underserved, these are all challenges that urban social workers confront on a routine basis.

Understanding the multiple dimensions and psychosocial implications of health problems that are endemic to urban populations allows social workers in any setting to work effectively with children, adolescents, and families. In order to directly address these health concerns with youth and their families, and to be influential in the promotion of social justice, a key tenet of the social work profession, social work practitioners must be actively engaged not only in clinical practice but also with the work of policy development, implementation, research, and analysis.

REFERENCES

Bartlett, H. (1975). Ida M. Cannon: Pioneer in medical social work. *Social Service Review, 49* (2), 208–229.

Battle, S. (2002). Health concerns for African-American youth. In J. L. Rozie-Battle (Ed.), *African-American adolescents in the urban community: Social services policy and practice interventions* (pp. 35–44). New York: Haworth Press.

Brindis, C., Klein, J., Schlitt, J., Santelli, J., Juszcak, L., & Nystrom, R. (2003). School-based health centers: Accessibility and accountability. *Journal of Adolescent Health, 32S* (6S), 98–107.

Block, J. P., Scribner, R. A., & DeSalvo, K. B. (2004) Fast food, race/ethnicity, and income: A geographic analysis. *American Journal of Preventive Medicine, 27* (3), 211-217.

Burlew, A. (2002). Empirically derived guidelines for assessing the psychosocial needs of children and adolescents with sickle cell. *Social Work in Health Care, 36* (1), 29–44.

Cohen, E., Mackenzie, R. G., & Yates, G. L. (1991). HEADSS, a psychosocial risk assessment instrument: Implications for designing effective intervention programs for runaway youth. *Journal of Adolescent Health, 12* (7), 539–544.

Centers for Disease Control and Prevention (2002). Childhood lead poisoning associated with tamarind candy and folk remedies–California, 1999-2000. *Morbidity and Mortality Weekly Report, 51* (31), 684–686.

Children's Defense Fund (2004). Lead poisoning prevention funding report, http://www.childrensdefense.org/childhealth/leadpoisoning.asp. Accessed July 26, 2004.

Diaz, A. (1998a). Educating the adolescent patient. In L. A. Wallis et al. (Eds.), *Textbook of women's health* (pp. 155–159). Philadelphia: Lippincott-Raven.

Diaz, A. (1998b). The adolescent partnership. In L. A. Wallis et al. (Eds.), *Textbook of women's health* (pp. 39–41). Philadelphia: Lippincott-Raven.

Diaz, A. (1998c). Comprehensive examination of the adolescent girl. In L. A. Wallis et al. (Eds.), *Textbook of women's health* (pp. 167–173). Philadelphia: Lippincott-Raven.

Epstein, H. (2003, October 12). Ghetto miasma: Enough to make you sick? *The New York Times Magazine,* pp. 74–81, 98, 102–105.

Federal Interagency Forum on Child and Family Statistics (2004). America's children in brief: Key national indicators of well-being. www.childstats.gov/americaschildren/pdf/ac04brief.pdf. Accessed July 26, 2004.

French, S. A., Story, M., & Perry, C. L. (1995). Self-esteem and obesity in children and adolescents: A literature review. *Obesity Research, 3,* 479–490.

Graham, L. (2004). All I need is the air that I breathe: Outdoor air quality and asthma. *Pediatric Respiratory Reviews, 5* (Suppl A), S59-S64.

Henry J. Kaiser Family Foundation (2000). *Abortion policy and politics.* [*Issue Update*]. Menlo Park, CA: Author.

Kaslow, N., & Brown, F. (1995). Culturally sensitive family interventions for chronically ill youth: Sickle cell disease as an example. *Family Systems Medicine, 13* (2), 201–213.

Kenney, G., Haley, J., & Tebay, A. (2003). Children's insurance coverage and service use improve. *Snapshots of America's Families III,* 1. Washington, DC: The Urban Institute.

Lloyd, C. (2002). A mother's work is never done: A critical analysis of low-income women's roles as financial provider and caretaker of children with special needs. (Doctoral Dissertation, University of Delaware, 2002). *Dissertation Abstracts International, 64* (01), 298A.

Lorey, F. W., Arnopp, J., & Cunningham, G. C. (1996). Distribution of hemoglobinopathy variants by ethnicity in a multiethnic state. *Genetic Epidemiology, 13,* 501–512.

McLean, D., Bowen, S., Drezner, K., Rowe, A., Sherman, P., Schroeder, S., Redlener, K., & Redlener, I. (2004). Asthma among homeless children: Undercounting and undertreating the underserved. *Archives of Pediatric and Adolescent Medicine, 158,* 244–249.

Millstein, S., & Litt, I. (1990). Adolescent health. In S. S. Feldman & G. R. Elliott (Eds.), *At the threshold: The developing adolescent* (pp. 431–456). Cambridge, MA: Harvard University Press.

Mitchell, D., & Murdock, K. (2002). Self-competence and coping in urban children with asthma. *Children's Health Care, 31* (4), 273–293.

Must, A., Spadano, J., & Coakley, E. H., (1999). The disease burden associated with overweight and obesity. *Journal of the American Medical Association, 282,* 1523–1529.

Nabors, L., Weist, M., Shugarman, R., Woeste, M., Mullet, E., & Rosner, L. (2004). Assessment, prevention, and intervention activities in a school-based program for children experiencing homelessness. *Behavior Modification, 28* (4), 565–578.

National Center for Health Statistics (2003). Prevalence of overweight among children and adolescents: United States, 1999-2002. http://www.cdc.gov/ncha/products/pubs/pubd/pubd/hestats/overwght99.htm. Accessed October 25, 2004.

Newacheck, P., Wong, S., Galbraith, A., & Hung, Y. (2003). Adolescent health care expenditures: A descriptive profile. *Journal of Adolescent Health, 32* (6), 3–11.

Perera, F., Rauh, V., Tsai, W., Kinney, P., Camann, D., Barr, D., Bernert, T., Garfinkel, R., Tu, Y., Diaz, D., Dietrich, J., & Whyatt, R.. (2003). Effects of transplacental exposure to environmental pollutants on birth outcomes in a multiethnic population. *Environmental Health Perspectives, 111* (2).

Phillips, N. P., & Straussner, S. L. A. (2002). *Urban social work: An introduction to policy and practice in the cities.* Boston: Allyn & Bacon.

Pietrobelli, A., Faith, M. S., Allison D. B., Gallagher, D., Chiumello, G., & Heymsfield, S. B. (1998). Body mass index as a measure of adiposity among children and adolescents: A validation study. *Journal of Pediatrics,* 132:204–210.

Polit, D., London, A., & Martinez, J. (2001). *The health of poor urban women: Findings from the project on devolution and urban change.* Manpower Demonstration Research Corp. Work Paper Series, ES-9, ES-17.

Redmond, H. (2001). The health care crisis in the United States: A call to action. *Health and Social Work, 26* (1), 54–58.

Schneider, D., & Northridge, M. E. (1999). Editorial: Promoting the health and well-being of future generations. *American Journal of Public Health, 89* (2), 155–157.

Schott, L. (2000). Issues for reconsideration as states reinstate families that were improperly terminated from Medicaid under welfare reform. Washington, DC: Center on Budget and Policy Priorities.

Shore-Sheppard, L. (2003). Expanding public health insurance for children: Medicaid and the State Children's Health Insurance Program. In R. Gordon & H. Walberg (Eds.), *Changing welfare* (pp. 95–118). New York: Kluwer Academic/ Plenum.

Stagg, E. V. (2004). Obesity weighs hard on urban kids. *American Medical News, 47* (18), 22–24.

Telfair, J., & Gardner, M. (2000). Adolescents with sickle cell disease: Determinants of support group attendance and satisfaction. *Health & Social Work, 25* (1), 43–50.

Washington State Department of Health. (2004, October 7). Lead poisoning. www.doh.wa.gov/topics/lead.htm. Accessed November 4, 2004.

Washington State Department of Health. (2000, April). Lead in folk remedies. www.doh.wa.gov/Topics/HomeRemedies.pdf. Accessed November 4, 2004.

Wood, P., Smith, L., Romero, D., Bradshaw, P., Wise, P., & Chavkin, W. (2002). Relationships between welfare status, health insurance status, and health and medical care among children with asthma. *American Journal of Public Health, 92* (9), 1446–1452.

Wright, R, Mitchell, H., Visness, C., Cohen, S., Stout, J., Evans, R., & Gold, D. (2004). Community violence and asthma morbidity: The inner-city asthma study. *American Journal of Public Health, 94* (4), 625–632.

Chapter 5

MENTAL HEALTH ISSUES AFFECTING URBAN CHILDREN

Dorinda N. Noble and Sally Hill Jones

Urbanization is a rapidly growing worldwide phenomenon. It is expected that by 2040, around two-thirds of the world's population will live in cities or large towns, thereby exposing more children to the unique stresses of living in urban environments (McMichael, 2000). During 2000, three-quarters of the population of the United States lived in urban centers; this included a majority of the 70.4 million children under 17 years of age (Marsella, 1991; UCLA Center Report, 2003). This chapter focuses on how the complex, interacting systems of cities affect children's mental health, how policies have responded to the need for mental health services for children, and how professionals attempt to prevent and treat mental health problems in children.

INTERACTIVE URBAN SYSTEMS

Cities are systems with many different components, all of which are interactive and affect each other. Physical characteristics of cities, such as size, the population's age and culture, transportation, the economy, political systems, educational opportunities, social and cultural aspects (such as religion and recreation), and the services systems (such as public health), interact and have a significant impact on the mental health of children. For example, between 1995 and 1996, the number of children in Baltimore born with syphilis, a disease with potentially devastating mental health complications, increased by 500 percent. Multiple factors seem to be behind this epidemic. According to the Center for Disease Control, the major culprit was crack cocaine. People came into poor areas of the city to buy crack, and some took both crack and syphilis back home with them. At the same time, Baltimore officials decided to save money by cutting back personnel at the city's sexually transmitted disease (STD) centers in poor areas of the city. Medical personnel dropped and patient visits declined. Consequently, syphilis moved from an acute, controllable condition to a more chronic, persistent disease because it was not treated early. Concurrently, Baltimore began dynamiting old public housing. Hundreds of families were displaced and moved to other parts of the city, in some cases taking their syphilis with them. So from the growth of the crack trade, to the down-sizing of STD clinics, to the dismantling of public housing, the epidemic of syphilis was spread across the city and exhibited itself in infected newborns (Gladwell, 2000).

THE DEMOGRAPHICS OF URBAN CHILD MENTAL HEALTH

It is estimated that from 12 to 22 percent of all children under age 18 in the United States need services for mental, emotional, or behavioral problems, and that approximately one out of every 50 children (1.3 million) receive mental health services (Latest Findings in Children's Mental Health, 2004; UCLA Center Report, 2003). Urban youth have been found to be more likely to have symptoms indicating a psychiatric disorder than rural youth (Offord et al., 1987). Most common disorders seen in urban youth are: *depression, posttraumatic stress disorder* (PTSD), *attention deficit hyperactive disorder* (ADHD), and *conduct disorder* (American Psychiatric Association [APA], 2000; Campbell & Schwartz, 1996; Offord et al., 1987). Exposure to urban violence increases behavior problems, such as aggressive behavior, memory impairment, withdrawal, and difficulty concentrating (Acosta, 2001; Schiff & McKay, 2003; Wiest, Acosta & Youngstrom, 2001).

Learning disorders are linked with several medical conditions prevalent in cities, such as lead poisoning and fetal alcohol syndrome. Toxic conditions such as environmental pollutants and lead poisoning are related to *pervasive developmental disorders* (such as autism,

Asperger's disorder, and others). Environmental toxins, infections, drug exposure in utero, and a history of child abuse and multiple foster care placements are related to ADHD. Conduct disorder is associated with inconsistent childrearing practices with harsh discipline, lack of supervision, large family size, frequent changes of caregivers, maternal smoking during pregnancy, and exposure to violence. Oppositional defiant disorder is more prevalent in children who have had a succession of different caregivers or who live in families with harsh, inconsistent, neglectful child-rearing practices (APA, 2000). Almost a third of all children receiving mental health services suffer from two or more psychiatric disorders, making treatment more difficult. The most common diagnostic combination is ADHD and mood disorders (Latest Findings, 2004).

While seen less frequently, other childhood disorders also have links to conditions found in urban centers. *Pica* and *rumination disorder*, both rare eating disorders, are linked with poverty, neglect, and lack of parental supervision. *Reactive attachment disorder*, in which children either cannot develop normal attachments to other people, or develop indiscriminate attachments, is related to extreme poverty, neglect, and multiple caregivers and foster placements (APA, 2000).

THE ROLE OF THE EDUCATIONAL SYSTEM

One constant in children's lives is school. In general, urban schools are more likely to be overcrowded and to have larger class sizes, employ beginning teachers and teachers with less education; at the same time, they have a higher percentage of children with mental health problems (Children's Defense Fund, September 2004). While disruptive behaviors are not confined to urban classrooms, when there are several disruptive children in a classroom, they tend to reinforce each other, magnifying the problem. Children in urban communities, particularly those from low income African American, Latino/a and Native American families, tend to be overrepresented in urban special educational classes, and are more likely to be classified as having mild mental disabilities and emotional and behavioral disabilities than children in nonurban communities (Oswald et al., 1999).

Like all students in the United States, urban children are often grouped and labeled by standardized tests—the results of which tend to shape students' careers. Historically, local school districts have made decisions about whether students have met graduation criteria, but by 2009, half of all states will use a single standardized test as the sole criterion to determine whether a student will graduate (Children's Defense Fund, September 2004). The mental health effects of this high-stakes testing on children and their families cannot be overstated, particularly as it affects a child's self-esteem. Standardized testing can be especially problematic for children in special education classes; exam scores have been found to be significantly lower among children with disabilities (Children's Defense Fund, September 2004). Testing also affects children's decision to stay in school. The most dramatic dropout problems are concentrated in 200 to 300 schools in the 35 largest cities in the U.S. (Kids Count Data Book, 2004).

HISTORY OF CHILDREN'S MENTAL HEALTH SERVICES

Modern mental health care for children grew out of the broader health care initiatives of the late 1800's and early 1900's, when American cities were flooded with foreign immigrants and rural young people looking for jobs. Poverty was a fact of life for many of them. Poor children were frequently moved into the work force at young ages, often at the cost of their physical and mental health (Noble & Ausbrooks, forthcoming).

Social workers such as Jane Addams were instrumental in reform movements that, among other things, worked to prohibit child labor, improve public health, and help create the U.S. Children's Bureau—an advocate of improving maternal and child health. These reform efforts were embedded in a larger societal progressive movement to improve public health in cities, where industrialization, immigration and population growth, and urbanization created serious sanitation and public health problems (Moniz & Gorin, 2003). The emergence of the U.S. Public Health Service in 1912 formalized the government's commitment to public health. As part of this public health movement, the Mental Hygiene Movement emerged, working to make mental hospitals and mental treatment more humane and effective. It also generated the creation, during the 1920s and 1930s, of child guidance centers in numerous cities to help children who were considered to be juvenile delinquents and emotionally disturbed (Horn, 1989).

It was World War II, however, that catapulted the mental hygiene movement forward. The common conception of the day that mental illness was only hereditary and not influenced by environment was hard to support in the face of soldiers who suffered mental health catastrophes in battle. Mental health professionals in the armed forces developed methods of alleviating stress (such as rest and rotation), and used battalion aid stations to treat mental issues (Moniz & Gorin, 2003).

These strategies were successful enough that many authorities thought they might work with the general population. In 1946, Congress passed the National Mental Health Act, which established the National Institute of Mental Health (NIMH) to research mental health treatments (Popple & Leighninger, 2005). The notion of treating the mentally ill in the community rather than in the hospital gained currency with the Community Mental Health Act of 1963, which established a network of community mental health centers. Currently, community mental health centers are overworked and underfunded, and consequently are hard-pressed to meet the challenges that urban areas present (Popple & Leighninger, 2005). Furthermore, people of ethnic groups that do not have a tradition of seeking mental health care may not usually use mental health centers (Snowden, 2003; U.S. Department of Health & Human Services, 2001).

It is noteworthy that the majority of mental health initiatives until the late twentieth century were aimed at treating adults, not children. In 1984, however, Congress established the Child and Adolescent Service System Program (CASSP) to help states develop local systems of care for children with serious emotional and behavioral disorders (New York Office of Mental Health, 2002). The Center for Mental Health Services, a component of SAMHSA (Substance Abuse and Mental Health Services Administration, an arm of the U.S. Department of Health and Human Services), has overseen, since 1992, block grants to states which help support mental health services, including integrated systems of community mental health services for children and adolescents (Leading the nation's mental health system, 2002). Various centers, such as the Research and Training Center on Family Support and Children's Mental Health (based at Portland State University), have been funded with federal dollars to generate better knowledge about children's issues, as well as more effective interventions to deal with children (Research and Training Center, 2003).

Treating children's mental health problems is expensive, and many children are not insured. The U.S. federal government has no broad mental health insurance coverage for all children. Some restricted mental health services are available to those who qualify for Medicaid, a program jointly funded by states and the federal government that provides health insurance to low-income groups, including poor children. In 1997, Congress created the State Children's Health Insurance Program (CHIP) to help states insure children whose parents were not able to afford private insurance but who were not poor enough to qualify for Medicaid; CHIP provides some mental health treatment coverage. Though Congress earmarked $40 billion to be distributed over a decade for state CHIP programs, many states have been slow to implement CHIP, both for financial and political reasons (Popple & Leighninger, 2005).

TRAUMA: A PERVASIVE THREAT TO CHILDREN'S MENTAL HEALTH

Environmental factors, such as crime, violence, poverty, and other conditions found in some urban communities can endanger children's mental health. The child's internal factors are also critical. A child's inborn genetic code predisposes him or her to certain responses, which, in turn, are shaped and molded by external influences. For example, the child who is frequently exposed to violence will become desensitized or "habituated" to violence, seeing it as normal. As an adolescent or adult, this person then may be more tolerant of violence, expect it, and be more inclined to resolve problems with aggressive action (Campbell & Schwartz, 1996; Cooley-Quille et al., 2001).

Experiences of violence are traumatic for many children. Trauma is an event or circumstance that overwhelms a person's internal and external resources. Not only can traumas trigger symptoms of mental illness, such as posttraumatic stress disorder (PTSD), but they can also interfere with the child's normal development. Children facing overwhelming difficulties tend to manifest their distress either as: (1) *Internalizing behavior* directed toward the self, such as depression, anxiety, dissociation, withdrawal, and self-injury; or (2) *Externalizing behavior* directed toward others, such as aggressive behavior (Pynoos et al., 1996).

Terr (1991) describes two levels of trauma: (1) *Type I trauma* is time-limited, such as a rape, a shooting, or sudden change in living situation. For many children, Type I traumas result in symptoms of PTSD. (2) *Type II trauma* results from chronic exposure to threatening situations, such as long-term incest, parental alcoholism, or war. It is cumulative in its effects, making the child vulnerable to additional psychopathology.

According to Steele (2004), traumatized children may experience: (1) *Cognitive dysfunction*, such as impaired memory; (2) *Hyper-vigilance*, a heightened state of fear or chronic readiness to flee; (3) *Survivor guilt*– an overwhelming guilt at having been spared, or suicide attempts to "even the score;" (4) *Recurrent memories* of the trauma or traumatic dreams about it; (5) *Regressive behavior*, such as a 14-year-old acting like a 6-year-old; (6) *Startle response*, such as marked response to sounds and sights and smells that occurred at the time of trauma; (7) *Emotional numbing*, which refers to the deadening of one's feelings; (8) *Aggressive responses* or assault on others; (9) *Limited future orientation*, as when children stop thinking of having a future; and (10) *Repetitive play or behavior*, in which the child tries to master or gain control over some aspect of the traumatizing event.

The traumatized child may have more trouble with family and social relationships and with academic achievement. In order to learn and to get along socially, a child must be able to regulate his/her emotions, focus attention, and control impulses. Those skills may be delayed or impaired in a child whose life is shaped by trauma. They often have trouble with memory and with acquiring language–skills that are necessary for learning to read, write, and communicate (Saigh et al., 1997).

Common Traumatic Events in the City

While children in every environmental context may experience trauma, city children face particular challenges. The population density in urban areas magnifies social conditions that contribute to the trauma, and density heightens the likelihood of a child's exposure to trauma, as well as the frequency and intensity of trauma.

Nearly eight children a day are killed by guns in the U.S. (Children's Defense Fund, January 31, 2005). Children who grow up with close proximity to sudden death have little sense of security about the future. This is reflected in a National Public Radio story (December 14, 2004) which described how in a particularly violent San Diego neighborhood, merchants have set up kiosks and prepare memorial t-shirts with the picture, name, and date of death of young people in this community who have died violently. One young man was quoted as saying that he knew several of these kids; he came to the kiosk to think about them and to wonder why he was not dead, too.

Children who see violent acts perpetrated in their home against someone they love feel helpless to stop it; yet, they may feel guilty that they cannot protect the loved one. It is chilling, then, to realize that between three million and 10 million children yearly witness domestic violence (Children's Defense Fund, June 2000). Because 85 percent of violent acts in the home are perpetrated against women (Children's Defense Fund, June 2000), children seeing those acts are more likely to develop skewed ideas about gender roles and interpersonal relationships.

When adults attack each other, children are in harm's way. When adults attack children, however, children are in grievous physical, mental, and emotional danger. About one million cases of child maltreatment are verified each year in the U.S. The most common form of maltreatment (52 percent) is child neglect, which has long-term effects on a child's physical and mental development. About a quarter of the cases of child maltreatment involve physical abuse. Around 12 percent involve sexual abuse, and the remainder involves medical neglect and emotional maltreatment. Most of the perpetrators of child maltreatment are parents (77 percent of perpetrators). Another 11 percent are other relatives (Downs et al., 2000).

Children who have survived abuse and neglect bear emotional and often physical scars. Their trust in adults is damaged, and they often have trouble forming healthy relationships. They may try to escape the pain of their abuse by using alcohol and drugs or by contemplating suicide. Some children bear the physical marks of their trauma in injuries they sustain. They also may display physical symptoms of their emotional distress: nightmares and night terrors, sleepwalking, anorexia and bulimia, and compulsive behaviors are only a few of the symptoms seen in maltreated children. Some develop serious mental illnesses, such as clinical depression or even dissociative disorder (in which the personality fragments) (Pynoos et al., 1996; Terr, 1991).

These disorders may be manifests as poor concentration, sudden changes in behavior, obsessive-compulsive behaviors, and hearing inner voices. It is easy for adults to misinterpret such behavior, and view the child being lazy, disrespectful, or even "crazy." The child who exhibits memory disturbances or actively avoids any reminders of the trauma can appear to adults to be lying or manipulating. The victim of sexual abuse who responds to others in sexualized ways may appear to be "immoral" or "loose."

Maltreated children are often moved into substitute care. On any given day, about 500,000 children in the U.S. are in out-of-home placement (Holody, this volume; Popple & Leighninger, 2005). Foster and residential care undoubtedly save many children's lives, but children in substitute care struggle with difficult emotions, thinking they are somehow responsible for the abuse, or feeling guilty when parents go to jail for abuse. Victimized children often exhibit behaviors such as anger, cruelty to animals or younger children, eating disorders, depression, or, in the case of sexually traumatized children, sexually inappropriate behaviors. Since the traumatized child feels more threatened and powerless, he/she may regress developmentally, exhibiting such behavior as anxiety at being separated from family members, or being unable to determine when a situation is physically dangerous and thereby putting him/herself at additional risk for trauma.

Trauma and the Brain

At birth, the average child's brain contains one hundred billion neurons (Buckingham & Coffman, 1999). The critical element about these brain cells, however, is not raw numbers, but the linkages, or synapses between them. These linkages between brain cells are created over time as a result of repeated experiences that carve out pathways in the brain. Chronic trauma can change a child's brain structure in many ways (van der Kolk, 1996): (1) *Psychophysiological change*, which leads to hyper-arousal in response states (meaning the child's emotional responses are stronger than the situation warrants); (2) *Neurohormonal change*, meaning the brain hormones that affect the child's psychological sense of well-being are altered; (3) *Neuroanatomical change*, referring to changes in the actual size of the brain (the brain, in other words, does not grow normally); and (4) *Immunological change*, referring to the brain's control of the child's immune system changes.

The traumatized child often tends to have a chronically disordered pattern of arousal, which means that the child's neurophysiological reactivity (the "*fight, flight,* or *freeze*" decision that people make in situations they perceive as dangerous) is heightened, and the ability to recover from the stress of perceived danger is slowed down (Pynoos et al., 1996; van der Kolk, 1996). Consequently, the traumatized child reacts more strongly to stimuli, anticipates danger by becoming hypervigilant, and tries to control perceived danger by developing ways to combat or escape it. Traumatized children, then, often appear to be hyperactive or withdrawn, and may seem limited in their abilities to pay attention, reflect on events, and control their behavior (Steele, 2004).

Since such children spend much energy on monitoring their situations and preparing to respond to the danger they expect, their neurological systems that regulate emotions may be underdeveloped. They do not learn to appropriately use emotions as signals; instead, they struggle to keep emotions from overwhelming them. Moreover, they tend to interpret their emotions in light of the trauma they have experienced, so they have trouble differentiating various emotions, identifying why they are experiencing those emotions, and finding appropriate ways of expressing their emotions (Pynoos et al., 1996).

DISRUPTIVE AND DELINQUENT BEHAVIOR DISORDERS

Some children who have suffered through long-term trauma, what Terr (1991) described as Type II trauma, exhibit disruptive behaviors, such as excessive aggression, poor impulse control and hyperactivity. A child's temperament may also predispose him/her to disruptive actions. Other factors common to urban settings, such as lack of supervision, homelessness, drug and alcohol abuse, incarceration of parents, poverty, and poor diet can contribute to behavior problems. Children with easy-going, cooperative temperaments are less likely to develop aggressive behaviors, but they may be more likely to be victimized by aggressive behavior of other children.

Attention deficit hyperactivity disorder (ADHD) is the most commonly diagnosed childhood psychiatric disorder, often co-occurring with diagnoses of conduct disorder, as well as anxiety, depression, and bipolar disorders (Harvard Mental Health Letter, 2004).

Poor diet and lack of exercise may exacerbate conditions such as ADHD and depression. Fast food chains, with their processed foods and high saturated fats, are concentrated in low-income urban neighborhoods (Children's Defense Fund, June 2004). Ironically, until 2004, McDonald's fast food restaurant was highly visible in the lobby of New York City's Harlem Hospital, and about 30 McDonald's outlets are still located in hospitals around the country (Connolly, 2004). The effects of poor diet are compounded by lack of exercise when children are not allowed to play outside because play areas are limited or unsafe. Lack of imaginative play with other children may increase a child's sense of isolation and decrease creativity, while limiting opportunities to "practice" socializing skills.

Poverty may lead to homelessness. Forty percent of the nation's homeless are families with children (Popple & Leighninger, 2005). The stresses of homelessness may lead to depression and contribute to behavior problems, including substance abuse. The abuse of alcohol and other drugs contribute to additional mental health problems. Many children are exposed to prenatal alcohol, which can result in Fetal Alcohol Syndrome, a condition which has profound mental health consequences. The use of drugs and alcohol by young people interfere with their normal development, as well as place children in risky situations (see Nadel & Straussner, this volume). Children with psychiatric problems may "medicate" themselves with drugs and alcohol to relieve their psychic distress. However, the use of drugs and alcohol in conjunction with psychotropic medications taken to treat psychiatric illnesses can be dangerous.

Children in families with a drug or alcohol-abusing parent often become "parentified," caring for and cleaning up after parents who stay up for days and act erratically. They may have to help protect and care for younger siblings and seek ways to bring money into the family (Winton, 2003). For example, a couple with two children ages five and one in a New Jersey city, taught the older child how to change the younger child's diaper. The parents then disappeared for several days on a drug binge (Summerhill, 2005).

Losing a parent, either through death, military deployment, or incarceration, also contributes to a child's mental health problems. In the U.S., 1,498,800 children had at least one parent in a state or federal prison in 2000 (see Mazza, this volume; Temin, 2001). Children tend to grieve the loss of their incarcerated parent and worry about the parent's well-being. Some mothers, when arrested, do not reveal that they have children, fearing that the state will remove the children from their custody. Consequently, their children may be left to fend for themselves or move between homes of relatives or acquaintances.

Some children respond to loss and mental distress by attempting suicide. Suicides can be triggered when children think of death frequently, suffer from depression, or experience the suicide of a peer. Suicide, in some cases, may be a way to externalize emotions and hurt others; in other cases, it may be a way to end their psychological pain. On an average day, four American teens die from suicide (Kids Count Data Book, 2004), and clusters of teen suicide are common. For every successful suicide, there may be 50 to 100 suicide attempts (Petr, 1998). The rate of suicide for African-American and American Indian teens is significantly higher than for other teens (Kids Count Data Book, 2004).

CHILDREN WITH INTELLECTUAL DISABILITIES

Children with intellectual disabilities (once called "mental retardation") often have accompanying psychiatric difficulties (Emerson, 2003). Intellectual disabilities can originate in biological factors; prenatal damage due to toxins; deprivation of nurturance or stimulation; fetal malnutrition; prematurity; viral infections and trauma during pregnancy; and childhood infections, traumas, or poisonings (APA, 2000). Children whose parents are poor get less frequent health care, more often live in unsafe environments (such as structures with lead paint), and are more likely to experience conditions or events that result in intellectual disabilities (see Mirabito & Loyd, this volume).

While intellectual disability is a physical and mental condition rather than a psychiatric illness, it is pertinent to mental health because these children are at increased risk for conduct and anxiety disorders, as well as pervasive developmental disorders (Emerson, 2003). The mental health of the primary caregiver, the functioning of the child's family, and the nature of the family's child management practices can all contribute to mental disorders that co-occur with intellectual disabilities (Hoare et al., 1998).

SOCIAL SUPPORT AND PSYCHOTROPIC MEDICATION

Urban children who have been traumatized by life events or who are predisposed to mental illness need positive, stable social support; such support, which can come from family, friends, schools, clergy, or social workers, is the biggest protection they have and can neutralize the effects of negative risk factors (Dulmus, 2003; Zimmerman et al., 2000). Religious belief and observance, and programs that teach children to make sense of and cope with trauma and its effects, can be effective as buffers against mental problems (Oman et al., 2004; Pearce et al., 2003).

Americans are used to treating most illnesses with medication, but using psychotropic medications to treat children is controversial. Most antidepressants, for instance, have not been widely tested on children, though physicians may still prescribe such medications "off-label," or for a use other than that approved by FDA (Antidepressant Medications for Children, 2005). Prescribing medications "off-label" for children requires physicians to guess about appropriate dosage and duration of treatment. Further, the effects of certain psychotropic medications on children has led some to blame drugs like Prozac (an antidepressant) for sparking suicidal or violent actions in children. The February, 2005 so-called "Zoloft Trial," in which authorities in Charleston, South Carolina prosecuted a child accused of murdering his grandparents when he was 12, is a case in point. This child, who had a history of aggression and suicide gestures, was prescribed Zoloft, an antidepressant. In an unsuccessful defense, his attorneys claimed that "Zoloft made him do it" (Teen Gets 30 Years, 2005).

British medical authorities recently banned prescribing antidepressants for children, while the U.S. Food and Drug Administration now requires that antidepressants commonly prescribed for children carry strong warning labels that the drugs can spur suicidal behavior (FDA Requires Warnings, December 10, 2004). Another concern is that psychotropic medications may be given to children to make life easier for caregivers (by controlling unwanted behavior) rather than addressing the systemic causes of the child's problems.

Despite these quandaries, one-third of all children in mental heath services are treated with psychotropic drugs, particularly if they suffer from more than one diagnosis (Latest Findings, 2004). The cost of treating children and adolescents for mental health concerns is estimated at nearly $12 billion (UCLA Center Report, 2003). Nevertheless, many children who need treatment do not get it on a timely or regular basis, as the President's New Freedom Commission on Mental Health, which studies and makes recommendations about American mental health care, has pointed out (Integrating Agendas for Mental Health in Schools, 2004). Many children in urban areas, particularly children of color, are less likely to get medical care in general, let alone psychiatric care and appropriate medication (Moniz & Gorin, 2003).

PREVENTIVE, SUPPORTIVE, AND CLINICAL SERVICES AND POLICIES

Applegate et al. (2005) studied how cumulative risk factors affected children's behaviors and found that there is no point beyond which services for children are hopeless. The Surgeon General's 2000 report on mental health echoed this sentiment, advocating that mental health services for children (1) need to be comprehensive and oriented toward preventing and treating mental conditions; (2) need to address both individual and societal issues; and (3) need to use innovative approaches involving community collaborations (U.S. Department of Health and Human Services, 2000).

Developing Preventive Programs

Many socioeconomic factors contribute to mental health problems. Addressing the scourge of poverty; making mental health care more equitable and comprehensive; providing adequate, safe housing; making communities environmentally and physically safe; ensuring that children are cared for and supervised; preventing unplanned teen pregnancies; eliminating substance abuse; and providing effective education are all societal goals that will improve urban children's mental health.

While such goals may seem very lofty, they can guide intervention efforts. Using comprehensive services specifically designed to meet targeted needs is an effective way to meet these goals. Services need to be structured so that different cultural groups can take advantage of them. One way to do so is to involve members of the cultural community in planning and implementing those services. Moreover, such services need to be long-term. The challenges to children's mental health took a long time to develop; effectively addressing them will take a long time. Although program funders demand accountability (as they should), effective programs require time to develop.

Children who have limited structure and supervision are more likely to be involved in risky behavior and to be victims of violence (Richards et al., 2004). Consequently, urban neighborhoods need more extensive after-school programs and supervised recreational facilities. Mentoring programs, such as Big Brother/Big Sister, need to be further researched and the activities and relationship elements that are shown to be effective need to be expended (Dulmus, 2005).

Another factor that protects children against risk of mental health disorders is parental support. Social agencies need to provide parents with training on how to monitor and discipline their children in effective and caring ways. They can also help families learn better communication skills and better ways to resolve conflicts without hurting each other. These skills, often taught in individual, family, or group therapies, have been shown to be associated with decreasing children's propensity for affiliating with violent peers and becoming involved with delinquency (Henry, 2001). Such parenting and family training is effective in intervening with children who have Oppositional Defiant Disorder or Conduct Disorder. Seattle's Raising Healthy Children is one such prevention program that has been show effective in working with teachers and parents to develop child management skills in the classroom and the family (Hawkins et al., 1992).

Children learn resilience by becoming more skilled at social interactions, controlling their emotions and behaviors, solving problems, and refusing to be involved in risky activities. Communities and schools can provide learning experiences to help children develop these resiliency skills. Programs such as Life Skills Training Program (Botvin et al., 1995), Promoting Alternative Thinking Strategies (Greenburg et al., 1995), and Problem-Solving Skills Training (Kazdin et al., 1992), as well as individual, family, and group therapy, help children become more personally competent and thus prevent disruptive behavior and the resulting negative consequences.

Urban schools can realize great benefits when they partner with local universities to meet children's educational and mental needs

(Ferguson, Kozleski, & Smith, 2001). Some school districts operate mental health units, and a few schools have established their own in-house mental health clinics. If that is not possible, schools can partner with community mental health clinics. Schools need to train their faculty in mental health issues, stressing that children with mental disturbances have rights that should be protected. Students should be screened for mental disorders, particularly substance abuse, and be linked to appropriate treatment resources. At the same time, in light of the accountability demands of the No Child Left Behind initiative, as well as the confidentiality mandates of the Family Educational Rights and Privacy Act (FERPA) and the Health Insurance Portability and Accountability Act (HIPAA), schools need to protect their computerized records of children with mental challenges and difficulties.

Positive Attitudes Toward Learning in School (PALS) is one example of a program which uses collaboration between schools, communities, and families to create a more effective learning environment and increase family support for learning (Atkins et al., 2003). Positive Behavioral Interventions and Supports (Sugai & Horner, 2002) is a model in which teams of professionals and family members determine what is triggering children's disruptive behavior, and develop positive alternatives to that behavior, such as supervised after-school activities, more parental involvement, peer social support, and specific classroom strategies aimed at helping children overcome disruptive behavior. Operation Positive Change, established in New Orleans, trained and supported parents in applying positive behavior support strategies. This project, developed by parents of an autistic child, engaged parents of disabled children in learning how to deal with their affected children, and how to support and encourage and teach one another (Markey et al., 2002).

CHAMP (Chicago HIV Prevention and Adolescent Mental Health Project) Family Program, developed and implemented by a community collaboration of parents, school staff, agency representatives, and university researchers, aims to help fourth and fifth grade students delay sexual activity. Parents learn to communicate with and monitor their children effectively, and work with their children to develop skills at refusing risky involvement and avoiding peer pressure (McKay et al., 2004).

Public and Private Service Partnerships

Collaborative programs will likely expand under the federal government's current push to fund more programs in faith-based institutions, which some policy-makers see as being efficacious in addressing family dysfunction. Faith-based interventions are part of a larger move to privatize governmental functions such as child welfare, mental health, education, poverty services, and prisons. Those who argue that privatizing services makes sense claim that since private services are more removed from political decision making, they can be more innovative and rational, less costly, more accountable, and offer consumers more choices. People who argue against privatizing public services claim that private organizations make choices based on costs and desire for profits; consequently, private organizations provide poorer quality care, fewer choices for consumers, and less cooperation and service integration among service providers (Petr, 1998). Regardless of the outcome of these arguments, it is clear that there is a growing partnerships between public and private entities. While effective cooperation and integration between entities is challenging and takes enormous time and energy, it involves more community people in addressing the problems in their midst, and opens more opportunities for thinking of new approaches to solving problems.

Noble and Gibson (1994) describe an innovative urban program in which the agency created foster homes for mothers and their children who were at risk of homelessness. This program, under the auspices of a religious service, partners with area food banks, schools, the housing authority, and day care centers to provide an environment in which mothers who are on the edge of disaster can begin to rebuild their lives. The entire family unit moves into the foster home. The foster parents work with the mother to help her develop financial skills, secure education or job training, find safe housing, secure protection from abusive boyfriends or husbands, and learn effective parenting skills. The mother is responsible for caring for her own children in the foster home, but has the foster parents' support in meeting her children's needs. The goal of the program is to help mothers move into independent living with their children, but with the safety cushion of the agency to help out in tough times.

Another example of a faith-based and community partnership is the Child and Family Program run in numerous southern cities, sponsored by Presbyterian Children's Home. This program places social workers in churches; the professionals then provide not only concrete items, but counseling and supportive services to families at risk for having to place the children outside the home. For example, while their mother was in prison, two young children lived in Shreveport, Louisiana with their grandmother, who worked long hours as a cab driver. One evening a drunk driver plowed his pick-up into the house, partially destroying it and injuring one child. The family had to vacate the house for repairs, and during their absence, the house was vandalized and all their possessions were stolen, including the children's hamster. The children were heart-broken. A local family service organization located resources to clean up the debris and refurbished the house. Church members contributed clothing, food, and furniture to the family. The family agency provided counseling—and another hamster (Gibson & Noble, 2002).

Clinical Services

Mental health services for urban youth need to encompass a wide range of interventions, including individual, family, and group therapy, as well as school and community-based interventions focusing on prevention and intervention. Innovative approaches are needed to address the lack of utilization of community mental health services by many ethnic families (Kataoka, Zhang, & Wells, 2002; Kazdin, 1996), as well as the need for multiple points of intervention for families and children with multiple problems.

Multisystemic Therapy

Multisystemic therapy is an intervention approach that has been successful with families struggling with complex challenges and with youth demonstrating severe disruptive behaviors (Cunningham & Henggeler, 2001). This approach, based on the family systems and social-ecological models, assumes that mental health and antisocial behavior is determined by multiple factors related to individual, family, peer, school, and neighborhood considerations. Services are intense and short-term. They are often offered in the home, focusing on the individual's and family's strengths. Professionals use parent training and cognitive-behavioral individual and family therapies, along with medications, if indicated. Multisystemic therapy has been used in inner-city neighborhoods, and research shows that it has been effective and cost-efficient in increasing family cohesion and effective parenting, while reducing criminal behavior, incarceration, substance use, inpatient hospital days, and out-of-home placements (Henggeler, 1999). The aim of this approach is to help individuals and families be more competent and empowered in dealing with their problems, and to build support for policies that increase family and community services instead of residential and institutional care. The approach holds promise for treating children with serious and chronic mental health and substance abuse problems.

Wraparound Process Approach

The wraparound approach, similar to multisystemic therapy, is an individualized, community-based intervention designed for youth with severe emotional and behavioral problems and their families. Unlike multisystemic therapy, the wraparound service is long-term, committed to provide services to the youth and family for as long as needed, and assumes gradual changes. The service team is headed by a resource coordinator who finds and develops an array of resources for the family. This approach appears to be effective (Burns et al., 2000).

An Example of Mental Health Intervention for an Urban Child

Cynthia grew up in Dallas. At a young age, her stepfather sexually abused Cynthia. The mother, Darla, protected Cynthia by reporting the abuse and divorcing the stepfather. Thereafter, though Darla provided basic necessities for Cynthia, she was also highly critical of Cynthia. Cynthia had low self-esteem, despite her above-average intelligence. A mental health practitioner diagnosed Cynthia with PTSD and depression.

At age 14, Cynthia became sexually involved with an older man and had a son with him. She continued to live with Darla, who criticized Cynthia for abusing the child, and in fact reported abuse to the child welfare authorities. As a result, Cynthia's son was placed in Darla's custody. Cynthia, by now age 16, then "fell in love" with another older man and became pregnant again.

At this point, her child welfare worker, Ms. Parker, placed Cynthia in a residence for pregnant teens in Fort Worth, 60 miles away. Ms. Parker believed that Cynthia needed some distance from her critical mother and her overbearing boyfriend. The social worker at the residential center, Ms. Bates, could detect that Cynthia was intelligent and was capable of gaining insight into why she was attracted to older men.

Ms. Bates and the residential center staff gave Cynthia intensive support while she finished her school year before delivering her child. Cynthia got a lot of feedback from Ms. Bates and other staff about how intelligent she was, and how to overcome her internal "you're no good" dialogue. Cynthia began to respond differently to Darla's negative letters and phone calls, and she started to think her mother's criticisms were incorrect. Cynthia also came to some conclusions about how she had been affected by the sexual abuse she suffered, as well as the steady stream of denigrating remarks from her mother and the loss of her baby's custody. She got to a point where she could discuss these traumas in her life and could explore alternate ways of framing them in her mind. Slowly Cynthia began to see herself in a different, more positive light.

Ms. Parker, the child welfare worker, assessed Cynthia's growing maturity and self-confidence and arranged for Cynthia's son to live with her. Ms. Parker and Ms. Bates helped Cynthia make realistic plans for continuing in school and staying at the facility after her second baby was born. They encouraged her to graduate from high school and helped her to get into a transitional living situation, where she had some moral support and therapeutic guidance as she learned to live on her own.

CONCLUSION

Urban children live in the multiple, interacting systems of cities, and their mental health is also shaped by multiple, external and internal interacting factors. Making sense of urban children's mental health, consequently, is complex. One clear factor is that urban children are subject to many life events and circumstances that may traumatize them, and trauma is a serious risk factor for children's mental health. Though U.S. mental health policy relating to children has lagged behind those directed toward adults, professionals' understanding of appropriate prevention and treatment strategies is growing. Numerous programs and initiatives offer hope that society can address the challenges that urban children face, particularly programs that involve collaboration between different entities which offer diverse perspectives and talents in solving mental health problems. Children are the future of society, and resolving their mental health concerns is worth a great deal of effort and money.

REFERENCES

Acosta, O. M., Albus, K. E., Reynolds, M. W., Spriggs, D., & Weist, M. D. (2001). Assessing the status of research on violence-related problems among youth. *Journal of Clinical Child Psychology, 30* (2), 152-161.

American Psychiatric Association (2000). *Diagnostic and statistical manual of mental disorders* (Fourth Edition, Text Revision). Washington, DC: American Psychiatric Association.

Antidepressant medications for children and adolescents (February 8, 2005). http://www.nimh.nih.gov/healthinformation/antidepressants_child.cfm. Accessed May 28, 2005.

Applegate, K., Egeland, B., van Dulmen, M. H. N., & Sroufe, L. A. (2005). When more is not better: The role of cumulative risk in child behavior outcomes. *Journal of Child Psychology & Psychiatry, 46* (3), 235-245.

Atkins, M. S., Graczyk, P. A., Frazier, S. L., & Abdul-Adil, J. (2003). Toward a new model for promoting urban children's mental health: Accessible, effective, and sustainable school-based mental health services. *School Psychology Review, 12* (4), 503-514.

Botvin, G., Schinke, S., & Orlandi, M. (1995). School-based health promotion: Substance abuse and sexual behavior. *Applied and Preventive Psychology, 4* (3), 167-184.

Buckingham, M., & Coffman, C. (1999). *First, break all the rules: What the world's greatest managers do differently.* New York: Simon and Schuster.

Burns, B. J., Schoenwald, S. K., Burchard, J. D., Faw, L., & Santos, A. B. (2000). Comprehensive community based interventions for youth with severe emotional disorders: Multisystemic therapy and the wraparound process. *Journal of Child and Family Studies, 9* (3), 283-314.

Campbell, C., & Schwartz, D. F. (1996). Prevalence and impact of exposure to interpersonal violence among suburban and urban middle school students. *Pediatrics, 98* (3), 396–402.

Children's Defense Fund (January 31, 2005). A moral outrage: One American child or teen killed by gunfire nearly every 3 hours. www.childrensdefense.org. Accessed June 24, 2005.

Children's Defense Fund (September 2004). High School Exit Exams. www.childrensdefense.org. Accessed January 15, 2005.

Children's Defense Fund (June 2, 2004). 13 million children face food insecurity. www.childrensdefense.org. Accessed January 15, 2005.

Children's Defense Fund (June 2000). Domestic violence and its impact on children. www.childrensdefense.org. Accessed January 13, 2005.

Connolly, C. (December 15, 2004). Head of Cleveland clinic is attacking Big Mac. Washington Post. www.washingtonpost.com. Accessed January 24, 2005.

Cooley-Quille, M., Boyd, R. C., Frantz, E., & Walsh, J. (2001). Emotional and behavioral impact of exposure to community violence in inner-city adolescents. *Journal of Clinical Child Psychology, 30* (2), 199–207.

Cunningham, P. B., & Henggeler, S. W. (2001). Implementation of an empirically based drug and violence prevention and intervention program in public school settings. *Journal of Clinical Child Psychology, 30* (2), 221-233.

Downs, S. W., Moore, E., McFadden, E. J., & Costin, L. B. (2000). *Child welfare and family services: Policies and practices* (6th ed.). Boston: Allyn & Bacon.

Dulmus, C. N. (2003). Approaches to preventing the psychological impact of community violence exposure on children. *Crisis Intervention, 6*: 185–201.

Emerson, E. (2003). Prevalence of psychiatric disorders in children and adolescents with and without intellectual disability. *Journal of Intellectual Disability Research, 47* (1), 51–58.

FDA requires warnings for use of antidepressants on children (December 10, 2004). *New York Times,* p. A 36.

Financial assistance for grandparents and other relatives raising children (July 2004). Children's Defense Fund. www.childrensdefense.org. Accessed February 15, 2005.

Ferguson, D. L., Kozleski, E. B., & Smith, A. (2001). Transformed, inclusive schools: A framework to guide fundamental change in urban schools. National Institute for Urban School Improvement. www.inclusiveschools.org. Accessed February 3, 2005.

Gladwell, M. (2000). *The tipping point: How little things can make a big difference.* Boston: Little, Brown.

Gibson, D. L., & Noble, D. N. (2002). Children and families who fly beneath the radar screen: One agency's mission. *Family Ministry, 16,* 4, 47–59.

Greenburg, M. T., Kusche, C. A., Cook, E. T., & Quamma, J. P. (1995). Promoting emotional competence in school-aged children: The effects of the PATHS curriculum. *Development & Psychopathology, 7* (1), 117–136.

Harvard Medical School (2004). An update on attention deficit disorder. *Harvard Mental Health Letter, 20* (11), 4–7.

Hawkins, D. J., Catalano, R. F., Morrison, D. M., O'Donnell, J., Abbott, R. D., & Day, L. E. (1992). The Seattle Social Development Project: Effects of the first four years on protective factors and problem behaviors. In J. McCord & R. Tremblay (Eds.), *Preventing antisocial behavior: Interventions from birth through adolescence* (pp. 139-161). New York: Guilford.

Henggeler, S. W. (1999). Multisystemic therapy: An overview of clinical procedures, outcomes, and policy implications. *Child Psychology & Psychiatry Review, 4* (1), 2-10.

Henry, D. B., Tolan, P. H., & Gorman-Smith, D. (2001). Longitudinal family and peer group effects on violence and nonviolent delinquency. *Journal of Clinical Child Psychology, 30,* 172-186.

Hoare, P., Harris, M., Jackson, P., & Kerley, S. (1998). A community survey of children with severe intellectual disability and their families: Psychological adjustment, career distress and the effect of respite care. *Journal of Intellectual Disability 42,* 218-227.

Horn, M. (1989). *Before it's too late, The child guidance movement in the United States, 1922-1945.* Philadelphia: Temple University Press.

Integrating agendas for mental health in schools into the recommendations of the President's New Freedom Commission on Mental Health (Winter 2004). UCLA Mental Health in Schools Center. http://smhp.psych.ucla.edu. Accessed February 13, 2005.

Kataoka, S., Zhang, L., & Wells, K. (2002). Unmet need for mental health care among U.S. children: Variation by ethnicity and insurance status. *American Journal of Psychiatry, 159,* 1548-1555.

Kazdin, A. E. (1996). Dropping out of child psychotherapy: Issues for research and implications for practice. *Clinical Child Psychology & Psychiatry, 1,* 133-156.

Kazdin, A. E., Siegel, T. C., & Bass, D. (1992). Cognitive problem-solving skills training and parent management training in the treatment of antisocial behavior in children. *Journal of Consulting & Clinical Psychology, 60* (5), 733-747.

Kids Count Data Book (2004). Baltimore: Annie E. Casey Foundation.

Latest Findings in Children's Mental Health (Winter 2004). Institute for Health, Health Care Policy, and Aging Research: Rutgers University. www.ihhcpar.rutgers.edu. Accessed February 13, 2005.

Leading the nation's mental health system into the 21st century (September 2002). http://www.mentalhealth.samhsa.gov/publications. Accessed May 28, 2005.

Markey, U., Markey, D. J., Quant, B., Santelli, B., & Turnbull, A. (2002). Operation positive change: PBS in an urban context. *Journal of Positive Behavior Interventions, 4* (4), 218-230.

McKay, M. M., Chasse, K. T., Paikoff, R., McKinney, L. D., Baptiste, D., Coleman, D., Madison, S., & Bell, C. C. (2004). Family level impact of the CHAMP Family Program: A community collaborative effort to support urban families and reduce youth HIV exposure. *Family Process, 43* (1), 79-93.

Marsella, A. J. (1991). *Urbanization and mental disorder: An overview of conceptual and methodological research issues and findings.* Report of the Urbanization Panel of the World Health Organization Commission on Health and the Environment. Geneva, Switzerland: World Health Organization.

McMichael, A. J. (2000). The urban environment and health in a world of increasing globalization: Issues for developing countries. *Bulletin of World Health Organization 2000, 78*: 1117–1126.

Moniz, C., & Gorin, S. (2003). *Health and health care policy: A social work perspective.* Boston: Allyn & Bacon.

National Public Radio (December 14, 2004). *All Things Considered.* Memorial t-shirts gain popularity in some urban areas. www.npr.org. Accessed January 2, 2005.

New York State Office of Mental Health (December 10, 2002). CASSP. http://www.omh.state.ny.us/omhweb/EBP/cassp.htm. Accessed May 13, 2005.

Noble, D. N., & Ausbrooks, A. (forthcoming). Serving children. In D. M. DiNitto & C. A. McNeece (Eds.), *Social work: Issues and opportunities in a challenging profession* (3rd ed.). Boston: Allyn & Bacon.

Noble, D. N., & Gibson, D. L. (December 1994). Family values in action: Family connectedness for children in substitute care. *Child and Youth Care Forum, 23* (6).

Offord, D., Boyle, M., Szatmari, P., Rae-Grant, N., Links, P., Cadman, D., et al. (1987). Ontario child health study II: Six-month prevalence of disorder and rates of service utilization. *Archives of General Psychiatry, 44*, 832–836.

Oman, R. F., Vesely, S., Aspy, C. B., McLeroy, K. R., Rodine, S., & Marshall, L. (2004). The potential protective effect of youth assets on adolescent alcohol and drug use. *American Journal of Public Health, 94* (8), 1425–1431.

Oswald, D. P., Coutinho, M. J., Best, A. M., & Singh, N. N. (1999). Ethnic representation in special education: The influence of school-related economic and demographic variables. *Journal of Special Education, 32* (4), 194-206.

Pearce, M. J., Jones, S. M., Schwab-Stone, M. E., & Ruchkin, V. (2003). The protective effects of religiousness and parent involvement on the development of conduct problems among youth exposed to violence. *Child Development, 74* (6), 1682-1697.

Petr, C. G. (1998). *Social work with children and their families: Pragmatic foundations.* New York: Oxford.

Popple, P. R., & Leighninger, L. (2005). *Social work, social welfare, and American Society* (6th ed.). Boston: Pearson Allyn & Bacon.

Pynoos, R. S., Steinberg, A. M., & Goenjian, A. (1996). Traumatic stress in childhood and adolescence: Recent developments and current controversies. In B. A. van der Kolk, A. C. McFarlance & L. Weisaeth (Eds.), *Traumatic stress: The effects of overwhelming experience on mind, body, and society* (pp. 331–377). New York: Guilford Press.

Research and Training Center (2003). http://www.rtc.pdx.edu/. Accessed May 13, 2005.

Richards, M. H., Larson, R., Miller, B. V., Luo, Z., Sims, B., Parrella, D. P., & McCauley, C. (2004). Risky and protective contexts and exposure to violence in urban African American young adolescents. *Journal of clinical Child and Adolescent Psychology, 33* (1), 138–148.

Saigh, P. A., Mroueh, M., & Bremner, J. D. (1997). Scholastic impairments among traumatized adolescents. *Behavior Research & Therapy, 35* (5), 429–436.

Schiff, M., & McKay, M. M. (2003). Urban youth disruptive behavioral difficulties: Exploring association with parenting and gender. *Family Process, 42* (4), 517–529.

Snowden, L. R. (2003). Bias in mental health assessment and intervention: Theory and evidence. *American Journal of Public Health, 93* (2), 239–244.

Steele, W. (2004). Helping traumatized children. In S. L. A. Straussner & N. K. Phillips (Eds.), *Understanding mass violence: A social work perspective* (pp. 41–56). Boston: Pearson Allyn & Bacon.

Sugai, G., & Horner, R. (2002). The evolution of discipline practices: School-wide positive behavior supports. *Child & Family Behavior Therapy, 24*, 23–50.

Summerhill, L. (2005). Personal communication. San Marcos, TX.

Teen gets 30 years in Zoloft case (February 16, 2005). http://www.cnn.com/2005/LAW/02/15/zoloft.trial. Accessed February 25, 2005.

Terr, L. C. (1991). Childhood traumas: An outline and overview. *American Journal of Psychiatry, 148*, 10–20.

Temin, C. (2001). Let us consider the children. *Corrections Today, 63*, 66–68.

UCLA Mental Health in Schools Center Report (December 2003). *Youngsters' mental health and psychosocial problems: What are the data?* http://www.smhp.psych.ucla.edu. Accessed January 25, 2005.

U.S. Department of Health and Human Services. (2000). *Report of the Surgeon General's Conference on Children's Mental Health: A national action agenda.* Washington, DC: U. S. Government Printing Office.

U. S. Department of Health and Human Services. (2001). *Mental health: Culture, race, and ethnicity—A supplement to mental health: A report of the Surgeon General.* Rockville, MD: Author

van der Kolk, B. A. (1996). The body keeps the score: Approaches to the psychobiology of posttraumatic stress disorder. In B. A. van der Kolk, A. C. McFarlane & L. Weisaeth (Eds.), *Traumatic stress: The effects of overwhelming experience on mind, body, and society* (pp. 214–241). New York: The Guilford Press.

Wiest, M. D., Acosta, O. M., & Youngstrom, E. A. (2001). Predictors of violence exposure among inner-city youth. *Journal of Clinical Child Psychology, 30*, 187–198.

Winton, C. A. (2003). *Children as caregivers: Parental and parentified children.* Boston: Allyn & Bacon.

Zimmerman, M. A., Ramirez-Valles, J., Zapert, K. M., & Maton, K. J. (2000). A longitudinal study of stress-buffering effects for urban African-American male adolescent problem behaviors and mental health. *Journal of Community Psychology, 28* (1), 17–33.

Chapter 6

URBAN YOUTH GANGS

Gregory Acevedo

The roots of gangs in the United States can be traced back through the history of the country (Branch, 1997). Since the early twentieth century, youth gangs "have ebbed and flowed, largely organized around class, racial, ethnic, and gender configurations" (Brotherton & Barrios, 2004, p. xiv). Gang involvement is largely an urban phenomenon and is highly prevalent in communities characterized by poverty and physical and social isolation (Vigil, 2002). These conditions are often associated with vulnerable and ineffective social institutions, atrophied local labor markets, failing schools, and distressed and problematic families.

Since 1975, the estimated number of youth gangs has increased more than 10 times (Howell, 2000). There has been a seven-fold increase in both the number of cities reporting youth gang problems and the number of gang members (Howell, 2000). In 2002, approximately 731,500 members were involved in 21,500 gangs nationwide (Egley & Major, 2004). Youth gangs were active in more than 2,300 U.S. cities (with populations of 2,500 or more), with larger cities and surrounding communities accounting for approximately 85 percent of the estimated number of gang members (Egley & Major, 2004).

This chapter presents a discussion and analysis of urban youth gangs and highlights current trends and issues related to them. Various perspectives that conceptualize the dynamics of urban youth gangs are surveyed. Risk and protective factors for youth gang membership are examined, and programs and strategies for preventing, intervening, and suppressing youth gang activity are reviewed. The Latino experience with urban youth gangs is presented in order to highlight key points and implications for discussion and analysis.

DEFINITIONS OF YOUTH GANGS

There is no consensus on the definition of "youth gang" (Branch, 1997). The term "street gang" is often used interchangeably with youth gang; however, some street gangs are actually adult criminal organizations (Howell & Decker, 1999). Other types of gangs, such as motorcycle gangs, prison gangs, and racial supremacist and hate groups, are distinct from youth gangs. Howell and Decker (1999) utilize Miller's (1992) definition of a youth gang:

> A youth gang is a self-formed association of peers, united by mutual interests, with identifiable leadership and internal organization, who act collectively or as individuals to achieve specific purposes, including the conduct of illegal activity and control of a particular territory, facility, or enterprise. (p. 21)

Typically, the age range of youth gang members is 12 to 24, with an average age of 17 to 18 (Howell, 1998). Gang membership is overwhelming male and often comprised of African-American and Hispanic youth living in urban areas (Howell, Egley, & Gleason, 2002). However, there is substantial gang activity among Asian-American and white youth, in suburban localities, and among females, including gangs whose membership is exclusively female (Branch, 1997; Campbell, 1984; Monti, 1994; Moore & Hagerdorn, 2001). Differences between ethnic groups have been noted in the literature. When compared at either the pan-ethnic level (e.g., Asian-American versus Latino) or by national origin group within a pan-ethnicity (e.g., among Hispanics, Puerto Ricans versus Mexican-American), the literature has identified differences in the type of crime perpetrated by certain ethnic-based youth gangs, and in their relationship to their co-ethic community (Branch, 1997).

Location is associated with the dynamics of gang activity. In areas with a longer history of youth gang activity, gangs are more likely to be highly developed and sophisticated. Long-standing gangs tend to have older members and intergenerational family legacies of membership. They tend to be larger and have changed their "mission" and activities over time. Some have experienced migratory expansion to new territories locally, regionally, nationally, and even transnationally (Howell, Egley, & Gleason, 2002; Thompson, 2004).

YOUTH GANGS AND VIOLENCE

Exposure to violent acts, whether observed or perpetrated, is endemic to youth gang activity and "is part of the everyday life of gang members, even when they are apart from the gang; it is in their neighborhoods and within families" (Howell & Decker, 1999, p. 8). Not all violent acts perpetrated by individual members are under the sanction of gang activity. The association of gangs with high levels of community violence and crime is often assumed in both the literature and media, but this assumption has been questioned (Branch, 1997; Klein, 1995). Further, there are differences in the level and type of violent acts, both between gangs and among their members. Conflict between gangs over territorial issues and disputes can lead to violence affecting bystanders in the community (LeDuff, 2004). Instances of intergang violence in the form of "drive-by shootings" are typical occurrences that have been exacerbated by the proliferation of increasingly more lethal firearms (Howell & Decker, 1999).

The conflation of the term gang with "drug gangs" has obscured the understanding of the nature of violence in gang activity (Howell & Decker, 1999). In fact, the number of youth gangs that can accurately be characterized as drug gangs is a minority (Howell, 1998). Klein (1995) notes that drug gangs differ from other types of gangs in their structure and functioning. The violence involved in drug gang activity may be substantially different from that of street gangs, and much of what occurs under the category of gang violence "is unrelated or only tangential to drug trafficking" (Howell & Decker, 1999, p. 8).

While not all gangs in and around schools are involved in serious criminal activity or are the direct cause of victimization and violence in schools, there is an association of youth gangs with violence in schools (Howell & Lynch, 2000). Although gangs vary in the proportion of their membership that is actively attending school, they have a significant presence in many urban schools, which serve as sites for recruitment of new members (Branch, 1997; Branch & Rennick, 1995; Horowitz, 1990; Howell & Lynch, 2000; Monti, 1994). The presence of gangs in schools is correlated with criminal activity and "is an important contributor to overall levels of student victimization" (Howell & Lynch, 2000, p. 6). Students who are not gang members may utilize self-protective measures such as carrying weapons, increasing the potential for violence within schools (Straussner & Straussner, 1997).

MEDIA AND PUBLIC PERCEPTIONS OF YOUTH GANGS

It is evident that simplistic conceptualizations do not capture the complex dynamics of youth gang activity. Portrayals of youth gang activity in film and the news influence public perceptions. At least in part, media structures the parameters of debate that determine policies and programs to address the problems associated with youth gangs, fostering images of gangs that lack substance and nuance, which at times do nothing more than glamorize youth gangs (Branch, 1997). For example, the "link between gangs, drugs, and violence . . . is strongly promoted in media representations of youth gangs," but does little to constructively educate the public about the issue (Howell & Decker, 1999, p. 8). The public response to media portrayals of youth gangs instigates "cycles of outrage" that lead to upsurges of heightened concern that eventually dissipate with time (Gilbert, 1986).

THEORETICAL PERSPECTIVES OF THE
YOUTH GANG PHENOMENON

Criminological, psychogenic, and sociological perspectives have guided scholarly investigation of the phenomenon of youth gangs over the last century.

Criminological and criminal justice views of youth gang activity have a long history. The initial public response to youth gang activity was law enforcement, and it became the principle institution of social control charged to combat youth gangs. This emphasis on law enforcement led to the viewing of youth gangs exclusively as a "crime problem" (Hagerdorn, 1988). This perspective has limited the study of the nature of youth gangs within a community perspective, or of their connections to broader social and economic structures. Nor has the criminological perspective accurately captured the symbolic reality of youth gang members and their full range of motivations, perceptions, and behavior (Brotherton & Barrios, 2004).

Psychogenic views of youth gang activity, typified in the classic work of Yablonsky (1963), have maintained a primarily individualized focus on youth gang members and their psychosocial development and socialization. The psychogenic perspective has emphasized the pathological nature of youth gang behavior and the emotional and cognitive deficits of their members. The social and emotional needs of members for a peer group are met almost exclusively within the gang, and, the youth gang becomes the members' primary reference group and the basis of their self-concept (Riester, 1993). Members internalize the antisocial conventions of the group. Lacking any substantive involvement with competing pro-social systems, the gang member's development of critical thinking, moral reasoning, and self-awareness is retarded.

The *sociological* view emphasizes the youth gang's social organization and its connection to community. Much of the early sociological literature on youth gangs, including the classic studies by Thrasher (1927), emphasized the changes brought about by such social forces as technology, immigration, and urbanization, and the influence of conditions of social disorganization, cultural conflict, and structural strain in the growth of gangs. From the sociological vantage, the youth gang phenomenon is viewed as functional social adaptation to dysfunctional social and economic structures. Ecological factors, especially poverty, and social and spatial segregation and isolation, may foster a sense of individual and collective marginalization. This corrosive social and material environment negatively affects community processes, including neighborhood social control mechanisms (Brotherton & Barrios, 2004).

During the 1950s and 1960s, sociological investigation focused on youth gang activity as a delinquent form of lower class or minority youth subculture. Gang members were viewed as adopting an alternative value system in reaction to the experience of status frustration and blocked opportunities within mainstream society (Cloward & Ohlin, 1960; Cohen, 1955; Miller, 1958). Scholarly works during this era also focused on the effects of formal "labeling" within the law enforcement and criminal justice systems (Becker, 1963; Werthman, 1969). Attention was paid to how gang members responded to official labels, such as "delinquent," and how their behaviors were shaped by their acceptance of these labels. They adopted deviant "career paths" and lived up to the socially expected behaviors of the delinquent role.

During the 1970s and 1980s, amidst an "epidemic" rise in youth gang and drug-selling activities, sociological study centered on the connection of youth gangs to the "underclass." This urban constituency resides in hyper-segregated racial and ethnic neighborhoods characterized by high levels of violence and crime, intergenerational poverty, limited academic achievement, and ineffectual family functioning (Wilson, 1987). Within the rubric of underclass theory, the subcultures of urban youth gangs came to be seen as "oppositional institutions" (Bourgois, 1995; Hagedorn, 1988; Klein, 1995; Moore, 1991; Padilla, 1993; Vigil, 1988), and youth gangs were seen as reproducing "behaviors and value systems . . . in opposition to those of the dominant culture" (Brotherton & Barrios, 2004, p. 35).

Jankowski (1991) conceived of longstanding urban youth gangs as sophisticated organizations that rationally respond to economic and social deprivation. He argued that youth gangs are fully integrated into their respective communities and serve a positive social function by managing to contain their members' defiant individualistic characters (Brotherton & Barrios, 2004).

The sociological literature of the 1990s adopted a less mechanistic and reductionistic analysis of the underclass connection to youth gangs, with multicausal frameworks emphasizing social and economic contingency (Sullivan, 1989; Venkatesh, 1997; 2000). Youth gang activity was seen as the net result of the interaction of various individual- and structural-level factors. These frameworks attempted to account for the variation that occurs between gangs and amongst their individual members. Varied outcomes resulted from aggregate and individual responses to local conditions. Every community maintained its own distinct local environment and socio-structural linkages between school, family, labor market, and the criminal justice system. Neighborhoods differed in terms of socioeconomic status, social networks, family structure, race and ethnicity, residential segregation, housing tenure, and impact of migration. Each neighborhood had its own specific patterns of employment and differences in the level of physical isolation from potential jobs and access to job opportunities. Neighborhoods also differed in their criminal activity along such dimensions as the role and amount of violence involved; the organization of markets for stolen or illegal goods; level of community acceptance of criminal activities; and the degree of recruitment, training, support, and direction supplied by adults or more established criminals.

Brotherton and Barrios (2004) broke new ground in the sociological conceptualization of youth gangs by viewing them as "street organizations." This theoretical approach recognizes that youth gangs and their members not only adapt to their ecological environment, they can also be agents of change within them. They have the capacity to foster critically conscious and constructive opposition to "the dominant culture and its structural foundations" (Brotherton & Barrios, 2004, p. 39). Youth gangs have the potential to transmute into social movements, manifested by street organizations, which are:

> formed largely by youth and adults of a marginalized social class...to provide its members with a resistant identity, an opportunity to be individually and collectively empowered, a voice to speak back to and challenge the dominant culture, a refuge from the stresses and strains of barrio or ghetto life, and a spiritual enclave within which its own sacred rituals can be generated and practiced. (Brotherton & Barrios, 2004, p. 23)

By introducing the concept of street organization, Brotherton and Barrios attempted to focus on the transformative power and the "dynamic social, cultural, spiritual, and political trajectory of some contemporary street subcultures" (Brotherton & Barrios, 2004, p. 23), instead of viewing the street gang from a purely criminal perspective.

Nature of Youth Gang Phenomenon

Although each theoretical perspective on youth gangs has formulated its own unique conceptualizations, there appears to be a consensus that recognizes a number of concepts regarding the nature of youth gangs. The accrued insights of the criminological, psychogenic, and sociological literature strongly suggest that youth gangs:

- Differ in their level and type of criminal activity;
- Are comprised primarily of working- or lower-class male youth but also have a significant representation among females and white middle-class youth;
- Typically emerge in areas with scarce economic, political, and social resources, and histories of racial and class segregation, in which ecological development has fostered social and spatial isolation;
- Tend to arise in communities engulfed by social disorganization and cultural conflict;
- Have experienced marginalization within mainstream institutions and systems, both at the collective- and individual-level;

• Are subcultures where some members collectively and individually express their racial, ethnic, and class identities.

RISK AND PROTECTIVE FACTORS

The majority of youth who are exposed to the risk factors for gang membership do not become involved in gangs. Although "there is no single cause for youth gang membership or delinquency" (Wyrick & Howell, 2004, p. 22), knowledge about risk and protective factors might contribute to constructing effective programs and services to prevent and reduce youth gang activity. The identification of risk and protective factors attracts much scientific attention, and one assumes that ultimately this knowledge can be translated into practical frameworks that can apply to clinical work with youth gangs members, their families, and communities. Solely identifying factors that contribute to gang involvement is not sufficient to the task of prevention and intervention. However, understanding how these factors operate will further these efforts.

Wyrick and Howell (2004) note that the major risk factors domains for gang membership are all related to various adolescent problem behaviors, including serious violence and delinquency. Research literature has demonstrated that "the accumulation of risk factors greatly increases the likelihood of gang involvement," and that "the presence of risk factors in multiple domains appears to increase the likelihood of gang involvement even more than the general accumulation of risk factors" (Wyrick & Howell, 2004, p. 22). Therefore, it is important to distinguish among the particular risk factors associated with each domain in order to identify those most vulnerable to gang involvement based on the accumulation of risk factors across domains.

Community, Family, School, Peer Group, and Individual Risk Factors

Howell (1998) provides an exhaustive literature review focusing on the main community, family, school, peer group, and individual risk factors for gang membership. *Community risk factors* include: poverty; limited economic and social mobility; high levels of residential mobility; the availability of drugs and firearms in the neighborhood; and the presence of gangs. Among the *family risk factors* are: family disorganization and management problems; parental drug/alcohol abuse and drug addiction; incest; family violence; having family members in a gang; sibling antisocial behavior; a lack of parental and adult male role models; and extreme economic deprivation. *School-based risk factors* involve: academic failure and frustration; low levels of commitment to school and low educational aspirations; high levels of antisocial behavior in school; negative labeling by teachers; being identified as having a learning disability; and the lack of teacher role models. Some of the *peer-group risk factors* are: commitment to delinquent peers rather than positive peers; exposure to street socialization; having friends involved in drugs or gangs; and the presence of gang members in class. *Individual risk factors* include: aggressive and defiant attitudes; having a fatalistic view of the world; hyperactive and externalizing behaviors; the need for excitement, acting in a daring and risky manner; social disabilities; early sexual activity; drug use or involvement in drug trafficking; a desire for group conferred status, identity, self-esteem, companionship, and protection; lack of refusal skills; and victimization.

Protective Factors

While the literature on risk factors is extensive, "few studies have addressed protective (resilience) factors that buffer children and adolescents from gang involvement" (Howell, 2000, p. 14). Some mental and social development processes may counteract trauma and stress and have a buffering effect against gang membership. Wyrick (2000) has suggested that protective measures that encourage adolescents to feel they have a stake in society could reduce and prevent gang involvement. These may include efforts to improve attitudes about school, reduce feelings of alienation, address family conflict, and modify perceptions that gangs are beneficial to their members.

PROGRAMS AND STRATEGIES TO REDUCE GANG INVOLVEMENT

Knowledge about risk factors and resilience contributes to the development of effective programs and intervention strategies. Given that risk factors across multiple domains increase the likelihood of gang involvement (Wyrick & Howell, 2004), programs and strategies need to target multiple risk factors across multiple domains. Comprehensive gang reduction programs and strategies should be developed along three primary dimensions: *prevention, intervention,* and *suppression.*

Prevention Programs

Prevention programs attempt to forestall youth gang activity by deflecting individual youths from gang involvement. They also attempt to quell the formation of gangs in the first place. Typical prevention strategies include *community organization* interventions aimed at improving neighborhood conditions, and *school-based programs.*

Community organization strategies "are designed to involve local community groups in improving neighborhood conditions . . . believed to foster the formation of gangs" (Howell, 2000, p. 5). Grass-roots efforts have led to programs that provide recreation, mediation and conflict resolution, advocacy, mentorship, "reparenting," and life-skills and leadership training. Some of these programs, such as the House of Umoja in Philadelphia, have proven to be effective (National Center for Neighborhood Enterprise, 1999), while others like the Chicago Area Project have not been empirically evaluated (Howell, 2000).

Strategies aimed at improving conditions and creating opportunities are exemplified in U.S. Department of Housing and Urban Development (HUD) supported programs, such as Empowerment Zone projects that revitalize economic and social services in high-risk communities, and Enterprise Communities, which promote physical and human development within these communities. Howell (2000) describes several programs that have targeted select low-income, inner-city areas. The Beethoven Project, based in a Chicago public housing complex, provides various health and social services to mothers and infants through a family drop-in center. The Neutral Zone, based in the state of Washington, provides recreation and service facilities for high-risk youth at several sites throughout the state. In St. Paul, Minnesota, the Community Outreach Program, run by the police department, is designed to divert first-time offenders from further delinquency and provide school liaison work in a Southeast Asian community experiencing gang activity. Overall, prevention efforts have demonstrated effectiveness (Office of Juvenile Justice and Delinquency Prevention, 1995).

School-based and early childhood programs based on the risk and protective factor model have included parent training and childhood skill development to target antisocial behavior, such as disruptive classroom behavior. A number of early childhood programs have proven effective (Howell, 2000). *School-based prevention programs* have included antibullying programs and protection programs that provide supervised routes for students traveling back and forth to school. Goldstein and Kodluboy (1998) have suggested that school-based prevention programs should address in-school safety and control procedures, provide in-school enrichment, and establish formal links to community-based programs. After-school activities, such as those provided through Boys and Girls Clubs of America, have offered alternatives to gang involvement through various recreational and leisure activities, social services, and case management. While there is some evidence that school-based efforts are effective, these programs have only recently begun to be adequately evaluated through large-scale, longitudinal assessments that are currently in process (Howell, 2000).

Intervention Programs

Intervention programs "seek to reduce the criminal activities of gangs . . . and . . . criminality among gang members" (Howell, 2000, p. 14). Since the 1940s, "detached worker" and "crisis intervention" programs have attempted to transform youth gangs into prosocial groups by providing social services, case management, advocacy, and group activities. Detached workers are "agency representatives dispatched from their offices to work directly with gangs in the community" (Howell, 2000, p. 5). When empirically evaluated, however, these programs have demonstrated little effectiveness as singular approaches, and in fact, such group work activities have been accused of potentially fostering gang activity by promoting the gang's cohesion (Klein, 1995). Detached worker programs may be more effective as part of broadly coordinated approaches (Spergel & Grossman, 1997).

Other gang intervention strategies have included programs that provide education, training, and employment services, including employing former gang members as workers. Life-skills training and mentorship programs have also been developed. Victim programs, have included emergency room intervention, providing counseling to victims of gang violence, and attempts to discourage retaliation. Training about gangs has been made available to hospital emergency room staff so that they are better able to aid in these efforts. Gang summits and truces been informally negotiated by local community residents, such as *Alliance for Concerned Black Men* in Washington, D.C., who intervened in an escalating conflict between warring gangs in their neighborhood. Treatment programs aimed at gang members in juvenile detention and correctional facilities have included interpersonal skills training, gang awareness curriculums, and aftercare programs developed for high-risk juvenile offenders (Howell, 2000). While all of these various programs show promise, for the most part, they have not been rigorously evaluated (Howell, 2000).

Based on his view of the family as the original agent of socialization, Branch (1997) has promoted a family-focused clinical intervention called the Family Intervention Project. This provides a psychoeducational approach that works with youth gang members and their families "to help the family find enough strength to start healing wounds while it helps its member who is 'in trouble' . . . using the resources that are already present" (Branch, 1997, p. xiv). Fleisher (1998), who based his studies of gangs in Kansas City, Missouri, has proposed a residential center approach to deliver education, training, and employment services, and life-skills training and mentorship programs.

Suppression Programs

Although intervention and suppression programs share the common goal of reducing criminal activities of gangs, suppression strategies "use the full force of the law, generally through a combination of police, prosecution, and incarceration" (Howell, 2000, p. 21). Suppression efforts often involve increased sanctions and enforcement through laws specifically targeting gang activity, or laws that have a wider scope. Suppressive methods also include the deployment of multiagency and multijurisdictional task forces that coordinate local, state, and federal law enforcement. Some suppression strategies use multiple techniques, such as community policing, networking and collaboration with neighborhood groups and officers specializing in gang activity, and problem assessment and program development (Howell, 2000).

Brotherton and Barrios (2004) have argued that the emphasis on suppressive law enforcement and punitive sanctions in policy formation has had a detrimental effect on the development of other gang intervention strategies and programs:

> In terms of social policies and fiscal budgets, this translates into far more resources being channeled into curfews, mass arrests, mandatory sentences, anti-combination laws [statutes barring gang members from associating with each other] and conspiracy indictments, than into social services that could support and empower gang-related youths or the kinds of information for schools, neighborhoods, political parties, churches, and family networks that promotes understanding and humanistic responses rather than fear and loathing. (pp. xiv-xv)

POLICIES

Legislation is an important foundation for the development of prevention, intervention, and suppression programs and strategies. Much federal and state legislation, as well as city ordinances and court injunctions, is related to enforcement. Through its distribution of federal funds to states and localities, the federal Juvenile Accountability Block Grants (JABG) wield a great influence over a wide range of anti-gang programming, including prevention, intervention, and suppression programs. However, JABG funding has been subject to political pressure, maneuvering, and partisanship. For example, in 2004 the White House requested massive cuts in the program, especially funding for its preventive measures. While the U.S. House subcommittee responsible for the legislation rejected the proposed cuts and additional funding was made available, the new funding was targeted for suppressive-oriented strategies (Jackman, 2004).

The current bias towards suppression strategies and programs reflects the appeal of solving the problem of urban youth gangs by policing, prosecuting, and incarcerating gang members. However, the historical evidence demonstrates that "war strategy" proposals have not been effective in eradicating such other social problems as drugs sales. The multisystemic nature of gang dynamics is not amenable to narrowly conceived intervention approaches. The lessons learned from the Latino experience with urban young gangs illustrate the difficulties in finding approaches to successfully address the "gang problem."

YOUTH GANGS AND THE BARRIO

Puerto Ricans and Mexican-Americans have figured prominently in the historical development of urban youth gangs in the U.S., with urban youth gangs in Latino communities dating back to at least the 1920s (Vigil, 2000). These two groups came to play major roles in youth gang activity in the barrios of cities such as New York, Los Angeles, Chicago, Philadelphia, and Hartford, Connecticut.

Barrio "refers to an urban neighborhood or group of neighborhoods in which Latinos are the predominant population . . . made up of ethnic networks, businesses, churches, civic organizations, and other social institutions" (Melendez, 1998, p. 105). Spanish Harlem in New York City, and East Los Angeles, California, are the most longstanding and visible barrios in the nation.

Youth gangs and drug trafficking among Latino youth have drawn significant attention among social scientists (Bourgois, 1995), and the relationship between barrio conditions and the formation of gangs have been studied at length. Incidents like the "Zoot Suit Riots" involving Mexican-American youth in Los Angeles in 1942, and the "Capeman Murders" involving Puerto Rican youth in New York in 1959, became iconic references of urban youth gangs in the press and film. Youth gangs in the barrio also attracted attention in the policy field. During the 1960s, for example, Mobilization for Youth, a well-known program of the War on Poverty, included Puerto Rican youth on Manhattan's Lower East Side in their target population.

Risk Factors in the Barrio

Barrios tend to be located in cities and states that have suffered most from disinvestment in social services such as mental health and substance abuse treatment. They suffer from shifting government priorities, for example the lack of civil rights enforcement and public employment, and shoulder an undue burden as a result of dysfunctional public school systems. The association of segregated urban public schooling and educational outcomes has not been positive.

The schooling of barrio children may be more at risk than ever. While "nationwide, the Latino share of public school enrollment has almost tripled since 1968" there has been "steadily rising segregation since the 1960s and no significant desegregation efforts outside of a handful of large districts" (Frankenberg & Lee, 2002, p. 2). In a study on community dynamics and the rise of Latino street gangs, Vigil (2002) notes that when segregation and isolation has been both social and spatial, it has undermined the rate and direction of acculturation, disrupted social networks, and bred dysfunctional forces. When barrios are cut off from mainstream social institutions, their social and economic development is likely to suffer. Economic indicators that today's barrios are stagnating are cause for concern.

Protective Factors in the Barrio

Barrios, while posing many of the community, family, school, peer group, and individual risk factors for gang membership, can also provide protective environments. Youth engagement in their ethnic immigrant culture promotes prosocial attitudes and behaviors. Ethnic identity can serve as a protective mechanism when associated with positive and constructive values and actions, and offers great potential benefits for Latino communities.

As noted earlier in this discussion, some theorists have perceived participation in street gangs as an attempt by gang members at affiliation and meaning. Branch (1997) notes that, "Latino gangs are much more pronounced in having ethnic identity as a part of their group's program than other ethnic gangs. Much of the activity of Latino gangs is affiliated with the barrio and *familia*. This seems to help in Latino adolescents' quest for a solid sense of identity, personal and group" (p. 59).

Among Latino youth, ethnic awareness and pride seem to work in tandem with deeply held cultural values and norms. The literature has identified Latino cultural tendencies toward "allocentrism," a sense of identity and commitment to collectives and groups rather than individuals, a focus on intergroup and intragroup harmony, and a preference for closeness in interpersonal space (Gutiérrez, Yeakley, & Ortega, 2002). Like most cultures, the family is the primary social unit of organization; however, Latino culture is characterized by "familism," the tendency to prize family matters above other institutions or activities. Familism and ethnic solidarity would appear to be solid grounds for protection against the risks for gang membership.

Gang intervention in the barrios requires that attention be given to actively changing the social structures, not just providing services; a fatal flaw that doomed, or at least undermined, efforts in the War on Poverty era. Focusing on social services, while almost exclusively relying on civil-rights legislation to alter social structures in the United States, has been unsuccessful (Valle & Torres, 2000, p. 37). It is the challenge of social workers and other helping professionals to discover other ways of offering opportunities for affiliation and meaning to youth in the Barrio; future research in this area is certainly merited.

Social Work and Youth Gangs

Social work has grappled with the youth gang problem for decades. In the early 1960s, Lloyd Ohlin at the Columbia School of Social Work developed Mobilization for Youth (MFY), which became the model for antipoverty programming during the Johnson Administration. MFY was designed as a comprehensive and well-coordinated strategy to reduce juvenile delinquency and youth gangs. MFY programming included the establishment of neighborhood service centers to provide concrete and social services, employment of local residents, both youths and adults, and community organizing strategies to foster civic engagement and community-led advocacy. As a pioneering agency, MFY emphasized the experimental nature of the program and the need to empirally evaluate its effectiveness.

Ultimately, under the weight of political pressure it experienced in response to its controversial community mobilization tactics, MFY strayed from its original comprehensive strategy and devolved into a highly scaled-back program focusing on vocational training and social service provision (Katz, 1989). There are important lessons to be learned from the MFY legacy for the current era of social work practice, most importantly, the need to structure comprehensive programs that will garner public support.

Social work is well poised to meet the challenge of intervening in the youth gang problem, especially in high-need areas such as the barrio. Through individual, family, and group work, practitioners have the opportunity to intervene with individual youth and their families within various agency and school settings. An important aspect of working with youth and their families would be to focus on fostering greater connectedness, communication, and limit setting.

Community and policy practice strategies can be directed towards crafting policies and programs that enrich the settings in which youth live, study, play, and work, and so enhance their wellbeing (Roth & Brooks-Gunn, 2000). These policies and programs could help these settings foster positive friendships and peer influences, create developmentally appropriate activities, and establish constructive connections between youth and adults. These interventions could target particular neighborhoods, assist in improving their physical environment and infrastructure, broaden economic opportunities, and promote community institutions and relationships that maximize networks of social support.

Social work research could direct more attention to the study of the risk and protective factors, and mechanisms and pathways that lead to youth gang involvement. In addition, evaluation research should generate evidence that confirms the effectiveness of various intervention strategies. Empirical validation of practices might increase public support for interventions that are potentially controversial, especially those involving community organizing.

CONCLUSION

Urban youth gangs are a social problem that will only find resolution through programs and strategies that target all the systems involved: individuals, families, communities, smaller scale social institutions like schools, and larger ones like the criminal justice system. According to Klein (1995), "Gangs are by-products of their communities: They cannot long be controlled by attacks on symptoms alone; community structure and capacity must also be targeted" (p. 147). The most difficult challenges in addressing this age old issue will be political and economic.

REFERENCES

Becker, H. (1963). *Outsiders—Studies in the sociology of deviance.* New York: Free Press.

Branch, C. W. (1997). *Clinical interventions with gang adolescents and their families.* Boulder, CO: Westview Press.

Brotherton, D. C., & Barrios, L. (2004). The almighty Latin King and Queen Nation: Street politics and the transformation of a New York City gang. New York: Columbia University Press.

Bourgois, P. (1995). *In search of respect: Selling crack in El Barrio.* New York: Cambridge University Press.

Burch, J. H., & Chemers, B. M. (1997). *A Comprehensive response to America's youth gang problem.* Fact Sheet #40. Washington, DC: U.S. Department of Justice, Office of Justice Programs, Office of Juvenile Justice and Delinquency Prevention.

Campbell, A. (1984). *The girls in the gang: A report from New York City.* New York: Basil Blackwell.

Cloward, R. A., & Ohlin, L. E. (1960). *Delinquency and opportunity: A theory of delinquent gangs.* New York: The Free Press.

Cohen, A. (1955). *Delinquent boys: The culture of the gang.* Glencoe, IL: The Free Press.

Egley, A., & Major, A. K. (2004). *Highlights of the 2002 National Youth Gang Survey.* Fact Sheet #1. Washington, DC: U.S. Department of Justice, Office of Justice Programs, Office of Juvenile Justice and Delinquency Prevention.

Fleisher, M. S. (1998). *Dead end kids: Gang girls and the boys they know.* Madison, WI: University of Wisconsin Press.

Frankenberg, E., & Lee, C. (2002, August). *Race in American public schools: Rapidly resegregating school districts.* The Harvard University Civil Rights Project. Cambridge, MA: Harvard University Press.

Gilbert, J. (1986). *A cycle of outrage: American's reaction to the juvenile delinquent in the 1950's.* New York: Oxford University Press.

Goldstein, A. P., & Kodluboy, D. W. (1998). *Gangs in schools: Signs, symbols, and solutions.* Champaign, IL: Research Press.

Gutiérrez, L., Yeakley, A., & Ortega, R. (2002). Educating students for social work with Latinos: Issues for the new millennium. *Journal of Social Work Education, 36,* (3), 541–557.

Hagedorn, J. M. (1988). *People and folks: Gangs, crime and the underclass in a rustbelt city.* Chicago: Lakeview Press.

Horowitz, R. (1990). *Sociological perspectives on gangs: Conflicting definitions and concepts.* In C. R. Huff (Ed.), Gangs in America (pp. 37–54). Newbury Park, CA: Sage.

Howell, J. C. (1998). *Youth gangs: An overview.* Bulletin. Youth Gang Series. Washington, DC: U.S. Department of Justice, Office of Justice Programs, Office of Juvenile Justice and Delinquency Prevention.

Howell, J. C. (2000). *Youth gang programs and strategies.* Summary. Washington, DC: U.S. Department of Justice, Office of Justice Programs, Office of Juvenile Justice and Delinquency Prevention.

Howell, J. C., & Decker, S. H. (1999). *The youth gangs, drugs, and violence connection.* Bulletin. Youth Gang Series. Washington, DC: U.S. Department of Justice, Office of Justice Programs, Office of Juvenile Justice and Delinquency Prevention.

Howell, J. C., Egley, A. K., & Gleason, D. K. (2002). *Modern day youth gangs.* Bulletin. Youth Gang Series. Washington, DC: U.S. Department of Justice, Office of Justice Programs, Office of Juvenile Justice and Delinquency Prevention.

Howell, J. C., & Lynch, J. (2000). *Youth gangs in schools.* Bulletin. Youth Gang Series. Washington, DC: U.S. Department of Justice, Office of Justice Programs, Office of Juvenile Justice and Delinquency Prevention.

Jackman, T. (2004, June 16). U.S. panel restores anti-gang funding. *The Washington Post,* p. B1.

Katz, M. (1989). *The Undeserving poor: From the War on Poverty to the War on Welfare.* New York: Pantheon.

Klein, M. W. (1995). *The American street gang.* New York: Oxford University Press.

LeDuff, C. (2004, October 15). In city numbed by violence, the death of a young boy stirs anguish. *The New York Times,* p. A6.

Melendez, E. (1998). The economic development of El Barrio. In F. Bonilla, E., Melendez, R. Morales & M. de los Angeles Torres (Eds.), *Borderless borders: U.S. Latinos, Latin Americans, and the paradox of interdependence* (pp. 105–127). Philadelphia: Temple University Press.

Miller, W. B. (1958). Lower class culture as a generating milieu of gang delinquency. *Journal of Social Issues, 14,* 5–19.

Miller, W. B. (1992). *Crime by youth gangs and groups in the United States.* Washington, DC: U.S. Department of Justice, Office of Justice Programs, Office of Juvenile Justice and Delinquency Prevention.

Monti, D. (1994). *Wannabe: Gangs in suburbs and schools.* New York: Oxford University Press.

Moore, J. W. (1991). *Going down to the barrio: Homeboys and homegirls in change.* Philadelphia: Temple University Press.

Moore, J. W., & Hagedorn, J. M. (2001). *Female gangs.* Bulletin. Youth Gang Series. Washington, DC: U.S. Department of Justice, Office of Justice Programs, Office of Juvenile Justice and Delinquency Prevention.

National Center for Neighborhood Enterprise. (1999). *Violence-free zone initiatives: Models of successful grassroots youth initiatives.* Washington, DC: National Center for Neighborhood Enterprise.

Office of Juvenile Justice and Delinquency Prevention (1995). *Delinquency prevention works.* Program summary. Washington, DC: Department of Justice, Office of Juvenile Justice and Delinquency Prevention.

Padilla, F. (1993). The working gang. In S. Cummings & D. J. Monti, (Eds.), *Gangs* (pp. 173–192). Albany, NY: State University of New York Press.

Riester, A. (1993). Creating the adolescent group therapy experience. In A. Alonso & H. I. Swiller (Eds.), *Group therapy in clinical practice* (pp. 219–236). Washington, DC: American Psychiatric Press.

Roth, J. L., & Brooks-Gunn, J. (2000). What do adolescents need for healthy development?: Implications for youth policy. Social Policy Report. *Society for Research in Child Development.*

Spergel, I. A., & Grossman, S. F. (1997). *Evaluation of the Little Village gang violence reduction project.* Chicago: The School of Social Service Administration, University of Chicago.

Straussner, J. H., & Straussner, S. L. A. (1997). Impact of community and school violence on children. In N. K. Phillips & S. L. A. Straussner (Eds.), *Children in urban environment: Linking social policy and clinical practice* (pp. 61–77). Springfield, IL: Charles C Thomas.

Sullivan, M. L. (1989). *Getting paid: Youth crime and work in the inner city.* Ithaca, NY: Cornell University Press.

Thompson, G. (2004, September 26). Shuttling between nations, Latino gangs confound the law. *The New York Times*, Section 1, p. 1.

Thornberry, T. P., Huizinga, D., & Loeber, R. (2004). The causes and correlates studies: Findings and policy implications. *Juvenile Justice, IX*(1), 3-19. Washington, DC: U.S. Department of Justice, Office of Juvenile Justice and Delinquency Prevention.

Thrasher, F. M. (1927). *The gang: A study of 1,313 gangs in Chicago.* Chicago: University of Chicago Press.

Valle, V. M., & Torres, R. D. (2000). *Latino metropolis.* Minneapolis, MN: University of Minnesota Press.

Venkatesh, S. A. (1997). The social organization of street gang activity in an urban ghetto. *American Journal of Sociology, 103*(1), 82–111.

Venkatesh, S. A. (2000). *American project: The rise and fall of a modern ghetto.* Cambridge, MA: Harvard University Press.

Vigil, J. D. (1988). *Barrio gangs: Street life and identity in Southern California.* Austin, TX: University of Texas Press.

Vigil, J. D. (2002). Community dynamics and the rise of street gangs. In M. M. Suárez-Orozco & M. M. Páez (Eds.), *Latinos remaking America* (pp. 97–109). Berkeley, CA: University of California Press.

Werthman, C. (1969). Delinquency and moral character. In D. R. Cressy & D. A.Ward (Eds.), *Delinquency, crime, and social processes* (pp. 613–632). New York: Harper and Row.

Wilson, W. J. (1987). *The truly disadvantaged: The inner city, the underclass, and public policy.* Chicago: University of Chicago Press.

Wyrick, P. A. (2000). *Vietnamese youth gang involvement.* Fact Sheet #200001. Washington, DC: U.S. Department of Justice, Office of Juvenile Justice and Delinquency Prevention.

Wyrick, P. A., & Howell, J. C. (2004). Strategic risk-based response to youth gangs. *Juvenile Justice, IX*(1), 20-29.

Yablonsky, L. (1963). *The violent gang.* New York: Penguin.

Section III

FAMILIAL FACTORS IMPACTING ON URBAN CHILDREN

Chapter 7

CHILDREN IN OUT-OF-HOME PLACEMENTS

RICHARD HOLODY

Foster care policy necessitates the separation of children from their families, if only temporarily; foster care practice seeks to limit and repair damage to the child through creative innovations that respond to the needs of the child and the dilemmas created by policy. Policy both frees and constrains the practitioner: it gives focus to the work but limits possible interventions and objectives. Further, foster care policy necessarily responds to the concerns of United States society at large and social welfare policy in general. And, like all social welfare policy, foster care policy is a creation of history, reflecting the often conflicting components of U.S. ideology. In short, it reflects tendencies that are wise and humane, as well as short-sighted and self-serving.

To understand the nature of practice with children in foster care, we must uncover the roots of foster care policy and their intimate connections with the history of American cities. Further, understanding contemporary foster care practice requires understanding child protective services (CPS), which, despite its overlapping historical concern with immigration, industrialization, and the rise of cities, nevertheless has a separate historical development.

Cities have always offered promise and threatened peril. Though tens and eventually hundreds of thousands of European immigrants seized the opportunities of freedom and resources available in the turbulent and largely unregulated cities in the late nineteenth century, their customs, languages, religions, and child-rearing practices were seen to the social elites as a challenge to what it meant to be an American. Current foster care policy, now intertwined with CPS policy, necessarily reflects the contradictions of capitalism and the challenges of democracy.

145

This chapter explores how foster care policy impacts on practice with children in care, with their substitute caregivers, and with their biological parents. It begins with a review of the histories of foster care and CPS, explores the development of "permanency planning," the philosophy that guides foster care practice, and considers the success and limits of that policy as society continues to struggle with the social problem of families being unable to raise children. It then explores typical cases encountered by the foster care practitioner to illuminate how policy structures not only the circumstances of the case but the possible intervention strategies of the worker as well.

A CENTURY OF FOSTER CARE: 1853-1959

From colonial days through the earliest years of the Republic, communities and local governments responded to the needs of abandoned, orphaned, and neglected children in a variety of ways: binding-out, indenture, and almshouses (Costin, Bell, & Downs, 1991). But in the first half of the nineteenth century, the United States, especially on the eastern seaboard, underwent a profound transformation that, in the minds of the elite and upper-class leaders, exposed the inadequacy of these earlier schemes for providing out-of-home substitute care for children.

Between 1800 and 1850, five million immigrants arrived in the U.S., primarily from Ireland and Germany, countries whose culture, language, traditions, and religions were different from what constituted America in the early days of the Republic. And these immigrants lived in something new in America: big cities. The population of Philadelphia quadrupled between 1790 and 1850; Baltimore became the second largest city in the country in 1850, following a more than tenfold increase in population in 50 years; and most dramatically, New York City, which then only included Manhattan and the Bronx, saw its population increase from 33,000 in 1790 to over 500,000 people by the start of the Civil War (Foner & Garraty, 1991). The immigrants lived in overcrowded tenements and worked in unregulated factories.

For Charles Loring Brace and other concerned Protestant leaders, this transformation was threatening the very fabric of American life.

Brace had worked with the poor in the Five Points Mission (an area of New York City that was the setting of Martin Scorsese's film, *Gangs of New York*), but quickly became frustrated by the limited progress at "curing" delinquency (O'Connor, 2001). In 1853, he and others founded the Children's Aid Society as a direct response to what he saw as the consequences of industrialization, urbanization, and immigration. It was, in Brace's own phrase, an attempt to control "the dangerous classes" of society (Brace, 1872).

Brace's solution was to "place-out" unwanted or uncared for urban children, most of whom were from Roman Catholic families, with farm families in the Midwest, usually Protestant families. They were expected to instill in the children the virtues of hard work, temperance, education, and respect. By the end of the nineteenth century, tens of thousands of children had been sent out of the city on "orphan trains" to be raised by these families. As Brace said of the thousands of immigrant children he sent to the Midwest, "happily, few, if any ever returned to New York" (Brace, 1873, p. 242). Catholics soon recognized the threat to their constituency posed by the success of this program and devised orphan trains of their own (Gordon, 1999). Foster care practice in the nineteenth century was a terminal service: its purpose was achieved once the child was removed from his or her home of origin—and from the pernicious influences of the city—and placed with the substitute family on a farm. Jacob Riis, the noted photojournalist and author of *How the Other Half Lives* (1890/1997), would later confirm the wide-spread acceptance of this approach: "Nothing is now better understood than that the rescue of the children is the key to the problem of city poverty . . .; that a character may be formed where to reform it would be a hopeless task" (p. 139).

However, by the end of the 1800s, child welfare leaders began reevaluating foster care, as the needs and rights of dependent childhood began to receive wider recognition (Folks, 1902). Between 1890 and 1930, the work of such leaders as Charles Birtwell, Homer Folks, and C. C. Carstens resulted in foster care being defined as a temporary service, rather than a permanent answer. Increased attention was given to the quality of care received by the child in the foster home or other out-of-home placement, the child's need for individualized assessment and services, and to the need to recruit, train, and monitor foster parents.

What was most striking about foster care policy and practice was how little it had been studied and how little was known over the years.

The first significant research about foster care, *Children in Need of Parents* by Maas and Engler, was published only in 1959 and began a tidal wave of studies and a reconceptualization that would result in significant federal statutory reform two decades later. But while this "permanency planning revolution" unfolded, other federal legislation was being enacted culminating a century of intermittent public concern about a related service: child protective services

THE RISE AND FALL AND RISE OF CPS: 1874-1974

While today the linkage between child protective and foster care services is a matter of daily practice—by far the majority of children in care are there for reasons of protection from the acts or neglect of their caregivers (www.nyc.gov/html/acs/home.html)—the history of the development of the these services is different and begins in 1873, in New York City, with the oft-told story of Mary Ellen Wilson (Stevens & Eide, 1990).

In brief, Mary Ellen was the out-of-wedlock daughter of Irish immigrants. Her father died in the Civil War shortly after her birth. (As in immigrant, he was conscripted because he likely lacked the $300 paid by men from elite families to avoid service in the war.) She was farmed-out (what we would now call an early form of family day care), went to a public orphanage, and was finally discharged from there to another immigrant family, Mary and Francis Connolly, where she was the oldest and only unrelated child. Mary Ellen was kept at home, forced to do onerous chores, and severely beaten. Her cries were heard by neighbors who contacted Etta Wheeler, who as a forerunner of social workers making home visits, made "errands of mercy" (Costin, Karger, & Stoesz, 1996, p. 52). When Mary Connolly refused her entrance, Mrs. Wheeler turned to her elite friends for help. They included Henry Bergh, founder the previous year of The Society for Prevention of Cruelty to Animals, who later helped file suit against Mary Connolly, and Elbridge Gerry, grandson of a former vice president of the United States, who represented the interest of Mary Ellen in courts. The story was widely reported in the press, largely prompted by Etta Wheeler's connections with the *New York Times*, even the court reporter who transcribed Mary Ellen's heartbreaking (if remarkably coherent) testimony was Jacob Riis. While Mary Ellen's safety was assured when the court removed her from the home and found Mary Connolly guilty of assault, this case awakened public concern about child abuse and had a profound impact on the development of child welfare services in the U.S. The case of Mary Ellen Wilson was instrumental in the establishment a year later, in 1874, of the first child protective services agency: the New York Society for the Prevention of Cruelty to Children (NYSPCC), headed by Henry Bergh. Though the NYSPCC required statutory approval (because, in part its agents carried firearms), the Society was a private entity.

Over the following four decades, SPCCs became popular responses to the newly-recognized problem of cruelty to children, especially in Atlantic seaboard states where, in the late nineteenth century, the demographics of the cities changed again with the arrival of immigrant families from Eastern European; almost 350 SPCCs were in existence by 1912 (Costin, Karger, & Stoesz, 1996). However, in the subsequent half-century, interest in saving children from cruel treatment from their parents abated, in large part because the strong social and legal presumption that shielded whatever happened within the family from outside—especially governmental—interference. Spanking and even harsher forms of corporal punishment were supported by Biblical injunction as well as the common-sense notion that the choices other parents made about discipline were probably reasoned and certainly well-intentioned. Only in 1962, with the publication of "The Battered Child Syndrome" (Kempe et al., 1962) in the prestigious *Journal of the American Medical Association*, and the subsequent extensive publicity given to those findings (and supportive editorial), did the idea that some parents intentionally harm their children become plausible to Americans.

In 1974, exactly one hundred years after the establishment of the first SPCC, the United States had its first federal child abuse legislation: the Child Abuse Prevention and Treatment Act (CAPTA) (P. L. 93-247). Within a few years, all states established and publicized 24-hour hotlines for the reporting of allegations of child abuse and neglect, as well as procedures for the investigation and disposition of these reports. Anonymous reporting was required, as was mandated reporting by professionals likely to have contact with children, such as teachers, doctors, and social workers. While most states had some procedure for investigating allegations of child abuse, within a few years of the passage of CAPTA legislation, over a million allegations were recorded nationally; through the years, that number increased, and in 2002, there were over 3,134,000 allegations (http://ndas.cwla.org).

It is worth noting that what was originally American society's concern about "cruelty" and later "battering" was transformed statutorily into a public policy of protecting children from parental abuse *and neglect.* While words such as battering and abuse suggest actual physical activities, neglect implies the absence or omission of care. This change significantly expands the policy basis for government intervention into family life and increases the likelihood that families who are poor, and thus cut off from resources that support parenting, will be the target of CPS investigations. And poor families in the United States remain disproportionately city-dwellers: in 2000, while the overall rate of poverty declined in cities over the previous decade, it nevertheless was 20 times greater in U.S. cities than in suburbs (www.hsbklyn.edu/urbansoc). A CPS policy that includes neglect has important implications for child welfare practitioners, for it forces all parties (client, practitioner, agency) to consider how the real dearth of resources available to some populations (e.g., quality of education in cities vs. suburbs), continuing patterns of oppression, and the insufficiency of government-supported services such a affordable day care, all affect individual case planning.

THE PERMANENCY PLANNING REVOLUTION IN FOSTER CARE

Maas and Engler's groundbreaking research of 1959 found that children languished in foster care for years, primarily because agencies had no other plan for them. This finding sparked twenty years of research and advocacy which had profound effects on child welfare policy and practice. From 1959 to 1979, various other research studies concurred that foster care had become a permanent status for the majority of children in care. These findings spurred several communities and states to experiment with a new model of service delivery–permanency planning. Most famous of these was the Oregon Project (Maluccio & Fein, 1983). This approach emphasized (a) regular visitation between biological parent and child in care; (b) early counseling with biological parents to devise both a goal-oriented plan identifying barriers to reunification and a service contract to overcome those barriers (Jones, 1978; Pike, 1980); and (c) "prompt and well considered decision making" by the agency to ensure that the child could be raised in a permanent home as soon as possible (Boyd, 1979, p. 609).

Giving weight to permanency planning was the concept of the "psychological parent," introduced by Goldstein, Freud and Solnit in their 1974 publication *Beyond the Best Interests of the Child.* The authors proposed that, from the perspective of the child, parenthood was defined not by biology or law, but by behavior. Whoever tended to the child's basic needs with affection and concern *was* that child's psychological parent. They posited that children who received such care from a consistent caretaker would develop an attachment to this psychological parent in a relatively short period of time: a year for infants, two years for school-aged children. The authors concluded that, from the perspective of the child, the "least detrimental alternative" for the child would be to remain with his or her psychological parent rather than be returned to the biological parent (Goldstein, Freud, & Solnit, 1974, p. 53).

While the concept of the "psychological parent" was hotly disputed (Bush & Goldman, 1982; Jenkins, 1981; Kadushin, 1976), it left its mark on the movement towards permanency planning (Maluccio & Fein, 1983). Following the logic of the "best interests of the child," permanency planning advocates emphasized the need for timely and decisive case decision making to ensure the child a permanent home quickly.

Time-limited, goal-oriented foster care practice received justification from another unexpected quarter: the judicial system. Beginning with the 1967 United States Supreme Court decision *In Re Gault* (387 U.S. 1), federal and state courts increasingly recognized the rights of the children and the biological parents served by the foster care system, including their right of legal representation at such judicial proceedings as placement extension, termination of parental rights, or adoption hearings (Stein, 1991).

Thus, research, advocacy, and support for the rights of children and biological parents from the legal system culminated in the 1980 passage of the federal Adoption Assistance and Child Welfare Act (P.L. 96-272), which institutionalized the guiding principles of contemporary foster care policy and practice. The goal of permanency planning was reinforced 16 years later with the passage of the Adoption and Safe Families Act (P. L. 105-89), which shortened the timeframe to 15 months during which birth families could work to regain their children.

The policy commitment to utilize foster care as a temporary service while the agency sought a permanent arrangement for the child—either reunification with the family of origin or adoption—profoundly affected foster care practice. Utilizing a problem solving model to operationalize policy objectives (Compton, Galaway, & Cournoyer, 2005), this approach includes: focusing on the here-and-now functioning of the parent client; starting with the client's strengths; drawing on the client's motivation to be reunited with his or her child; and making the goals and objectives of the work explicit through written contracts and frequent case conferences. The problem-solving model may be utilized similarly with other permanency planning outcomes: adoption or independent living.

PERMANENCY PLANNING, CPS, THE CRACK EPIDEMIC: THE LIMITS OF POLICY REFORM

Between the late 1970s and 1985, the nationwide foster care population dropped almost in half, from an estimated 502,000 to about 275,000. Many factors contributed to this decline, including the aging out of an older foster care cohort and the reduction in average births per family following legalization of abortion; certainly, the institutionalization of permanency planning principles also changed agency practices and was a factor. In the mid-1980s, permanency planning was a policy success.

But a variation of an old problem then hit American cities. Where nineteenth century elites saw a connection between the "reign of rum" and inadequate care of children in the cities (Riis, 1890), child welfare experts at the end of the twentieth century responded to the crack epidemic and considered what society's response should be "when drug addicts have children" (Besharov, 1994). There was a spurt in neglect allegations concerning illegal use of substances (i.e., parents were said to be unable to provide minimum standards of care because of their addiction to crack cocaine), and during the decade beginning 1987, the number of CPS investigations increased by 45 percent (NCPCA, 2000), resulting in a dramatic rise in the foster care population, especially in cities. Where nationwide over 500,000 children were again in foster care by 1990, the number of children in care rose from 28,000 in New York State to over 51,000 in New York City alone during the same time period. Despite the ebbing of the crack crisis in cities since the early 1990s (as evidenced by the decline in other social indicators such as the murder rate), nationwide foster care figures remained over a half a million at the beginning of the twenty-first century (http://nccanch.acf.hhs.gov) and less than half had a permanency goal of reunification with parents (www.cwla.org).

CLINICAL PRACTICE WITH CHILDREN IN OUT-OF-HOME PLACEMENTS

The goals of permanency planning provide the framework for case decisions and can be achieved only through the application of sound clinical skills. The following case vignettes illustrate the intersection of foster care policy and practice. They represent, though hardly exhaust, the range of typical problems that confront foster care workers.

The Rosado Case: Contradictions of Permanency Planning

Following a Child Protective Services investigation of a report that she was neglecting her children, Mrs. Rosado, a 26-year-old widow, was informed that her six-year-old son and four-year-old daughter were being placed in foster care. This family of three had no home of its own in the three years since they arrived in Baltimore from their native country in Central America. Mrs. Rosado's relatives in the United States wrote to her of the opportunities that existed here—each family had its own home!—and the promise of opportunity exceeded the reality of life in her country. By moving, even to a country she didn't know and where they spoke in a foreign language, Mrs. Rosado believed that she could do well for her children and herself.

But for three years, she had experienced continued frustration. Unable to find affordable housing, she and her children had to "double-up" in the apartments of different relatives, as she tried to learn English and look for work. The last relative that Mrs. Rosado lived with complained to Protective Services that while she baby-sat, Mrs. Rosado "partied" and used alcohol and drugs with her new friends.

So CPS took away her children because Mrs. Rosado had been missing for five days without making suitable arrangements with the aunt who acted as babysitter; because she had not enrolled her son in school; because she had not obtained vaccinations for either child; and because her alleged dependency on alcohol and cocaine absorbed the time and energy that parenting her children required.

At the foster care agency, Mrs. Rosado was told by her (non-Spanish-speaking) worker that she needed to rehabilitate within 15 months or the agency would begin legal proceedings that could result in the adoption of her children by another family.

Abstracted from its contemporary details, the story of Mrs. Rosado is remarkably similar to the stories of nineteenth century European immigrants. It is a story of strangers in a strange land; of hope, promise, and harsh reality; of the challenge of assimilation and the dangers of urban life. A hundred years ago, the foster care agency may have made minimal efforts, if any, to help such a parent reclaim her children who likely were sent to a farm family in the Midwest. While permanency planning now mandates the practitioner to make diligent efforts to help the biological parents resume their parental responsibilities, it also mandates that the practitioner initiate adoption proceedings for the foster child if the rehabilitative work fails within the specified time-limit.

Assume that Mrs. Rosado and her worker have a year and a half to develop and achieve the permanency goal of returning the children to her. Where do they begin? The skills of partialization and setting priorities need to be utilized to bring order to this complicated family situation. Mrs. Rosado might well insist that housing is her family's primary goal: that the stress she experienced from years of doubling-up in the homes of others resulted in her own need to escape, to hang-out and even take drugs, as she struggled with her increasing sense of failure.

While the practitioner might agree with Mrs. Rosado about the need for housing, such a prioritization may be unrealistic. Where would Mrs. Rosado live with her children? Without income beyond public assistance—which she might not qualify for due to her immigration status—Mrs. Rosado could afford only to live in poorly maintained, low rent housing. Waiting lists for most public housing projects are very long. While she may be given housing priority status because her children are in foster care, in fact hundreds if not thousands of urban parents are given "priority" for scarce public housing because they experience fires or other disasters, or because they are homeless, or because their children too are in foster care. Were Mrs. Rosado to find an inexpensive apartment in a private building, she likely would be moving into a neighborhood where drugs were readily available and crime pervasive—conditions that would make it difficult for her to overcome her cocaine and other substance use.

Thus, the practitioner must focus on Mrs. Rosado's substance abuse problem. Assuming Mrs. Rosado is able to acknowledge her need for help for her substance use, she and the worker now face significant choices. Inpatient treatment is preferable if the cocaine use has impaired the client's judgment or if the client had demonstrated a priory inability to achieve abstinence (Straussner, 2004). But such programs may not be available for her, or have lengthy waiting lists. And Mrs. Rosado may resist the referral if she is not to have contact with her children while she is in treatment. Out-patient drug treatment raises other problems for Mrs. Rosado. Since "recovery from cocaine use" requires no less that "the pursuit of a different life style" (Smith & Wesson, 1988, p. 18), the practitioner must help her restructure her days, and even her personal relationships, to better withstand the inevitable daily pressures to return to drug usage (Straussner, 1989). The practitioner must explore and help develop the client's natural support systems: relatives who will need to understand the nature of substance abuse and provide support, even for efforts that may fail; church members who may help her find housing or assist her with transportation; and trusted friends who can accompany the client to the foster care agency or drug treatment center. Finally, the practitioner must guard against making referrals for more generalized counseling or therapy that does not begin by challenging the client's substance use, even if preferred by the client. Such therapies have been describes as "almost universally unsuccessful and potentially hazardous" (Smith & Wesson, 1988, p. 22) for clients with such presenting problems.

Child welfare practitioners typically err in understanding the problem-solving process with clients like Mrs. Rosado to be a brisk, cognitive, directional process: "This is what you have to do to get your children back." One source of this error is policy: the urgency implied in the timeframes proscribed by permanency planning, especially as narrowed by ASFA. The practitioner knows that, from the perspective of foster care policy, either reunification or adoption—as long as the result is achieved in a timely way—is a satisfactory outcome. In addition, the practitioner may be constrained by another policy consideration: inadequate funding for foster care services, which likely results in increased caseloads and thus less time available for each client. Remember too that Mrs. Rosado speaks Spanish and in the vignette her practitioner did not. Here again, enlightened funding policy may encourage the hiring of practitioners who are able to converse with clients in their primary language whereas funding cuts increase the likelihood that immigrant clients—now arriving from increasingly diverse cultures—will be served in a language and in a milieu that is equally alien to them.

Directive work with clients, however, overlooks the necessity of relationship, especially with involuntary clients, and the need to establish conditions of trust through empathetic understanding. Nowhere is the need to consciously reach for the client's thoughts and feelings more important than in the practitioner's first meetings with the client. The practitioner must expect the client to be confused and angry, and to be far more concerned with seeing her children than with beginning permanency work. When working with involuntary clients, it is important that the practitioner begin with clear statements of purpose (Hepworth, Rooney, & Larson, 1997). At the same time, the practitioner must allow and even encourage the client to ventilate her feelings of loss at her children being in care, and reframe the expression of these feelings into a tentative agreement to work together toward family reunification.

Following the Adoption and Safe Families Act, permanency planning makes it even more imperative that the practitioner focus on the issue of engagement with the biological parent, because that foster care policy reform reduced the timeframe for parental rehabilitation. Partializing the problem, setting priorities, and maintaining focus on contractual work are critical skills that need to be used repeatedly. The more the practitioner succumbs to the overwhelming global quality of

Mrs. Rosado's life situation, the greater the probability that the time-frames for permanency planning will elapse—resulting in Mrs. Rosado losing her children to adoption.

The Clarke Case: Independent Living and Permanency Planning

Toni Clarke is like most 17-year-olds: she's confused. She has some friends and is now part of a new crowd; she performs slug-gishly in school—good enough to be promoted and to graduate next year, not well enough to be really engaged in studying; she has no life goals as mostly she says she wants to "get through the next few weeks." She gets along well with her siblings "all things considered," and has never been in trouble with the law.

What's different about this adolescent is that Toni is in foster care and found herself there almost by chance. Her mother abandoned Toni, her two younger siblings, and their father six years ago. Mr. Clarke, Toni always believed, did a pretty good job as a single parent. But when Toni's 12-year-old sister arrived at school with bruis-es on her face and the back of her thighs, and Mr. Clarke's explanations to CPS were deemed unsatisfactory, all three children were placed into care, even though there was no particular concern that the then 15-year-old Toni had been the target of Mr. Clarke's physical rage. After earlier losing his wife, losing his family to foster care was an overwhelming burden for Mr. Clarke and apart from occasional visits with the agency, he did not participate meaningfully in any plan of reunification. The foster care agency began proceedings to find adoptive homes for the two younger children.

Toni expressed anger whenever the word adoption was spoken and, on one occasion, ran away from the foster home because she feared her foster care worker was "going to make me say I wanted to be part of another family." She returned in two days and though otherwise fairly open and cooperative about other matters, would shut down on the subject of adoption.

After entering care, Toni felt differently; she was less sure of who she was than before. At school she drifted away from former friends and toward other kids who seemed to feel "different" about them-selves as well, though not because they were in foster care. Instead, this "in crowd" consisted of kids who said they were gay or lesbian, or maybe even they were simply questioning their sexual orientation. Toni wasn't sure either, but did know that she was more comfortable with friends who were nontraditional, whatever the reason.

Toni's agency knew little about her social life. Instead it tried to answer its own question: how to devise a permanency plan for a 17-year-old who can't return home and refuses to be adopted. Toni agreed with her worker when told that the goal for her was "independent living," though she had no idea what that meant.

There are always anomalous situations that fit uneasily in policy, outliers that require a policy response yet defy simple categorization. Teens, especially those in the mid- to later-adolescent period, are almost by definition anomalous: no longer children, not yet adults; needing support for their decision-making, but limited in the choices they are allowed; needing to form their identity, risking identity confusion; and can there be any agreement as to when adolescence ends? From the perspective of the foster care system, adolescents are outliers, especially when family reunification is impossible. Though innovative outreach efforts have found prospective adoptive homes for even older teenagers with emotional, behavioral, and physical problems, the cooperation of the teen to a plan of adoption remains crucial: younger adoptive children may rebel through acting-out and older teens by running away, completely undermining the purpose of insuring a safe, substitute home for a child who has already experienced neglect or abuse. In an urban area, the teen who runs away will easily find places to hide.

In 1985, the federal government recognized the risks facing teens in foster care. Through the Independent Living Initiative (P.L. 99-272), Washington supported a policy of providing services to teens to transition from foster care to life on their own—independent living. A decade later, the Government Accounting Office (1999) found that "[t]he transition from the foster care system to self-sufficiency" remained "difficult" because too many teens exiting care lacked adequate education, finances, housing, and other supports and so became homeless, in receipt of public assistance, or were otherwise dependent on society (p 3). In 1999, these services were expanded through the Foster Care Independence Act. Federal policy now includes the mandate to provide services through workshops around daily life issues (budgeting, job hunting, etc.) as well as augmented counseling prior to the teens exit from care.

Given Toni's age, family circumstances, and sense of identity, she will likely age-out of foster care (at, depending on the state, age 18 or 21). Her practitioner, then, faces the daunting task of fulfilling not only a federal mandate but a fundamental commitment of the society to her well-being: to help her live on her own; "daunting," because it is the very nature of adolescence to be a period of turbulence, questioning, rejecting, challenging, and testing, especially of authority figures such as social workers and foster parents. Clinical work with Independent Living teens such as Toni requires not only that the practitioner be knowledgeable about expected transitions experienced by teens, but also have a personality that fits comfortably in working with the language, behaviors, moods, and thinking of adolescents; working with teens is not for everyone.

One key challenge for teens is, of course, identity. For Erikson (1982), this resulted from a process by which old and family values and allegiances are challenged; peer relationships, with their mutual strivings and concerns, become privileged; and finally, the first answer to the question "who am I" is found. This psychosocial developmental process is self-evidently more complex for teens in foster care, as they are deprived of the daily interaction (no matter how tense and oppositional) with their birth family. The clinician needs creative ways of helping teens like Toni find their way to their identity.

Workshops and activities become especially important interventive tools. Self-sufficiency requires the familiarity with the considerable number of daily adult tasks whose importance is often unknown or underestimated by teens. Managing a bank account, budgeting an income, contacting various utilities to set up one's own living arrangement, maintaining a steady and healthy diet, assuring that clothes are clean; these and many other such quotidian details are for most people learned in the course of a consistent home life with caregivers that have a deep connection with them. Teens in foster care, on the other hand, have had a broken relationship with their birth family and perhaps a contentious one with their substitute parents. If the practitioner attempted to address these daily living skills only through one-to-one counseling, a teen such as Toni might likely find the approach stigmatizing: "Why do you think *I* need this help?" Ongoing, regularly-scheduled workshops are more appropriate settings for such topics.

Independent living also suggests heightened self-awareness and so teens need to find ways of self-expression that are comfortable and challenging. Here again, teens such as Toni may feel more comfortable exploring their identity in peer activities, especially those that are more artistic than therapeutic in nature. Toni's practitioner might bring her to an organization such as UrbanWord, which encourages teens and young adults to express their feelings, examine their experiences, and discover their talents through poetry (written and "slammed" or performed) with and in front of peers (www.urban-wordnyc.org). Or, organizations can be found that encourage other forms of writing (www.youthcomm.org) or other art forms such as photography (e.g., www.kids-with-cameras.org). Lifebooks (Holody & Maher, 1995) also provide teens with the opportunity to organize and create their own versions of who they are. Practitioners should remember the special importance assigned by Gilligan (1982; Gilligan et al., 1992) to girls finding their own voice as they struggle through the special gender and social dimensions of adolescence.

Part of one's identity, of course, includes sexuality. It is not clear from Toni's story if she is attracted to gay and lesbian schoolmates because she feels a commonality with their sexuality, or if she is intrigued by their outsider status within the school and community—a status she feels though for different reasons. Assume that Toni is discovering that she is a lesbian. She would face challenges in finding adult acceptance for her sexuality as researchers have found that teens have difficulty discussing or disclosing their gay or lesbian identity, in no small part because of larger societal ambivalent and oppressive attitudes toward homosexuality (Saltzburg, 2004). The special experiences of teens that are both "in the system and in the life" have found increased attention in peer (Youth Communication, 2002) and professional writings (Mallon, 2000); practitioners need to maintain an active and up-to-date familiarity with this literature.

The practitioner may well assess that Toni needs additional therapeutic services. A coginitive-behavioral approach is appropriate to reinforce the developmentally increased, decision-making capacity of the teen: to consider the future, to plan, to weigh consequences including on others, to make decisions, to think about thinking. However, there are practical limits to this approach. Toni may well be misinterpreting words or behaviors of her birth or foster parents; she, like other teens, may be experiencing great stress over what is in reality a minor event (www.cornerstonebh.com). Under such circumstances, the practitioner may prefer family therapy which may be held separately with the foster teen's birth family (for issues surrounding loss and understanding) and the foster family (to minimize current communication problems and to reinforce the caregivers' commitment).

As with many policy goals, "independent living" may describe an ideal rather than a reality: how many 18- or 21-year-olds, even with the benefit of a stable home, can be said to be able to live with full self-sufficiency? That goal, nevertheless, structures the practitioner's goal with teens such as Toni; achieving it requires the practitioner to be flexible, creative, self-aware, and patient.

The Robinsons: Dilemmas of Kinship Care

Eunice Robinson had raised her four children with little help from her husband—he frequently deserted her and now was dead. Though she was often on welfare and lived in a public housing project apartment, she felt pride in her parental accomplishments. Her three older children had jobs, lived in good neighborhoods, and gave her grandchildren who respected their grandmother. But her youngest, 19-year-old Louise, told a different story.

Louise had already lost one child to adoption, a child she gave birth to six years ago. Eunice could not understand how Louise didn't learn her lesson, but Louise gave birth a year and a half ago and now was pregnant again. Worse, Louise had dropped out of school, never had any employment lasting more than a week, and was made pregnant by three different men. Louise was never home—often leaving Eunice to care for the baby, and she worried that Louise was using drugs and was risking the health of her expected child.

Louise was arrested for possession and sale of drugs. After Louise told the police her address and said she had a baby at home "probably alone," a police officer and a child protective service worker went to the apartment and found Mrs. Robinson and the baby. The CPS worker obtained some information, verified that the baby was safe with her grandmother that night, and said that a representative of the foster care department would contact her about putting Louise's baby into foster care, where Louise's newborn would be sent after she gave birth.

Eunice Robinson was 59 years old and was anticipating that her next years would be dominated by her church work and playing with her grandchildren. But to her, blood was blood, and the thought of Louise losing two more children to the system was both distressing and contrary to what she believed was essential to her African-American heritage: black folk and families must protect their own.

Tired, angry at Louise for what she did, angry at herself for not raising Louise better, Eunice Robinson asked to be named foster parent for her grandchildren. She reasoned: why should strangers be paid to raise my kin when the children would be better off with me? Using an accelerated process devised for assessing possible kinship homes, the foster care worker approved Mrs. Robinson to be a foster parent.

The migration of African-Americans from the rural South to the "promised land" of northern cities after the two World Wars was fueled in part by the promise of opportunity and renewal that cities have always represented (Lemann, 1991). But in these cities, the migrants encountered obstacles to justice and opportunity: de facto discrimination in housing, employment, and education.

Contemporary foster care policy also discriminates against non-white and particularly African-American service recipients. The values of permanency planning, as translated into law and regulation, necessarily reflect the values of the dominant class of society (Giddens, 1979). Permanency planning requires that foster care be a short-term, time-limited solution to an individual's family problem. It is based on the ideal of a nuclear family, viewing adoption of a child as satisfactory as the return of the child to his or her family of origin.

But the historical experience of African-Americans in American cities challenges each of these foundations for permanency planning. African-Americans ascribe far more importance to the extended family than does the dominant white culture (Billingsley, 1992); African-Americans have utilized formal adoption procedures less frequently (Hill, 1975); and many African-American families continue to face challenges related to historical and present-day discriminatory practices.

Bridging the conflict between the values of the foster care delivery system and the values of many of the clients of the system in urban areas is the use of kinship foster homes. Placement of children in foster care with their eligible relatives as the placement of first choice began in the mid-1980s, especially in such cities, as New York, Chicago, and Los Angeles. Placement of children with extended family members meets all of the underlying values of permanency planning except one—the eventual removal of the child from the foster care system. Children placed with kin tend to have longer stays in foster care than those placed in traditional homes. Efforts to encourage kinship caregivers to adopt the children in their care has met with mixed results, primarily because the kinship caregivers see no need to create, for example, a legal mother-child relationship when a biological grandmother-grandchild relationship already exists (Thornton, 1991). At the same time, relatives who provide foster care may resist agency monitoring efforts, often viewed as intrusions into their family life.

In this context, the practitioner's first challenge with kinship caregivers is to develop a working relationship that both respects the integrity of the values of the caregiver and reflects society's interest in monitoring out-of-home care. The practitioner needs to examine his or her own biases and assumptions about what "family" means to guard against unconscious cultural interpretations of case events. The second challenge is to promote the goal of establishing a permanent home for the child, which may mean working to encourage a grandmother/foster parent to adopt her grandchild/foster child.

Foster care agencies and practitioners must recognize and accept that kinship care is qualitatively different from more traditional foster care arrangements. For example, when monitoring the ongoing health and welfare of a child in a kinship home, the practitioner may need to give more weight to the natural relationship between caregiver and child than to a technical violation of a regulatory standard of care, such as the child's having a crowded bedroom

Or in another typical example, the biological parent, especially in the early stages of placement, will usually not know the location of the foster family home and is able to visit with his or her child only through the arrangements made with the foster care worker. Such secrecy does not exist with kinship families. Louise knows where her mother and child live and has a longer and deeper relationship with Mrs. Robinson than the practitioner ever will. While Louise may formally agree to work through the agency to reunite with her child; in reality, she understandably may circumvent the agency to achieve what she really wants—contact with her child at a time of her own choosing. Mrs. Robinson in turn may agree with the practitioner that her daughter should have only limited access to her child, both out of concern for the safety of the child and to help Louise confront the effects of her drug usage. But actually saying no when her daughter unexpectedly arrives at the apartment on a Saturday morning is quite another matter, one where the ties of blood may well take precedence over the foster parent's contractual agreement with the agency.

The practitioner must also be aware of the effects of Louise's drug usage on the relationship between herself and her mother. And adult child's drug abuse typically renews issues of separation and loss for a parent who may unconsciously "tend to protect [her child] from outside agencies" and even "covertly encourage [her] return" (Stanton, Todd, & Associates, 1982, p. 13). Ironically, the agency's use of Mrs. Robinson as a kinship caregiver unintentionally reinforces a common dynamic of enabling in substance abuse relationships—she has taken over her daughter's parental responsibilities, in effect giving her more time and freedom to use drugs.

The foster care practitioner needs to help the parties confront the extent of Louise's drug use and the meaning of that usage in the Mrs. Robinson-Louise dyad. It is likely that Mrs. Robinson's feelings about her daughter's life style—including perhaps guilt, disappointment, frustration, and anger—may distort her perception of Louise's parental capabilities or the extent of Louise's drug use. Or, Mrs. Robinson's commitment to the primacy of family and her possible suspicion of agency rules may limit her candor and cooperative working with the practitioner. The practitioner needs to discuss Louise's drug use with all family members and provide appropriate referrals to 12-step and other support groups.

Should family reunification fail, the practitioner and the kinship caregiver face the thorniest dilemma of kinship foster care: should the agency require that, in this case, Mrs. Robinson adopt her own grandson, thereby removing him from care and giving him a "permanent" home? State policies may vary on this question. A new policy initiative, tried in several states but lacking full federal support, is to create a new category of relationship, guardianship, removing the child out of the foster care system (thus saving administrative costs) but leaving the kin caregiver with legal authority to make decisions in the child's behalf as well as a stipend comparable to the foster care monthly grant.

It is clear, however, that one purpose of permanency planning was to reduce the number of children in care and both adoption and guardianship (where this option is possible) meet that goal. That goal would be missed if Louse's child remains in long-term foster care, although an assessment of the case may well indicate that the "best interests of the child" are best met when the child is with the grandmother rather than be adopted by a stranger. What makes for good case-by-case practice sometimes will contradict the goals of policy.

CONCLUSION

Because policy shapes practice, it is no surprise that the urban foster care practitioner can feel frustrated, overwhelmed, inadequate, confused, impatient, tired, and even dazed. Derived from this country's complex reaction to nineteenth century immigration and urbanization, child welfare policies–foster care and protective services–have become even more complex at the beginning of the twenty-first century as the United Sates continues to struggle with the implication of continued and even more diverse immigration, as well as the violence and decay present in the inner-cities. Both services, then and now, begin dramatically–an allegation that results in government intrusion into family; the separation of child from family of origin–and so seek to end a threatening situation. Then, and only under these crisis circumstances, does the work of the practitioner begin.

Though permanency planning seeks to direct and structure outcome of foster care practice, it is not a substitute for clinical skills: the practitioner must effectively focus on engagement skills, use such skills as ventilation and setting priorities, act as broker and teacher, and be creative and resourceful. Though foster care policy regarding the integration of permanency planning with the preferential use of kinship foster homes remains unsettled, as the policy of establishing guardianship as an outcome is being explored, the practitioner can still utilize the contracting process to help clients better understand their wants and needs. Working with teens and children in foster care can be most effective when the practitioner begins by recognizing the child's developmental stage and the importance of continuity of experience, and by devising creative ways to develop working relationship with those in care.

And foster care practitioners must use their practice experience to help shape policy. In the case vignettes concerning Mrs. Rosado and the Robinson family, for example, the workers sought to provide services to drug and alcohol abusing parents (predictably, a long-term process) within the framework of permanency planning (reflecting the child's need for a psychological parent, which is intended to be a short-term process). In the past, proposals to reform foster care policy to meet the needs of situations where the biological parents are chronic drug and alcohol abusers have included devising new programs for long-term foster care (Barth, 1994) and integrating the child welfare and drug treatment service systems (Horn, 1994). Alas, the only significant reform of foster care in the last decade, the Adoption and Safe Family Act, shortened the time available for biological parents to undergo rehabilitation. Foster care practitioners know first-hand the importance of family to the child in care—even when that family may be dysfunctional, they remain the child's primary source of identity and the parents, whatever their individual problems, retain a uniqueness and dignity. Whatever tomorrow's foster care policy becomes, workers must accept the responsibility to advocate for policy change that realistically reflects both the needs of the culturally diverse children and families they serve, as well as the resources needed by agencies to fulfill their social mandate.

REFERENCES

Aust, P. H. (1981). Using the life story book in treatment of children in placement. *Child Welfare, 60,* 535-536, 553-560.

Barth, R. P. (1994). Long-term in-hme services. In D. J. Besharov (Ed.), *When drug addicts have children* (pp. 175-194). Washington, DC: Child Welfare League of America and American Enterprise Institute.

Billingsley, A. (1992). *Climbing Jacob's ladder.* New York: Simon and Shuster.

Boyd, P. E. (1979). They can go home again! *Child Welfare, 58,* 609-615.

Brace, C. L. (1872). *The dangerous classes of New York.* New York: Wynkoop and Hallenbeck (Reprinted: Silver Springs, MD: NASW Classics Series, 1973).

Bush, M., & Goldman, H. (1982). The psychological parenting and permanency principles in child welfare: A reappraisal and critique. *American Journal of Orthopsychiatry, 52,* 223-235.

Compton, B. R., Galaway, B., & Cournoyer, B. R. (2005). *Social work processes* (7th ed.). Belmont, CA: Brooks/Cole.

Costin, L .B., Bell, C. J., & Downs, S. W. (1991). Child welfare: Policies and practice. White Plains, New York: Longman.

Costing, L. B., Karger, H. J., & Stoesz, D. (1996). *The politics of child abuse in America.* New York: Oxford University Press.

Folks, H. (1902). *The care of destitute, neglected, and delinquent children.* New York: Macmillan.

Foner, E., & Garraty, J. A. (Eds.). (1991). The reader's companion to American history. Boston: Houghton-Mifflin.

Giddens, A. (1979). *Central problems in social theory.* Berkely, CA: University of California Press.

Gilligan, C. (1982). *In a different voice: Psychological theory and women's development.* Cambridge, MA: Harvard University Press.

Gilligan, C, Taylor, J. M., Tolman, D., Sullivan, A., Pleasants, P., & Dorney, J. (1992). *The relational world of adolescent girls considered to be at risk.* Monograph. Cambridge, MA: Harvard Graduate School of Education.

Goldstein, J., Freud, A., & Solnit, A. (1973). *Beyond the best interests of the child.* New York: Free Press.

Gordon, L. (1999). *The great Arizona orphan abduction.* Cambridge, MA: Harvard University Press.

Government Accounting Office. (November, 1999). *Foster care: Effectiveness of independent living services unknown.* Washington, DC: Author.

Hepworth, D. H., Rooney, R. H., & Larson, J. A. (1997). *Direct social work practice: Theory and skills* (5th ed.). Pacific Grove, CA: Brooks/Cole.

Hill, R. (1977). *Informal adoption among black Americans.* Washington, DC: National Urban League.

Holody, R. (1993). *Reforming foster care: A history of New York's Child Welfare Reform Act.* Unpublished doctoral dissertation, Yeshiva University, New York.

Holody, R., & Maher, S. (1996). Using lifebooks with children in family foster care: A here-and-now process model. *Child Welfare, 75,* 4.

Horn, W. F. (1994). Implications for policy-making. In D. J. Besharov (Ed.), *When drug addicts have children.* Washington, DC: Child Welfare League of America and American Enterprise Institute.

http://nccanch.acf.hhs.gov. Accessed on 8/18/04.

http://ndas.cwla.org. Accessed on 1/12/05.

Jenkins, S. (1981). [Review of the book *Beyond the best interest of the child].* Social Casework, 62, 316-317.

Jones, M. (1978). Stopping foster care drift: A review of legislation and special programs. *Child Welfare, 57,* 571–580.

Kadushin, A. (1976). Beyond the best interests of the child: An essay review. *Social Services Review, 48* (4), 508–516.

Kempe, C. H., Silverman, F., Steele, B., Droegmueller, W., & Silver, H. (1962). The battered-child syndrome. *Journal of the American Medical Association, 181,* 17–24.

Lemann, N. (1991). *The promised land.* New York: Knopf.

Lindsey, D. (1994). *The welfare of children.* New York: Oxford University Press.

Maas, H. S., & Engler, R. E. (1959). *Children in need of parents.* New York: Columbia University Press.

168   *Children in the Urban Environment*

Mallon, G. (2000). *Let's get this straight: A gay- and lesbian-affirming approach to child welfare.* New York: Columbia University Press.

Maluccio, A, (1991). The optimism of policy choices in child welfare. *American Journal of Orthopsychiatry, 61,* 606-609.

Maluccio, A., & Fein, E. (1983). Permanency planning: A redefinition. *Child Welfare, 62,* 195-201.

Nelson, B. J. (1984). *Making an issue of child abuse.* Chicago, IL: University of Chicago Press.

O'Connor, S. (2001). *Orphan trains.* New York: Houghton Mifflin.

Pike, V. (1980). Permanency planning for foster children: The Oregon project. *Child Welfare Training.* Washington, DC: U.S. Department of Health and Human Services.

Riis, J. A. (1890). *How the other half lives.* New York: Charles Scribner's Sons.

Saltzburg, S. (2004). Learning that an adolescent child is gay or lesbian: The parent experience. *Social Work, 49,* 109-118.

Smith, D. E., & Wesson, D. R. (1988). *Treating cocaine dependency.* Center City, MN: Hazelden Foundation.

Stanton, M. D., Todd, T. C., & Associates (1982). *The family therapy of drug use and addiction.* New York: Guilford.

Stein, T. J. (1991). *Child welfare and the law.* White Plains, NY: Longman.

Stevens, P., & Eide, M. (1990) The first chapter of children's rights. *American Heritage,* July/August, 84-91.

Straussner, S. L. A. (Ed.) (2004). *Clinical work with substance abusing clients* (2nd ed.). New York: Guilford Press.

Straussner, S. L. A. (1989). Intervention with maltreating parents who are drug and alcohol abusers. In S. M. Ehrenkranz, E. G. Goldstein, L. Goodman & J. Seinfeld (Eds.), *Clinical social work with maltreated children and their families: An introduction to practice* (pp. 149-177). New York: New York University Press.

Thornton, J. (1991). Permanency planning for children in kinship foster homes. *Child Welfare, 70,* 593-601.

Wheeler, C. (1978). *Where am I going? Making a child's life story book.* Juneau, AK: The Winking Owl Press.

www.cornerstonebh.com. Accessed on 1/4/05.

www.cwla.org. Accessed on 8/18/04.

www.kids-with-cameras.org. Accessed 1/12/05.

www.nyc.gov/html/acs/home.html. Accessed on 1/12/05.

www.urbanwordnyc.org. Accessed on 11/18/04.

www.youthcomm.org. Accessed 1/12/05.

Youth Communication. (2002). *In the system and in the life.* New York: Author.

Chapter 8

CHILDREN IN SUBSTANCE-ABUSING FAMILIES

MERYL NADEL and SHULAMITH L.A. STRAUSSNER

Sixteen-year-old Tasha and her 13-year-old brother Mark live in a low-income housing project in Chicago with their maternal grandmother, Mrs. N, who is a kinship foster parent. Tasha's father, whom she barely remembers, is currently serving time for drug-related charges. Her mother was a drug abuser who died from AIDS six years ago. While Tasha is in an honors program in school, Mark is in special education classes and appears to exhibit symptoms of attention deficit hyperactivity disorder. Mrs. N, a widow, whose alcoholic husband died many years ago, depends on Tasha for help with housework, in dealing with Mark's frequent school problems, and with her own numerous medical needs. Mark displays bullying behavior toward other children and, after being confronted by a teacher, he has refused to attend school anymore. He told his sister that he has been smoking blunts and plans to become a drug dealer so he can have money to move out. When questioned by the social worker from the foster care agency, he stated that he didn't plan to hang around and see grandma die and that he didn't like being bossed by Tasha. When the worker explored this further, he revealed a family secret: "Grandma drinks every night and then passes out." Tasha then expects him to make sure that grandma is OK and to help get her to bed.

Suzette is a 15-year-old adolescent who lives with her parents, Mr. and Mrs. T, on Beacon Hill in Boston. Her father is a banker and her mother is a lawyer who works for an old, prestigious Boston law firm. Now that Suzette is older, the family housekeeper functions less as a nanny and more as a maid and cook. Suzette takes a bus to her private school in the city and chooses her own after school activities. Older schoolmates on her bus have offered her cigarettes and a few months ago, marijuana. Her parents are often at work until 7:00 P.M. or later and frequently have evening commitments as well. Mrs. T has been prescribed Xanax by her psychiatrist to control her anxiety; her prescription is renewed regularly. When they arrive home, Mr. T likes to relax with a cocktail while Mrs. T eagerly pours herself a glass of white wine, which she refills throughout the evening. Some evenings she misses dinner, "falling asleep" after several glasses of wine. Mr. T. tells Suzette that her mother "just works too hard and needs her rest." The parents often go away for weekends to their country house and recently have begun to allow Suzette to remain in the city alone. Suzette feels free to invite friends to her home, where they have begun to explore her parents' well-stocked liquor cabinet. Suzette and her friends have recently bought false identification cards and have begun to frequent Boston dance clubs where they often buy and use "club drugs" such as ecstasy and Special K.

As reflected in the above vignettes, substances of abuse are ubiquitous in the urban environment and their detrimental impact is felt by many children. Whether in affluent neighborhoods or impoverished ones, access is easy (Johnston, O'Malley, Bachman, & Schulenberg, 2005), and experimental use can slide subtly into abuse and addiction. This chapter explains the nature of substance abuse problems and their impact on children and families, and discusses the policy, programmatic, and clinical practice issues related to this urban social problem.

SUBSTANCE USE, ABUSE, AND DEPENDENCE

Potential substances of abuse most commonly used by young people include such legal substances as alcohol, tobacco, and caffeine; various forms of inhalants, such as glue, paint, and aerosols; and prescription medications, such as OxyContin, Vicodin, Ritalin, and

Adderall. Some young people also abuse illicit drugs, such as heroin, cocaine or crack, methamphetamine, known as "ice" or "crystal meth;" hallucinogens, such as LSD; and marijuana. Anabolic steroids and "designer" or "club" drugs also lend themselves to abuse, particularly by adolescents. Designer or club drugs are synthetically-produced compounds that mimic other psychoactive substances; they include MDMA, known as ecstacy; GHB; and Rohypnol, the "date rape" drug (National Survey on Drug Abuse and Health [NSDUH], 2004).

The use of substances can range on a continuum from *experimentation* to substance *use* to *abuse* and then to *dependence* or addiction (Straussner, 2004). The 2000 edition of the American Psychiatric Association's *Diagnostic and Statistical Manual of Mental Disorders*, referred to as DSM-IV-TR (APA, 2000), divides all substance-related disorders into two major categories: *Substance-Induced Disorders* and *Substance Use Disorders*. The former comprises conditions such as substance intoxication, withdrawal, and substance-induced psychosis. The latter includes two categories: *Substance Abuse* and *Substance Dependence*. While *substance abuse* may result in a variety of negative psychosocial consequences, such as drunk driving, the more serious condition of *substance dependence* refers to a *compulsive* use of alcohol or other drugs, commonly referred to as alcoholism or drug addiction, and may include physical dependence manifested by withdrawal symptoms.

SCOPE OF SUBSTANCE ABUSE PROBLEMS

About 18 million Americans (more than 16 percent of those 12 and over) have a problem with alcohol, and over 9 million (approximately 8 percent) abused illegal drugs in 2003 (NSDUH, 2004). Many of these individuals are parents whose use of alcohol and other drugs (AOD) has a detrimental impact on their children. An estimated "11% of U.S. children, 8.3 million, live with at least one parent who is either alcoholic, or in need of treatment for the abuse of illicit drugs. Of these, 3.8 million live with a parent who is alcoholic, 2.1 million live with a parent whose primary problem is with illicit drugs, and 2.4 million live with a parent who abuses alcohol and illicit drugs in combination" (U.S. Department of Health and Human Services [USDHHS], 1999).

The U.S. General Accounting Office (GAO) found that parental substance abuse was the major factor for 78 percent of the children entering foster care in Los Angeles, New York City, and Philadelphia County (U.S. GAO, 1994), while a national survey of all states conducted in 1995 and again in 1996, found that more than three-fourths of states indicated that substance abuse was one of the top two conditions for families reported for child maltreatment (Wang & Daro, 1997). Each year, approximately 8,000 babies are born with Fetal Alcohol Syndrome to mothers who abuse alcohol (CASA, The National Center on Addiction and Substance Abuse at Columbia University, 2005).

Children not only live with substance-abusing adults; many are also substance users or abusers themselves. The annual *Monitoring the Future* (Johnston et al., 2005) surveys of high school students indicate a general decline in substance use between 2002 and 2004, particularly of marijuana, ecstasy, and amphetamines (including methamphetamine). On the other hand, the use of LSD and other hallucinogens, heroin, cocaine and crack, tranquilizers, Rohypnol, and GHB have remained stable, while the use of inhalants and the narcotic OxyContin have increased. Although tobacco use has not increased significantly, it is worrisome that nationally 53 percent of high school youth have tried cigarettes, and that 25 percent of 12th graders are current smokers. Alcohol use also remains high, with 77 percent of high school students having consumed alcohol by graduation (Johnston et al., 2005). According to government data, amongst teenagers between 12 and 20 years, over 19 percent binge drink, and over 6 percent were described as "heavy drinkers" (USDUH, 2004).

Despite the stereotype of the high prevalence of drug use in the cities, it has been found that the difference in drug use between urban and nonurban areas has been minimal, and "in recent years, the use of a number of drugs declined more in the urban areas than in the nonurban ones" (Johnston et al., 2005, p. 40). In particular, the use of crack, heroin, and methamphetamine is more prevalent in nonurban areas. In terms of ethnicity, overall, the rates among young Native Americans are the highest among all ethnic groups in the U.S., while the rates among Asian-Americans are the lowest (Johnston et al., 2005). When comparing white, black, and Hispanic youth, white youths tend to have the highest rates of substance use and African-American youths the lowest; rates of use among Hispanic youth usually fall in between—however, it is equal to or exceeds the rates of whites for some substances, such as inhalants (Straussner, 2001). African-American and Latino youngsters, however, are most likely to witness the use of crack and heroin, reflecting the more *public* usage of these substances in inner-city communities (CASA, 2005).

UNDERSTANDING THE EFFECTS OF SUBSTANCE ABUSE: A BIOPSYCHOSOCIAL PERSPECTIVE

Familial substance abuse can affect children in many ways. It is therefore important to examine the biological, psychological, and social consequences of parental substance abuse for children and adolescents.

Biological Factors: Maternal Substance Abuse During Pregnancy

While there are some indications that *paternal* substance use is detrimental to the fetus and newborn child, such impact has yet to be fully explored (Purvis, 1990). On the other hand, there is a growing knowledge about the consequences of maternal substance abuse during pregnancy. Drugs and alcohol ingested by the pregnant woman pass through the placenta into the bloodstream of the fetus, thus raising the risk for birth defects (Behnke & Eyler, 1993; CASA, 2005). Children whose mothers drink during pregnancy are at risk for Fetal Alcohol Effects, and 6 percent are born with the more serious condition of Fetal Alcohol Syndrome (Streissguth, Aase, Clarren, Randels, LaDue, & Smith, 1991). The use of substances during the third trimester of pregnancy appears to have the most significant impact on brain development (Azmitia, 2001).

After birth, some babies appear, at least in the short-term, to suffer no ill effects from prenatal drug exposure, while others may be premature or small for gestational age and have complications, such as respiratory problems that are often associated with these conditions. Some newborns suffer from drug withdrawal and have symptoms such as excessive crying and irritability; hypertonia (stiff muscles); tremors; sleep disturbances; and increased sensitivity to light, sound, and touch.

As the child develops, other physiological effects may become evident. These can include developmental delays of various kinds, such as failure to thrive, cognitive deficits, and speech, language, and motor delays. Physical problems, such as asthma, may develop in connection with respiratory deficiencies. During the school years, learning disabilities and behavioral problems, such as attention deficit hyperactivity disorder and conduct disorder, may become evident (Azmitia, 2001; CASA, 2005; Coles & Platzman, 1993).

Psychological and Social Factors

Parents who are preoccupied with obtaining and using alcohol and other drugs are unlikely to provide their children with an environment conducive to optimal psychological and social development (Markowitz, 2004). Abuse of all substances can be found in families of all socioeconomic groups and can affect the lifestyle of all members of the family. In middle- and upper-class homes, where economic issues might not be a concern, emotional neglect and psychological rejection remain potent risks, as exemplified by the case of Suzette. Although considerable variability is found, the home environment of the child of the substance abuser is often characterized by an inconsistent, absent, abusive, or neglectful parent who lacks parental empathy.

It is not unusual for the entire family to organize itself around the substance abuser, resulting in such dynamics as role confusion and unclear boundaries, denial, secrecy, and shame (McIntyre, 2004). The pervasiveness of the defense mechanism of denial by the substance abuser is often reinforced by the denial of family members, who may view the erratic behavior of the abuser as normative. In the effort to maintain family homeostasis, family members may attempt to compensate by assuming additional responsibilities. For example, a husband such as Mr. T, Suzette's father, may minimize his wife's drinking problem or cover up its effects, while a child such as Tasha may assume a parental role. Even when children are placed in kinship foster care, as seen in the case of Mark and Tasha, they may find themselves with relatives who also have an alcohol or drug problem (Straussner, 1994).

These familial dynamics also impact on children's performance in school and the community. Studies have found that children with substance-abusing parents, regardless of socioeconomic background, exhibit higher levels of behavioral problems and lower levels of adaptive functioning than other children (Prelow, Martin, Brick, & Burke, 1993).

UNDERSTANDING YOUTHFUL SUBSTANCE ABUSE

Suzette, now 17, has moved from her flirtation with cigarettes, alcohol, and marijuana to weekend binging, smoking marijuana on a regular basis after school, and using "designer drugs" at the clubs that she patronizes. Her circle of friends has narrowed mainly to others immersed in this life style. Her arguments with and alienation from her parents have increased. Her poor schoolwork and increased absenteeism resulted in a referral to Ms. M, the school social worker. Suzette's use of substances at her favorite club has also changed as she and her peers, concerned about the negative effects of using ecstasy, stopped using it at the club. However, with her false ID, Suzette has no problems ordering bar drinks. One night an acquaintance laces her fifth drink with Rohypnol and, taking advantage of her intoxicated state, rapes her while driving her home. The next day Suzette tells the social worker at her school and the only person in school with whom she has established a positive relationship, about the rape. Ms. M helps Suzette to call her parents and obtain immediate medical attention followed by referral to a rape crisis clinic. She also recommends that the family see a substance abuse counselor for ongoing therapy. Ms. M had previously identified Suzette as a student at very high risk —a "disaster waiting to happen."

Tasha is now 18 and in her first semester of college. Ever the achiever, she has won a scholarship that enables her to attend and reside at a college in another part of the state. She knows she must attain high grades to keep her scholarship and is concerned about her ability to perform well on her finals. She shares this concern with her roomate who tells her about another student who sells "study drugs." Tasha has heard that these drugs (nonmedical use of Ritalin and Adderall) can help students concentrate for extended periods of time and is thinking about getting some.

Experimental use of substances is commonplace during adolescence. However, for some, due to a combination of genetic, familial, social, and intrapsychic dynamics, experimentation moves into problematic substance abuse and possibly dependence. It is important to understand the risk factors and to identify warning signs when assessing youth for risk of substance abuse.

Risk factors exist on many levels: *at the individual level* they include young age at first use of drugs, the intensity of feelings of alienation from family, and high levels of anxiety or depression; *at the family level,* they include unclear family roles and expectations, inadequate parental monitoring, and lack of consistency in parenting; *at the peer group level,* associating with peers who use drugs is a critical risk factor; *at the school level,* academic failure, low commitment to school, and difficulties with school transitions need to be taken into account; and *at the community level,* permissive community law and norms and availability of drugs are important risk factors (Freshman, 2004).

The case of Suzette exemplifies how the use of substances that is ignored at home may lead to serious consequences, including significant trauma, for a vulnerable adolescent. Such problems are compounded when they are ignored by other adults, such as teachers and health professionals, or misdiagnosed and mistreated by well-meaning clinicians who lack knowledge about addictions. The case of Tasha illustrates how even young people who have avoided involvement with substances in the past can become vulnerable as they transition to a new environment with new stressors.

THE POLICY–PRACTICE RELATIONSHIP

Social problems lead to policies that, in turn, lead to programs and treatment approaches. These policies, and therefore programs and approaches to interventions, tend to reflect the dominant attitudes of the time.

Historical Approaches: Changing Attitudes Over Time

A brief historical review of substance use, abuse, and control efforts in the United States shows that substance abuse policies are generally consistent with prevailing ideology and tend to parallel public attitudes, rather than actual drug use patterns.

In Colonial America and during the early 1800s, drinking and even drunkenness were acceptable behaviors. In fact, during the 1800s, opiates and cocaine were legal and widely used, particularly as patent medicine by middle-class women (Straussner & Attia, 2002). It was only during the latter part of the nineteenth century that any use of alcohol was perceived as problematic, resulting in the growth of the temperance movement (O'Dwyer, 2004).

Beginning in 1906 with the Pure Food and Drug Act, the federal government instituted controls on the use of drugs as patent medicine ingredients. The Harrison Narcotic Act of 1914, the Volstead Act which ushered in Prohibition in 1919, and the 1937 Marijuana Tax Act further restricted the use of drugs and alcohol. Court decisions prohibited even physicians from maintaining individuals on addictive substances, such as heroin (Friedman, 2004). Public policies thus criminalized the users of various substances while at the same time limited their access to treatment for their addictions.

Following the repeal of Prohibition in 1933, the social use of alcohol once again became widely acceptable, while problematic alcohol use was seen as a sign of an individual's moral shortcoming. Treatment for alcohol problems, in line with the widespread popularity of Freudian theories, tended to focus not on abstinence but on understanding the underlying causes. Unlike alcohol, illicit drug use, particularly heroin and marijuana, continued to be seen as dangerous (as reflected by the government film "Reefer Madness") and drug use remained relatively low through the 1950s–used mainly by low-income adolescent and young adult males in a few large cities, and by subgroups such as musicians and nightclub performers. Formal treatment for drug problems remained almost nonexistent with the exception of the two federal hospitals–at Lexington, Kentucky and Fort Worth, Texas–first established during the 1930s in order to conduct research and to provide detoxification for some drug-addicted prison inmates (O'Dwyer, 2004). The long-term rate of abstinence for addicts who left these facilities was close to zero, a finding that later provided the rationale for the development of methadone maintenance treatment programs. Moreover, some important neurochemical and brain research studies were first initiated in these government hospitals.

During the 1960s, experimentation by middle-class youth with drugs of all kinds was initially regarded as avant-garde and "on the fringe," but rarely criminally punishable. However, by the 1970s, as usage became more widespread in inner-city communities and federal administrations became more conservative, the "war on drugs" was proclaimed and policies of law enforcement and punishment became increasingly dominant—a pattern continuing today.

At the same time, the passage of the Hughes Act in 1970, authorizing the establishment of the National Institute on Alcohol Abuse and Alcoholism (NIAAA) and the National Institute on Drug Abuse (NIDA), had a profound impact on the treatment of both drug and alcohol abusers. This Act resulted in increased federal funding for substance abuse research and model treatment programs; in the establishment of occupational alcoholism programs, the precursor of employee assistance programs (Straussner, 1990); and in the increased coverage by health insurance companies of alcohol and other drug treatment facilities. It also provided the impetus for the decriminalization of public drunkenness by all state governments.

Another significant piece of legislation impacting on many urban children was the 1991 Individuals with Disabilities Education Act or IDEA (Public Law 99-457), which expanded the Education for All Handicapped Children's Act of 1978. This law mandated that all states must "provide a continuum of educational services for disabled students with additional therapeutic and other medical-related services necessary for them to participate in and benefit from an appropriate education" (Smith, 1993, pp. 1442–1443). Many children of substance abusers qualify for such assessment and interventive services. In fact, according to Smith, "some states have developed criteria which permit documentation of maternal use of drugs or alcohol during pregnancy as making them eligible to receive services" (p. 1444).

Another important policy change was the passage of the 1997 Adoption and Safe Families Act (ASFA), P.L. 105-8.9. This law addressed the need for children in out-of-home placements to be placed in a permanent home and not be moved from one foster home to another. Child protection workers are required to work with and find treatment for parents with drug abuse problems. However, the law provided few new resources to meet this need. In spite of the lack of resources, if the substance-abusing parent does not recover, workers are mandated to terminate the clients' parental rights and free their children for adoption after 15 months (O'Gorman & Diaz, 2004). Consequently, many substance-abusing parents, particularly mothers, are caught between trying to work on their recovery at the same time that they are facing losing their parental rights.

CURRENT FEDERAL POLICIES AND PROGRAMMATIC IMPLICATIONS

Federal policy efforts, under the auspices of The White House Office of National Drug Control Policy and the Substance Abuse Mental Health Service Administration (SAMHSA), may be conceptualized as consisting of a three-pronged approach: domestic and international law enforcement or interdiction, focusing on the "supply" side of drugs to the U.S. public, and two approaches focusing on the "demand" side: (1) drug prevention and prevention research, and (2) drug treatment and treatment research.

The Supply Side: Enforcement and Punishment

The federal drug control budget has increased annually as the government has attempted to control the massive costs of drug abuse to society, estimated at $160.7 billion in 2000 (includes health care costs, productivity losses, and other costs). The "supply side" approach tries to prevent drugs from reaching current or potential consumers and focuses on foreign crop eradication, border and marine interdiction, and arrests of drug distributors and dealers. These programs get the largest percentage of the federal drug-related budget—more than the other two areas, treatment and prevention, combined (Office of National Drug Control Policy, 2003).

Enforcement and punishment efforts within the U.S. involve legal activities usually carried out by police, military, court, or corrections personnel. Their aim is to eliminate the substances in question and punish those involved. Unfortunately, when the punishment includes imprisonment of a parent whose sole crime is the selling or using drugs, the whole family, and particularly the children are profoundly impacted (see Mazza, this volume).

Various efforts have been made to protect the fetus and newborn children of substance- abusing women. Reports in the popular press of the variety of effects of drug use on the newborn have influenced policy makers and judges to attempt to control the behavior of pregnant substance abusers through legal measures. These attempts involve "creative" uses of existing family, criminal, and civil laws and regulations, rather than the establishment of new ones (Garcia, 1993). In some Family Court cases, the fetus has been considered a person, while in others definitions of child abuse and neglect have been written or interpreted to include the impact of substance abuse by pregnant woman on the fetus and newborn child (Andrews & Patterson, 1995; Garcia, 1993).

In some cases, women have been criminally charged with distributing a controlled substance to the fetus. For example, in a California case, the drug abusing mother of an infant who died was convicted of child endangerment after the prosecutor argued that the death resulted from the baby's nursing on breast milk which contained methamphetamine ("A mother's drug use," 1994). By 1997, 240 women in 35 states have been criminally prosecuted for using illegal drugs or alcohol during pregnancy (Marwick, 1998).

The Demand Side: Treatment and Prevention Approaches

Treatment and prevention policies aim to prevent or decrease the use of drugs. These policies have led to the development of various education/prevention activities, treatment programs, and research studies on treatment effectiveness and program evaluation (Office of National Drug Control Policy, 2003).

Treatment Approaches

In spite of the Hughes Act of 1970 and the resulting increase in federal funding for research and treatment, the proportion of substance abusers who obtain appropriate treatment today is small relative to the total number of people in need of such treatment. As pointed out by a survey conducted by the Child Welfare League of America (1997), "Approximately 67% of the parents with children in the child welfare system required substance abuse treatment services, but child welfare agencies were able to provide treatment for only 31% of them" (p. 3).

Although methadone maintenance clinics serve thousands of clients in urban areas and provide lifelong access to methadone for heroin addicts (Friedman, 2004), most other substance abuse treatment programs are relatively short-term and tend to focus on the "disease-model" concept of substance abuse emphasizing an alcohol- and drug-free existence (O'Dwyer, 2004). For many urban parents experiencing multiple social, economic, and emotional problems, recovery from AOD abuse is a lifelong struggle necessitating extensive social and emotional supports–supports that are not always readily available.

HELPING FAMILIES OF SUBSTANCE ABUSERS. Although treatment of the substance abuser is usually necessary, family members can benefit from treatment for themselves even when the substance abuser refuses it. Family members can also serve as a motivating force in getting a reluctant substance abuser into treatment through the process known as "Intervention"–an approach that utilizes supportive confrontation to break through the denial common to substance abusers (McIntyre, 2004). For example, Tasha's and Mark's concern for their grandmother could be channeled to confront, or "intervene," and motivate her to seek help for her drinking. While "interventions" are often conducted by specially trained clinicians, many of the techniques can be learned and utilized by other practitioners.

Once the substance abuser is in recovery, family therapy focusing on dysfunctional family roles and communication patterns can be valuable for all family members (McIntyre, 2004). However, the timing of family therapy is crucial since some substance abusers may not be able to tolerate and benefit from such an approach during the early stages of their recovery.

HELPING THE PREGNANT SUBSTANCE ABUSER. Pregnancy can be a significant factor in motivating substance-abusing women to accept AOD treatment. However, many substance-abusing women do not receive prenatal care and consequently are not referred for treatment. The causes are undoubtedly complex; if one's daily behavior is focused on obtaining and using a substance, limited energy is left for other activities, including seeking prenatal care. Moreover, some substance-abusing women are too dysfunctional or too immature even to notice that they are pregnant, while others are too afraid of being arrested and/or losing their children to reveal their pregnancy and seek help. Lack of health insurance can also play a role. Homelessness, likewise, increases the difficulty of obtaining consistent care.

Even when a pregnant substance-abusing woman is willing to seek treatment, she may face obstacles since many AOD rehabilitation programs will not admit pregnant women. Moreover, some in-patient programs that do admit pregnant women will not allow them to bring their other children, or will accept only women with preschool-age children, forcing some mothers to put their older children into foster care.

In order to be effective, treatment programs for pregnant substance-abusing women must provide both tools for recovery as well as hope for a better life for themselves and their children. Individual counseling, group treatment and peer support, parenting and communication skills, and assertiveness training are essential components of treatment for pregnant substance-abusing women (Wong, 2006). Many substance-abusing-women also need help in other areas of their lives such as housing, income support and financial planning, education and vocational training, and understanding the nature of their often problematic relationships with drug-abusing men.

HELPING INFANTS AND CHILDREN OF SUBSTANCE ABUSERS. Early assessment of and intervention with infants and young children from substance-abusing families is critical. Children of AOD abusers frequently are at risk for physical, emotional, and sexual abuse and a comprehensive assessment of these issues is required. Children should also be evaluated for learning disabilities and other psychosocial concerns and appropriate referrals should be made as early as possible. Needless to say, medical care is essential.

During the 1980s, alarms were raised over symptoms displayed by the so-called "crack babies." Although many of these concerns were later viewed as a societal overreaction, some of these children have been found to have attention deficit and problems with organization as they grew up (Azmitia, 2001). More recently, similar concerns have been voiced about babies exposed in utero to methamphetamines, sometimes referred to as "crank babies." While the long-term effects of methamphetamine exposure on these children is yet unknown, such babies should be evaluated and observed for birth defects and other problems that may be related to this exposure (Jewett, 2005).

School-age children may benefit from group treatment that can help them to realize that they are not alone in their plight, enables them to utilize support from other group members, and learn that expression of their feelings regarding parental substance abuse can be helpful. Services such as Student Assistance Programs focus on identifying troubled students, such as Suzette, based on cues like deteriorating academic performance, behavioral changes, excessive lateness or absences, sleepiness in class, or neglected appearance. After meeting individually with the child to further assess his/her situation, the practitioner may then refer the student to appropriate school- or community-based services (Morehouse, 1979).

The most widely available and free community-based programs for teenage children of substance abusers, particular alcoholics, are the Alateen self-help groups provided under the auspices of Al-Anon Family Groups. Utilizing the principles of Alcoholics Anonymous and of Al-Anon, Alateen teaches children about the progressive nature of alcoholism and to "detach" from the alcoholic's pathological behavior and focus on their own functioning. Other self-help groups for older children of alcohol and drug abusers exist in numerous communities under varied sponsorships.

Children of AOD abusers may also be helped through group treatment in both outpatient and in-patient substance abuse programs. In these settings, children are readily identified through a parent's involvement in treatment but may never have had the opportunity to discuss their own issues in relation to familial substance abuse. Such programs are typically multifaceted, involving education around substance abuse, sharing feelings and mutual support, problem-solving and group activities which serve to reduce isolation (Markowitz, 2004). Unfortunately, most children of substance abusers who are in foster care and group homes, or those seen in community-based family and mental health clinics for a variety of psychological or behavioral problems, are not provided with such specialized, but highly valuable treatment. Screening instruments such as the Children of Alcoholics Screening Test (CAST) have been found to be useful in identifying such children (Pilat & Jones, 1985). Books, pamphlets, and videotapes issued by the *National Association for Children of Alcoholics, Al-Anon*, and individual authors offer useful information for children of substance abusers at various age levels and can be easily provided by schools, foster care agencies and treatment facilities.

HELPING SUBSTANCE-ABUSING ADOLESCENTS. Mark, now 16, still lives with his grandmother but has been expelled from school after several suspensions. His grandmother feels helpless to discipline or guide him and he spends time on the streets with other high school dropouts. He has begun doing "errands" for local drug dealers and is often rewarded with marijuana. Recently the police have picked him up, charging him with possession of marijuana. He is referred to drug court.

Use of any substances during preteen or early adolescent years, as exemplified by Mark and Suzette, can interfere with healthy resolution of the various biopsychosocial changes and struggles arising during adolescence. Furthermore, adolescent substance abuse can begin or continue an intergenerational cycle in which children of substance abusers become parents of drug-exposed infants. In order to recover, substance-abusing adolescents need the support of their family members or, when this is not feasible, may need to be removed from a dysfunctional environment (Straussner, 1994).

Adolescent substance abuse treatment programs have been developed in a variety of inpatient and outpatient settings. Cognitive-behavioral treatment, family-involvement, and attention to the multiple systems in the adolescent's life are critical components when working with this population (Freshman, 2004). In recent years, there has been a growing recognition of the special needs of adolescents with co-occurring mental health and substance abuse disorders (Center for Substance Abuse Treatment, 2005).

Practitioners working with substance-abusing adolescents need to help them focus on age-appropriate developmental tasks. For most teenagers, social maturation stops when drug use starts. During their recovery, adolescents need to be taught alternative ways of dealing with stress and anxiety, of resisting social pressures, and of reducing impulsivity. Viewing substance abuse by inner-city adolescents as a "socially" or "culturally" acceptable behavior minimizes their pain and need for help.

HARM REDUCTION. Harm reduction is an increasingly popular set of tactics that seek the short-term goal of reducing the harm resulting from substance abuse, rather than the long-term goal of abstinence (Seiger, 2004). As applied to adolescents, harm reduction approaches include information about drugs and their impact, beverage server training, the use of designated drivers, needle exchange programs for those injecting drugs, and even the reduction of criminal penalties to minimize the impact of a criminal record.

DRUG COURTS AND DIVERSION PROGRAMS. Drug courts and other alternatives to incarceration programs offer treatment as an option to incarceration (Office of National Drug Control Policy, 2005).

Although such treatment is clearly coerced, it is far more successful than imprisonment. For our adolescent, Mark, drug court holds the promise of changing his path from one heading toward increasing drug use to one heading toward recovery.

Prevention Approaches

Prevention-oriented programs are generally aimed at those who have not yet begun to use substances or those in situations in which alcohol or other drug use endangers others, such as driving under the influence. The science of prevention has moved, in a fairly short time period, from simply educational programs to increasingly sophisticated, evidence-based multifaceted approaches based on utilization of risk and protective factors (National Institute on Drug Abuse, 2004). A wide range of evidence-based prevention programs focusing on children, adolescents, their parents, and their community are available.

Prevention programs are based on the current public health model and range on a continuum from *Universal* to *Selective* to *Indicated*. This section discusses several universal and selective prevention efforts. Indicated programs are aimed at youth who have already begun to use substances, as described in the section on youthful substance abuse.

UNIVERSAL PROGRAMS. Universal programs are those aimed at the general population. At their most basic, they include information regarding potential substances of abuse and reach students, parents, and others through textbooks, lectures, warnings (such as on liquor bottles, in bars, on cigarette packs), and the mass media. While some of these programs appear to be effective, overall, there has not been a significant decrease in substance abuse problems over the years.

Some universal programs are based on the federal Drug-Free Communities Act of 1997, since expanded and extended. This Act provided grants to communities that agreed to mount comprehensive alcohol and drug prevention programs. Each community is required to mobilize and maintain a coalition that includes representatives of multiple segments of the community, such as youth, parents, school officials, media, business, faith organizations, and healthcare professionals. The coalition assesses the community's needs, chooses appropriate programs, implements them, and evaluates outcomes. One example of a universal effort is the National Youth Anti-Drug Media

Campaign. Supported by federal funds, the campaign utilizes a variety of mass media to reach parents and youth. The campaign employs a website and booklets to provide models for communicating productively with one's children (Office of National Drug Control Policy, n.d.). Its slogan, "Parents. The Anti-Drug," has become ubiquitous.

The social norms approach is another universal prevention strategy—one that uses an environmental, strengths-based approach. It is based on the believe that young people overestimate the degree to which peers have permissive attitudes and behavior with respect to use of alcohol and other drugs, and underestimate the extent to which their school peers actually engage in healthy, or risk-reducing behaviors (see www.socialnorm.org). For example, after conducting a student survey, a college will publicize the information about the percentage of students who admit to drinking alcohol during a weekend—a figure that is typically much lower than that assumed by the majority of the students. This provision of information about normative behavior among their school peers makes students feel less pressure to engage in unhealthy activities. Although some questions regarding the effectiveness of social norms approach have been raised, some researchers found that this approach has shown success in changing the drinking norms on high school and college campuses (Perkins, Haines, & Rice 2005).

SELECTIVE PROGRAMS. Selective programs are those addressing the needs of higher risk youth. It is estimated that 55 percent of 12- to 17-year-olds are at medium to high risk for substance abuse and require specialized efforts (CASA, 2005). Youth considered "high risk" for experiencing alcohol and other drug problems include offspring of alcoholics and drug users, the economically disadvantaged, victims of sexual abuse, runaway and homeless youths, gay and lesbian youths, school dropouts, pregnant teenagers, and children in out-of-home care (CWLA, 1992; Johnson, 1991). High-risk factors for individual children include "inadequate life skills; lack of self-control, assertiveness and peer-refusal skills; low self-esteem and self-confidence; emotional and psychological problems . . . school failure (and) early antisocial behavior" (Gardner, Green, & Marcus, 1994, p. 5). Of course, many adolescents fall into more than one high-risk group, putting them at even greater risk. Overall, prevention services to youth at high risk for use and abuse of substances aim to help them to clarify values, improve decision-making skills, learn to choose appropriate peers, and understand the dynamics of their own families (Smith, 1993). A variety of programs aimed at such youth have been funded through the federal Center for Substance Abuse Prevention (Johnson, 1991).

CONCLUSION

The use and abuse of alcohol and other drugs is a pervasive national problem that is highly visible in urban areas and its effects on children are profound and sometimes even tragic. The stories of Suzette, Tasha, and Mark personify the variety of ways in which substance abuse may affect urban children. Often buffeted by circumstances beyond their control, they and their families are in dire need of appropriate services provided by informed professionals.

The goal of clinical intervention is to maximize the resiliency of the children and their families by means of a combination of cognitive, affective, and behavioral approaches so that these highly vulnerable children can have a chance at a fulfilling future. It is the responsibility of practitioners to become knowledgeable about effective practices with this population and to develop an understanding of interrelationships between problems, policies, programs, and clinical practice. They need to advocate to ensure that appropriate help is available to all those impacted by substance abuse in our cities. The increased emphasis on evidence-based prevention and intervention programs will allow clinicians to maximize the strengths of children, parents, and communities in the hope of minimizing current and future substance abuse problems and their traumatic sequelae.

REFERENCES

A mother's drug use, an infant's death and then a conviction (1994, September 11). *The New York Times*, p. 36.

American Psychiatric Association. (2000). *Diagnostic and statistical manual of mental disorders* (5th ed., text rev). Washington, DC: Author.

Andrews, A. B., & Patterson, E. G. (1995). Searching for solutions to alcohol and other drug abuse during pregnancy: Ethics, values, and constitutional principles. *Social Work, 40,* 55-64.

Azmitia, E. C. (2001). Impact of drugs and alcohol on the brain through the life cycle: Knowledge for social workers. *Journal of Social Work Practice in the Addictions, 1*(1), 41-63.

Behnke, M., & Eyler, F. D. (1993). The consequences of prenatal substance use for the developing fetus, newborn, and young child. *International Journal of the Addictions, 28,* 1341-1391.

CASA, The National Center on Addiction and Substance Abuse at Columbia University. (2005). *Family matters: Substance abuse and the American family.* http://www.casacolumbia.org/absolutenm/articlefiles/380-family_matters_report.pdf. Accessed June 1, 2005.

Center for Substance Abuse Treatment. (2005). *Definitions and terms relevant to co-occurring disorders.* COCE Overview Paper No. 1. Rockville, MD: Substance Abuse and Mental Health Services Administration, and Center for Mental Health Services.

Child Welfare League of America. (1997). *Survey of state and public child welfare agencies.* Washington, DC: Child Welfare League of America

CWLA North American Commission on Chemical Dependency and Child Welfare. (1992). *Children at the front.* Washington, DC: Child Welfare League of America.

Coles, C. D., & Platzman, K. A. (1993). Behavioral development in children prenatally exposed to drugs and alcohol. *International Journal of the Addictions, 28,* 1393-1433.

Freshman, A. (2004). Assessment and treatment of adolescent substance abusers. In S. L. A. Straussner (Ed.), *Clinical work with substance-abusing clients* (2nd ed.) (pp. 305-329). New York: Guilford.

Friedman, E. G., & Wilson, R. (2004). Treatment of opiate addiction. In S. L. A. Straussner (Ed.), *Clinical work with substance-abusing clients* (2nd ed.) (pp. 187-208). New York: Guilford.

Garcia, S. A. (1993). Maternal drug abuse: Laws and ethics as agents of just balances and therapeutic interventions. *International Journal of the Addictions, 28,* 1311-1339.

Gardner, S. E., Green, P. G., & Marcus, C. (Eds.). (1994). *Signs of effectiveness II.* Washington, DC: U.S. Department of Health and Human Services.

Jewett, C. (2005, April 17). New drug wave delivers 'crank babies.' Earlier alarm over cocaine's effects could limit aid for meth abuse. *Sacramento Bee,* p. A1.

Johnson, J. L. (1991). Preventive interventions for children at risk: Introduction. *International Journal of the Addictions, 25,* 429-434.

Johnston, L. D., O'Malley, P. M., Bachman, J. G., & Schulenberg, J. E. (2005). *Monitoring the future, national results on adolescent drug use: Overview of key findings, 2004.* http://www.monitoringthefuture.org/pubs/monographs/overview2004.pdf. Accessed June 1, 2005.

Markowitz, R. (2004). Dynamics and treatment issues with children of drug and alcohol abusers. In S.L.A. Straussner (Ed.), *Clinical work with substance-abusing clients* (2nd ed.) (pp. 284-302). New York: Guilford.

Marwick, C. (1998). Challenging report on pregnancy and drug abuse. *Journal of the American Medical Association, 280* (12), 1039-1040.

McIntyre, J. R. (2004). Family treatment of substance abuse. In S.L.A. Straussner (Ed.), *Clinical work with substance-abusing clients* (2nd ed.) (pp. 237-263). New York: Guilford.

Morehouse, E. R. (1979). Working in the schools with children of alcoholic parents. *Health and Social Work, 4,* 144-162.

National Institute on Drug Abuse. (2004). Preventing drug abuse and addiction. *NIDA NOTES, 19,* S-7.

O'Dwyer, P. (2004). Alcoholism treatment facilities. In S. L. A. Straussner (Ed.), *Clinical work with substance-abusing clients* (2nd ed.) (pp. 171-186). New York: Guilford.

O'Gorman, P., & Diaz, P. (2004). *The lowdown on families who get high: Successful parenting for families affected by addiction.* Child Welfare League of America. Washington, DC, http://www.cwla.org. Accessed January 17, 2005.

Office of Management and Budget (Fiscal Year 1995). *Controlling illicit drug use, Excerpts from budget of the United States government.* Washington, DC: Congressional Research Service, Library of Congress.

Office of National Drug Control Policy. (2005). *Healing America's drug users: Getting treatment resources where they are needed.* http://www.whitehousedrugpolicy.gov/publications/policy/ndcs05/healing_amer.html. Accessed June 3, 2005.

Office of National Drug Control Policy. (2003). *Drug data summary.* http://www.whitehousedrugpolicy.gov/publications/factsht/drugdata/index.htm. Accessed May 25, 2005.

Office of National Drug Control Policy. (n.d.). *Keeping your kids drug-free.* Washington, DC: National Youth Anti-Drug Media Campaign.

Perkins, H. W., Haines, M. P., & Rice, R. (2005). Misperceiving the college drinking norm and related problems: A nationwide study of exposure to prevention information, perceived norms and student alcohol misuse. *Journal of Studies on Alcohol, 66*(4): 470-478.

Pilat, J. M., & Jones, J. W. (1985). A comprehensive treatment program for children of alcoholics. In E.M. Freeman (Ed.), *Social work practice with clients who have alcohol problems* (pp. 141-159). Springfield, IL: Charles C Thomas.

Purvis, A. (1990, November 26). The sins of the fathers. *Time,* pp. 90-92.

Sieger, B. H. (2004). The clinical practice of harm reduction. In S.L.A. Straussner (Ed.), *Clinical work with substance-abusing clients* (2nd ed.) (pp. 65-81). New York: Guilford.

Smith, G. H. (1993). Intervention strategies for children vulnerable for school failure due to exposure to drugs and alcohol. *International Journal of the Addictions, 29,* 1435-1470.

Straussner, S. L. A., & Attia, P. R. (2002). Women's addiction and treatment through a historical lens. In S.L.A. Straussner & S. Brown (Eds.), *The handbook of addictions treatment for women* (pp. 3-25). San Francisco: Jossey-Bass.

Straussner, S. L. A. (2004). Assessment and treatment of clients with alcohol and other drug abuse problems: An overview. In S.L.A. Straussner (Ed.), *Clinical work with substance-abusing clients* (2nd ed.) (pp. 3-36). New York: Guilford.

Straussner, S. L. A. (2001). Ethnocultural Issues in substance abuse treatment. In S. L. A. Straussner (Ed.), *Ethnocultural factors in the treatment of addictions* (pp. 3-28). New York: Guilford

Straussner, S. L. A. (1994). The impact of alcohol and other drug abuse on the American family. *Drug and Alcohol Review, 13,* 393-399.

Straussner, S. L. A. (1990). Occupational social work today: An overview. In S. L. A. Straussner (Ed.), *Occupational social work today* (pp. 1-17). New York: Haworth Press.

Streissguth, A. P., Aase, J. M., Clarren, S. K., Randels, S. P., LaDue, R. A., & Smith, D. F. (1991). Fetal alcohol syndrome in adolescents and adults. *Journal of the American Medical Association, 265,* 1961-1967.

Substance Abuse and Mental Health Services Administration. (2004). *Overview of findings from the 2003 national survey on drug use and health* (Office of Applied Studies, NSDUH Series H-24, DHHS Publication No. SMA 04-3963). Rockville, MD: Author.

U.S. General Accounting Office. (1994). GOA/HEHS-94-89: Foster care: Parental drug abuse has alarming impact on young children. Washington, DC: Author. http://161.203.16.4/t2pbat3/151435.pdf. Accessed February 11, 2005.

U.S. Department of Health and Human Services, Substance Abuse and Mental Health Services Administration, (1994). *National household survey on drug abuse: Population estimates 1993.* Rockville, MD: U.S. Department of Health and Human Services.

U.S. Department of Health and Human Services, (1999). *Blending perspectives and building common ground: A report to Congress on substance abuse and child protection.* Washington, DC: Government Printing Office. http://aspe.hhs.gov/ hsp/sub-abuse99. subabuse.htm. Accessed June 20, 2005

U.S. General Accounting Office. (1994). GOA/HEHS-94-89: Foster care: Parental drug abuse has alarming impact on young children. Washington, DC: Author. http://161.203.16.4/t2pbat3/151435.pdf. Accessed February 19, 2005.

Wang, C., & Daro, D. (1997). *Current trends in child abuse reporting & fatalities: The results of the 1996 Annual Fifty State Survey.* Chicago: National Center on Child Abuse Prevention Research, National Committee to Prevent Child Abuse.

Wong, J. (2006, in press). Social support: A key to positive parenting outcomes for mothers in residential drug treatment with their children. *Journal of Social Work Practice in the Addictions,* 6(1/2).

Chapter 9

CHILDREN OF INCARCERATED PARENTS

CARL MAZZA

On any given day, over two million American children have a parent who is incarcerated in prison or jail. Ninety-three percent of these incarcerated parents are fathers (U.S. Department of Justice [USDOJ], 2000). Black children are nine times and Latino children are three times more likely to have an incarcerated parent than are white children, and, according to government data, over 750,000 black children, 300,000 Latino children, and 400,000 white children have a parent in prison (USDOJ, 2000). In general, incarceration is not only an urban, but also a neighborhood phenomenon. For example, close to 75 percent of all incarcerated people in New York City come from only seven distinct neighborhoods; the same neighborhoods that are experiencing a myriad of urban social problems associated with poverty, alienation, disempowerment, and social neglect (Prisoners' Alliance with Community, 1997).

Parental incarceration can have a profound effect on children, including the trauma of witnessing parental arrest and the stigma and shame that results from it. The issue of stigma and the resulting secrecy about parental imprisonment may be so strong that it is quite possible that many social workers and other professionals who are currently working with children and adolescents are seeing children of incarcerated parents and do not know it (Mazza, 2002).

This chapter will discuss the criminal justice policies affecting families with an incarcerated family member, and the impact of parental incarceration on children. Case examples will be utilized to illustrate this impact and several innovative intervention programs around the country will be described.

CRIMINAL JUSTICE POLICIES AND INCARCERATION

The United States incarcerates a higher percentage of its population than any other Western nation. Between 1980 and 2002, the prison population has quadrupled, from half a million to two million men and women (Benko & Peugh, 2005). Women are the fastest growing group of incarcerated people in the United States. Between 1980 and 1995 there was a 417 percent increase in the number women in prison (Maura, 1999).

While there are a variety of causes as to why so many people, particularly from urban communities, are imprisoned, the major factors are drug-related crimes and the abuse of substances (Benko & Peugh, 2005). Beginning in the 1970s through the 1980s, the federal government declared a "war on drugs," which was followed by the passage of a series of stringent antidrug laws by individual states. The intent of these laws was to make the penalty for drug involvement so severe that people would refrain from drug trafficking and use (Irwin & Austin, 2001). One-third of all women and more than one-fifth of all men incarcerated in the U.S. are imprisoned directly because of drug policies (Mauer, 1999).

Impact of the "Broken Windows" Theory

Another factor contributing to the increase in the prison population has been the changing philosophy related to tolerance of antisocial behaviors, known as the "Broken Windows" theory. This concept was first formulated by James Q. Wilson and George L. Kelling and published in the March 1982 issue of the *Atlantic Monthly*. This new theory about crime fighting, which they titled the "Broken Windows" theory (Wilson & Kelling, 1982), postulates that communities deteriorate when small problems are not dealt with immediately. It uses the analogy of a broken window, which, if it is not quickly repaired, results in other small blemishes being tolerated in the building. Within a short amount of time, the building's condition begins to deteriorate, and those who can afford it move out into better housing. At the same time, the deteriorating building begins to attract people who use the building for illegal and illicit purposes. The neighboring buildings begin to be neglected, and the neighborhood gradually deteriorates.

Indeed, Broken Windows takes the cliché "a stitch in time saves nine" and transforms it into social theory. During the mid-1980s, the Broken Windows theory became the basis for law enforcement in New York City under the leadership of Mayor Giuliani. Expanding upon this theory, Giuliani began to use it as the basis for "Quality of Life" law enforcement. Following New York City's lead, other major cities in the U.S. embraced the Broken Window/Quality of Life policy of policing (Harcourt, 2001; Taylor & Taylor, 2000).

In order for the Broken Windows practice to be effective, it demands close police monitoring. Police have to notice and arrest people for minor infractions, such as graffiti writing or holding an open container of beer. Unlike suburban neighborhoods where police are more likely to have the authority to practice with more discretion in making arrests, strict adherence to such policing in urban communities is particularly harsh on low-income urban neighborhoods that do not have the economic or political clout to protest this potentially smothering police presence.

Once a person is arrested, prosecutors have an enormous amount of discretion in deciding who gets charged with a crime and/or who enters a plea bargain. In a plea bargain, the person who was arrested enters an agreement with prosecutors to avoid a court trial and possible conviction of a more serious offense. In order to obtain a plea bargain, the defense attorney must be an effective advocate, well connected with the prosecutor's office, and/or be willing to work hard on behalf of his/her client. Obviously, a well-paid experienced private attorney might very well be more successful in reaching a plea bargain for the client than would a less experienced, overburdened public defender. Consequently, poor urban citizens, particularly people of color, comprise a disproportionately high percentage of incarcerated people. In some low income urban communities, close to one-quarter of men of color have been convicted of a felony and/or are on probation or parole (Mauer, 1999).

The Prison Industry in the U.S.

In order to provide for the growing prison population, during the years 1985 to 1995, the federal governments and the individual states opened a new prison at the rate of one a week (Mauer, 1999). Prisons have in effect become a growth industry, and like any other industry, it has created lobbying forces within individual state capitals as well as Congress dedicated not just to its survival, but also its growth. Prisons have also become an enormous source of economic growth in rural communities throughout the United States. With high rates of unemployment and vast land holdings, rural communities have learned to depend on prisons for employment and their economic well-being (Mauer, 1999). It is in these rural communities' best interests to ensure the continued existence of their prisons. Locating prisons in rural areas has a profound impact on the children of incarcerated parents, as they are separated geographically and the families of most children with incarcerated parents do not have the resources to arrange for the children to visit. This issue will be discussed later in the chapter.

Furthermore, the U.S. Census counts people in their location at the time of the census itself. Therefore, these rural communities receive the extra benefit of counting the inmates as members of their local communities without having to provide them with any local services. Likewise, the urban areas lose out since these men and women (most of who will eventually transition back) are not counted in the census, and consequently urban communities with incarcerated individuals receive less federal aid.

Another policy impacting on urban communities is the denial of voting rights: forty-six states in the U.S. deny voting rights to people in prison. In addition, 32 states deny voting rights to those on parole or probation and 14 states deny voting rights to anyone ever convicted of a felony (Mauer, 1999). The denial of voting rights to so many adults in some communities has an enormous negative impact on the political power of a community, weakening their power to demand justice and change.

Another major policy impacting incarcerated people far away from their homes and their families is the high cost of telephone calls. In the majority of states, the departments of corrections award phone contracts to private companies who bid for them. The winning bid is awarded a monopoly contract for all of the correctional facilities in a state. The inmates cannot bypass the winning contractor for a less expense phone company (Hairston, 1998). Reviews of the telephone bills of the families of incarcerated people indicate that inmate initiated collect phone calls costs at least three times more than collect calls from a pay telephone outside prison, and is five to ten times more expensive than a collect call from someone's home (Hairston, 1998). For example, in her memoir about her marriage to an incarcerated man, the author asha bandele (sic) states that her collect call telephone bill from her husband was often more than $500 a month (bandele, 1999). Moreover, when they do speak, the exorbitant cost of the calls frequently creates, or regenerates, arguments and hostilities between the prisoner and family members regarding the financial toll the incarceration is having on the family (Hairston, 1998).

"Invisible" Punishments

The numerous social policies and discriminatory practices affecting individuals with a history of incarceration result in what Travis (2002) calls "invisible punishments." In addition to restrictions on voting rights, discussed above, there are various civil restrictions that are placed on individuals being released from prison, including, lack of access to educational grants and loans, restrictions on professional licenses and certifications, difficulties securing employment and disqualifications for financial bonding services needed for some jobs. Further, the 1996 federal legislation, the Personal Responsibility and Work Opportunity Reconciliation Act (PRWORA) restricts access to welfare benefits to anyone convicted of a drug offense. This policy is particularly damaging to women since it is estimated that over 50 percent of women in prison are there due to drug-related offenses. In addition, in some states, people recently released from prison for drug offenses are barred from living in public housing, and if a family member in a public housing apartment is found housing a recently released person from prison, that family can be evicted from their home.

IMPACT OF PARENTAL INCARCERATION ON CHILDREN

Over 75 percent of incarcerated women and almost 70 percent of incarcerated men have children (Bloom & Steinhart, 1991: U.S. Department of Justice, 2000). Children who have/had a parent in prison are five times more likely to be incarcerated than other children (Schneller, 1978; U.S. Department of Justice, 2000). Since one in every eight American children will have had a parent in prison or jail sometime during their childhood and/or adolescence (Mazza, 2002; San Francisco Partnership for Incarcerated Parents, 2003), without intervention, they are highly likely to replicate their parents' histories.

For children, there are three discrete stages involved in parental incarceration, each of which presents its own set of challenges. These are: the time of the arrest, the time of incarceration, and the transition from prison to the home and community. These stages are discussed below.

Impact of Parental Arrest

How the arrest of a parent is carried out, and therefore, how it impacts on his or her children, is driven by criminal justice policies. Traditionally, many cities had policies to protect children from witnessing the arrest of their parents. With such policies, it was common practice for an officer to escort children out of the room before a policeman handcuffed a parent and took him or her away. However, in the effort to "get tough on crime," since the early 1990s many cities have changed their arrest policies and no longer attempt to shield children from witnessing the arrest (Bernstein, 2005).

Witnessing the arrest of a parent puts a child in the position of viewing the parent both as a criminal and a victim; while the parent is being openly accused of committing a crime, seeing the parent being handcuffed and driven away by the police is also experienced as an assault on the parent (Mazza, 2002). Witnessing the arrest process is very frightening and confusing to children who often find that there is no one with whom they can talk about it. On the other hand, if children are not present at the time of the arrest, they may experience a sense of abandonment. Suddenly the parent has disappeared. Where did he/she go? Why did he/she go? When will he/she return? Children may respond to the confusion and sense of abandonment by blaming themselves for their parents' disappearances. Moreover, if the parents resided with the children at the time of arrest, the equilibrium of the households is disrupted as household dynamics and family income are changed. The sense of security may be shaken, if not destroyed. In some cases, the children may have to leave their homes and move to live with relatives or friends, or enter the foster care system. This is particularly common when it is the mother who is arrested. Given the current federal government's policy of permanency planning resulting from the Adoption and Safe Families Act of 1996, eventual termination of parental rights becomes a real possibility (see Holody, this volume).

Even if the parents resided outside of the children's homes, confusion and concerns remain. Family members may lie to children about what has happened to the parent for "their own good." The children are often told that their parents moved away, that they took jobs in other parts of the country, or that they decided to go back to school far away. These explanations do nothing but increase a sense of abandonment, which in turn can lead to depression and anger.

The issue of family secrets arises: everyone knows the truth about the parents, but no one dares mention it. Children know to "go along" with maintaining the family secret, yet there is often confusion, shame, and anger in doing so. Maintaining a family secret can be stifling, and children cannot begin to understand their feelings and resolve pertinent issues if they are not allowed to talk about what is happening around them.

Karpel (1980) differentiates between *internal family secrets*, in which two or more people keep a secret from at least one family member, and *shared family secrets*, in which all of the family members know the secret but pledge to keep it from others outside of the family. Both types of secrets affect the children of incarcerated parents who know the truth long before the adults in their lives admit it to them. The families often develop shared family secrets in which a verbal or nonverbal pact is made never to discuss the incarceration of the parents with anyone outside of the family. Often the incarceration is a taboo subject even within the families, and therefore is not discussed at all. Secrets, by their very nature, create anxiety, tension, shame, and fear within those who hold them (Boszormenyi-Nagy & Spark, 1973; Ou & Katz, 1999). Holders of secrets feel uncomfortable when certain subjects arise; they must keep track of their deceptive comments and excuses, and live in fear of eventually being "found out." Secrets tend to erode trust within relationships because either someone is left out or someone eventually discloses the secret and is viewed as a traitor (Imber-Black, 1993). The sense of anxiety, tension, fear, shame, guilt, and erosion of trust frequently leads to a lessening of self-esteem among secret-keepers.

Issues for Children During the Time of Parental Incarceration

Parental separation because of incarceration is unlike any other parental separation. Typically, when a couple is usually separated, one of the parents moves out of the home. That parent may not be welcomed back in the home, but he/she still can maintain contact with the children. The noncustodial parents can have his/her children visit in the new residence, often spending the night. The noncustodial parent and the children can go places together and communicate freely. But when a parent is imprisoned there are unique dynamics impacting the relationship between parents and children. A powerful and complex bureaucracy now has ultimate control of the frequency, quality, and length of the contact between the now incarcerated parents and their children.

Visitation Issues

With incarceration comes the issue of visitation. Incarcerated parents can be assigned to any correctional facility within a state. Often parents are incarcerated hundreds of miles away from their children, making visitation very difficult. Transportation becomes the key issue in parental visitation. According to Bloom and Steinhart (1993), transportation issues were given as the primary reason why over 50 percent of mothers and fathers who are incarcerated do not receive visits from their children. Without a car, travel is restricted to public transportation. As previously discussed, due to economic incentives many rural communities within a particular state may vie for a prison to be built in their communities. Given the remote location of some of these rural communities, public transportation may not exist. In some states, several times a year, the Department of Corrections will charter buses to take families from urban areas to the prisons. In order to get a seat on these chartered buses, the incarcerated parents must apply for tickets, register their family members as approved visitors, and send the tickets to the family members. In order to reach the prisons by 9:00 or 10:00 A.M., the buses must leave the designated urban departure spots at 3:00 or 4:00 A.M. Having the children's caretakers get the children ready and transporting them to the departure spot by 3:00 A.M. is an ordeal. Furthermore, the departure spots are often in highly commercialized, high-crime neighborhoods. Even if the family has access to a car, the expenses associated with the trip are often enormous. In addition to fuel, there are expenses associated with food and very probably motel expenses. Few families can afford such costs on a regular basis.

Prison visits are time limited and the family often spends much more time traveling to and from the visits than they do with their loved ones in prison. Spending 14 hours roundtrip on a bus or in a car for a two hour visit is not an idea that most people look forward to. Even though most prisons have weekend visits, that assumes that caregivers do not work on weekends or have other obligations, and there are some prisons that have only weekday visits, meaning that the children would have to miss school and caregivers would have to miss work in order to see their family member.

In most prisons, children under 16 years of age must be accompanied by their guardian. In most cases when fathers are incarcerated, the children remain with their mothers. If the mothers and fathers have a strained or no relationship with each other, the caretaking parents often do not want to see their former partner so visits do not take place. If other relatives serve as caregivers, such as grandparents and aunts and uncles, as is frequently the case when mothers are incarcerated, they may need to have legal documentation that these adults have guardianship over the children. If the children are in foster care, visitation is usually arranged through the child welfare authority designed to oversee the foster care placement. Because of bureacratic policies, limited staffing (especially true on weekends), limited financial resources, and prejudical attitudes against incarcerated parents, many child welfare authorities are reluctant, if not outrightly refusing to facilitate visitation.

When the children are allowed visitation, they enter a strange and confusing world. Prison visitation involves long lines and detailed, invasive physical searches. Depending on the facility in which the parent is housed, the amount of physical contact with the parent may be limited. Although most prisons allow "contact" visits and mothers are allowed to hold their children on their laps, many prisons do not allow incarcerated fathers to hold their children (Hairston, 2000). Incarcerated parents are often assigned seats by the correctional staff at the visitation table, usually in the seats facing the front of the visitation room, thereby facing the correctional officers who are stationed in the front of the room. The assigned seating arrangement and the awareness of being constantly watched results in an artificial and tense atmosphere that discourages spontaneity within the family. In addition, children may not be permitted to bring paper into the visiting room; consequently, they may not be able to share their drawings, report cards, homework, or art projects with their parents resulting in a greater gap between the daily lives of the children and their parents (Mazza, 2002).

The visiting rooms themselves are often dank and uninviting places. The furniture is institutional, often old and mismatched. The walls are usually cinderblock and void of decorations. In a few prisons, there are decks of playing cards and old Bibles that can be used to pass the time during visits. Paper towels are sometimes taken from the restroom, and parents and children use their creativity to devise games and activities with them (Mazza, 2004).

Restrictions that are commonly imposed on incarcerated parents may lead to a role reversal between parent and child. For example, in most prisons inmates are not allowed to touch money or to move beyond certain markings on the floor. Children, however, may walk up to the vending machines located in a corner of the room, insert money, and choose the food. If the food needs to be heated up, the children may insert it into a nearby microwave oven and wait until it is ready, while the parents can only look on helplessly. This parentification of children can be quite confusing. The children often sense that they have more power than their parents. Furthermore, the parents' interactions with their children are always under surveillance; therefore, interactions between parents and children often have a surreal quality to them.

Communication Issues

The parentification of children often continues through the use of telephone calls and letters. As previously discussed, while incarcerated parents are at certain times allowed to make collect phone calls home, the high cost of these collect calls makes it impossible for most children to talk often to their parents. Moreover, many prison telephones have timing mechanisms whereby the calls are automatically disconnected after a certain amount of minutes have passed. Therefore children and parents can be in the middle of a sentence when the telephone call is cut off. This can further increase a child's sense of rejection, anger, sadness, and isolation (Hairston, 1998).

Incarcerated parents can also write letters to their children. In some states, however, there are limits as to how many letters can be written in a given month. In other states, the incarcerated parents must supply their own postage and therefore must have access to at least some funds. In the majority of states, letters emanating from prison are stamped, often in red ink, clearly identifying that the letter was sent from a prison. This can make some families and children self-conscious and embarrassed about receiving letters (Hairston, 1998). As with telephone calls, incarcerated parents are dependent on their children responding to their letters. Moreover, letter writing can only occur when the incarcerated parents are confident in their writing abilities. Given the low educational level of many of those incarcerated, they often have poor writing skills. Consequently, some parents may be reluctant to write. Children, on the other hand, may see writing as a chore, an extension of homework and far from a fun activity. Consequently, letter writing becomes a problematic form of communications for many incarcerated parents and their children.

As previously mentioned, in the visit rooms, physical contact is often restricted. Fathers may not be able to hold their children in their laps and kissing and hugging may be restricted. In addition, children witness the imbalance of power between their parents and the correctional officers working in the visiting rooms. They sense that their parents must obey the rules or orders given by the officers. They realize that the officers can come over to the table any time and tell their parents to stop doing some activity and that their parents must comply. Moreover, in many prisons, a "count" is taken several times a day, during which all inmates are counted to ensure that no one is missing. In the visiting rooms during a count, all of the inmates must stand silently while everyone else remains seated. This can be a humiliating, fearful, and/or anger-inducing experience for some parents. These feelings can be communicated to the children nonverbally and can have a profound impact on the children's own views towards authority figures. These views may have dangerous, if not deadly, consequences for the children back home in their urban communities.

A unique aspect of communication between incarcerated parents and their children relates to issues related to passage of time. Children have a different sense of time than adults. To children, time passes more slowly than for adults (Goldstein, Freud, & Solnit 1973). For example, when incarcerated parents are asked by their children "When are you coming home?" the parents respond by saying "soon." Children may view such a comment as meaning "right away." When met, these expectations are not met the sense of sadness and anger becomes reenforced. Incarcerated parents say "soon" for different reasons. This term may be used as an alternative to giving the children a specific time. In fact, many incarcerated people truly do not know when they will be home. That decision is not up to them; it is a decision often made by parole boards of which they have little influence. To incarcerated parents "soon" seems a better choice than "I don't know." Moreover, the notion of time in prison often takes on a different dimension than in the rest of the world. In prison, someone is "short" if he has a short amount of time left on his/her sentence. Yet, being "short" can mean several years. Certainly two years of prison time is closer to release than twelve years, but two years is still a good deal of time, particularly to children.

Other frequent comments made by incarcerated parents to their children are, "I'm innocent," "I didn't do anything," or "They made a mistake." Whether these statements are true or false, they dramatically undermine the children's sense of safety and security. If their parents can be picked up and put in prison for doing "nothing," so can they, and so can other members of their families. No one is safe. No one is secure, and tomorrow they run the risk of being abandoned by another loved one. This again, reinforces the children's focus on living day-to-day with no real sense of security and safety.

Emotional Issues

Incarceration often leads to depression expressed through isolation and social withdrawal. Additionally there is frequently a sense of shame experienced by the incarcerated parent. This shame and depression can lead to further withdrawal from contact with their children, increasing the children's sense of abandonment, as well as feelings of responsibility and guilt for the incarceration. In children and adolescents, depression is often masked by anger, irritability, and disruptive behavior (American Psychiatric Association, 2000). The ramification of this depression frequently is seen in a drop in the children's school performance, use of substances, an increase in behavior problems, and a lessening of appropriate social skills.

Transitioning Out of Prison

Once they are released from prison, most people reentering the larger society are placed on parole. The amount of time people spend on parole is usually linked to their initial sentencing in court. For example, if a person was sentenced to 10 to 15 years and was released from prison after nine years, then he/she would be placed on parole for the remaining six years of his/her sentence. In some states, after doing well on parole for several years, people can apply for "early release," meaning that they request through their parole officer to be released from parole. The parole officer can either recommend early release or deny it. If the officer recommends it, an administrative review takes place and a decision is made as to whether the request should be granted.

Parole officers have discretion to approve or disapprove employment, to institute restrictions such as curfews and to limit travel even within a community. In New York City, for example, a parolee living in the borough of the Bronx may be banned by parole from entering the borough of Brooklyn. Parolees are often subjected to random drug screenings even if they were not convicted of a drug offense. They may also be mandated to attend specific programs, such as anger management.

Getting Out

Many men and women who have been released from prison feel overwhelmed with everything in the larger society and exhaust all of their energy trying to adjust to life "outside." The communities may look the same, but things have changed. If they have been incarcerated for a number of years, they may not be familiar with cell phones, DVDs, or video games. They often feel like strangers in their own neighborhoods.

The quality of life for families of people leaving prison is largely impacted by the "invisible" punishments, discussed earlier. Restrictions on employment and lack of access to public assistance, educational grants, or public housing, for example, severely limit the options available. Further, if the family is already living in public housing, the policy prohibiting the parolee from living there prevents the chances of restoring the family unit. These policies are particularly damaging for women, since it is estimated that over 50 percent of women in prison are there due to drug-related offenses, which invoke many of the "invisible" punishments. To transition from prison without employment or work experience and then be barred from any type of public assistance gives these women little chance of succeeding (Women's Prison Association, 2003).

Parents transitioning from prison may lack housing and enter the shelter system, where they must immediately learn how to navigate systems leading to emergency assistance. Parents with children in foster care must immediately engage themselves with the child welfare system in order to prevent the termination of their parental rights. Even if they do engage themselves in the child welfare system and their parental rights have not yet been terminated, their options for the future are limited, based on lack of employability, housing, and finances.

Parents and Children

Serving a number of years in prison obviously impacts on one's availability to parent children. With the federal Safe Families and Adoption Act, the chances of losing parental rights during their incarceration have increased dramatically. The Act mandates the termination of parental rights after the children have remained in foster care for fifteen months. The fact that the mothers were incarcerated and therefore could not parent the child at the time does not exempt them from this Act. Consequently, many of the mothers transitioning from prison have to come to terms with the fact that they are no longer the legal mothers to their children. Even when a maternal relative has been raising the children, either as a kinship foster parent or as a relative outside the child welfare system, the children see the aunt or grandmother as "mom," leaving the newly paroled mother feeling alone, alienated, and self-hating.

Over the years, many men lose their connections with their children, as the custodial parent either moves away, making visits more difficult, or becomes involved with other partners and subsequently lessens or terminates the communications between the incarcerated parent and the children. Even when grandparents or aunts and uncles are raising the children, daily life responsibilities eventually make visiting the incarcerated parent very difficult, and such visits become less and less frequent.

For those who have not lost parental rights, once they are released from prison, many feel like strangers to their children. They feel guilty for not being available to see the children grow, and most feel inadequate that they did not have any financial resources to contribute to the children's well-being. Often, the newly released parent lives in a separate household and must work extremely hard to develop a meaningful relationship with the children.

Case Example

Michael Holland, 39 years old, served seven years in an Illinois State Prison for a drug-related crime. During his incarceration, he had consistent contact with both his wife Della and his two children, Jonathon and Michelle, now ages 15 and 12. Della and the children reside in a two bedroom apartment in a public housing complex on the south side of Chicago. Della works as a waitress for a chain restaurant. The family's income is supported with food stamps. While incarcerated, Michael received his general equivalency diploma. His family would visit him once every two weeks, generally on Sunday. Letters to the children would occur on a weekly basis. Early in his incarceration, Michael would make collect calls to his family several times a week. Given the expense associated with the collect telephone calls, Michael eventually began to call home just once a week.

Michael is currently on parole. Unless he obtains an early release, he will be on parole for the next eight years. He is mandated to attend drug treatment support groups three times a week. Even though Michael does not have any substance abuse history, because he was convicted of a drug offense, his parole officer made the groups a condition of parole. Also, because of his drug conviction, he is barred from living with his family in public housing. Michael therefore has been paroled to his mother's home about three miles away from Della and the children. He has a 9:00 P.M. curfew. For the first three months, he has kept the curfew. He has now begun to spend evenings, sometimes even sleeping at Della's apartment. He knows that this is a potential violation of his parole and he runs the risk of his parole officer making an unannounced visit at his mother's home. If this were to occur, his parole officer could recommend return to prison.

During the day, while Della is working and the children are at school, Michael, when he is not in the drug support groups or looking for employment, stays at Della's apartment doing housework, shopping for groceries, and cooking.

As he entered adolescence, his son, Jonathon, began to exhibit behavioral problems. His grades dropped and he began to miss curfews. Although not a member of any street gang, he increasingly uses gang gestures and wears gang related colors. For most of her life, Michelle was strongly attached to her mother; preferring to spend free time with her mother rather than her friends. Although Della generally likes spending time with Michelle, she sometimes felt Michelle is too "clingy."

When Michael was released from prison the family initially celebrated "Daddy's return." Michael thought that Della had too many rules for Jonathon and began to give Jonathon longer curfews and extra privileges without consulting Della. Jonathon's behavior continued to deteriorate while arguments between Michael and Della escalated. When her parents were arguing, Michelle would often cry and run to wrap her arms around her mother. After several weeks, Michelle would state how she wished "Daddy would just go away and stay away."

Michelle's teacher noticed that she was more withdrawn socially and referred her to the school social worker, who recommended that they start family counseling at a community mental health agency. During counseling, both Michael and Della discussed their fears. Della was frightened that the consistency and stability she had worked so hard to achieve was being disrupted by Michael. While she was glad to have Michael back home, she saw herself being "set up" as the "bad guy" in relations to Jonathon's behavior. Della also admitted to feeling the loss of power within the home, explaining that while Michael was incarcerated, she was the sole voice of authority in the house. Currently she is feeling ambivalent about sharing the control. She felt that Michael saw himself as superior to her since he received his high school equivalency diploma while Della herself never completed high school or a G.E.D. program.

Michael felt emasculated because he wasn't employed yet and relied on Della's salary. While he didn't mind helping around the house, he felt that Della was taking advantage of and disrespecting him by leaving lists of chores to do while she was at work. Michael couldn't help feeling that while he was incarcerated Della should have been able to secure a better paying job and move the family to a safer neighborhood; while he took responsibility for "holding the family back," he also felt that Della was underachieving. As he felt more emasculated by Della, he granted Jonathon more freedom, both in terms of "getting back" at Della as well as vicariously living through some of Jonathon's youthful behaviors. While he certainly didn't want Jonathon to join a gang or follow his path to prison, he was concerned that Della was making Jonathon "too soft."

Jonathon tended to idealize his father, putting the blame for the family problems, including Michael's initial arrest, on Della's shoulders. Jonathon was drawn to the "streets" in part because he didn't feel any real connections at home. Jonathon senses that his mother tended to project her angry feelings towards Michael unto him. Michelle liked the way things "use to be." Michael's return has changed the family dynamics. Now she felt that she had to compete with Michael for some of Della's attention and affection.

Although the family had several rough patches they remained in counseling. As this reconstituted family began to settle down, and after Michael found full-time permanent employment, they moved into an apartment where they could begin to come together as a family. The Holland family reflected great strength, as seen in their willingness to seek help, their openness to discuss their feelings, and in their underlying bonds; these were the dynamics that kept this family together.

Working with Children of Incarcerated Parents

In working with children of incarcerated parents, social workers must provide an accepting, nonjudgmental climate. Anger and distrust are often the two strong emotions experienced by children of incarcerated parents, and these feelings may be displaced toward the social workers (Weissman & LaRue, 2001). The concepts of nonjudgmental attitude, controlled emotional involvement, and purposeful expression of feelings as outlined by Biestek (1957), are important to the growing therapeutic relationship. Social workers also need to be culturally competent and their office settings must be inviting and reflect cultural sensitivity, and respect for diversity. The staff of an agency should reflect the cultural diversity of the clients. Programs must be careful not to label the children, for example never referring to an intervention group as "Children of Incarcerated Parents." The children already feel labeled, marginalized, and rejected, and the staff must be very sensitive to this issue.

The issue of stigma may be so strong that it is quite possible that many social workers who are currently working with children and adolescents are working with children of incarcerated parents and not know it. It is also imperative that social workers conduct careful assessments including the family history and current dynamics. Due to the strong social stigma, children may initially deny that their parents are incarcerated. The denials may take the form of inconsistent or illogical tales regarding the whereabouts of their parents, such as stating that a parent is working in Texas or going to school in California while the family lives in Baltimore. It is recommended that social workers try to obtain accurate information about both parents from the caregivers. The children should not be confronted with the fact that the social workers know that the parents are in prison. Rather, as the relationship builds, the subject of incarceration should be introduced gradually.

Let's look at the example of Malcolm. Malcolm's father is incarcerated but Malcolm never mentions this in sessions, although he was referred to a social worker due to behavioral problems following the arrest of his father. After several months of weekly individual sessions, the social worker found an opportunity to interject the subject of prison into an existing discussion about news events.

Malcolm: A teacher in my school was arrested over the weekend for drunk driving.

S.W.: Wow, how do you know that?

Malcolm: Everybody was talking about it in school and Tina, this girl in my class, brought in this newspaper article about it. He's still not in school. They have a substitute teacher for his class.

S.W.: Did you ever have him as a teacher?

Malcolm: No, but when the gym teacher was out sick, he covered basketball practice, so I know him a little bit.

S.W.: How do you feel about him?

Malcolm: He was always cool with me. I hope he's okay. It's hard to believe that he's in jail now with all of those bad people.

S.W.: Well, in jail, the people aren't necessarily bad. Good people can make bad decisions.

Malcolm: You telling me that not everyone in jail is bad?

S.W.: You tell me. You don't feel that the teacher is a bad person, yet he's in jail.

Malcolm: Yea, I never thought about it like that.

Malcolm thought that prison was a place for "bad people," consequently he never talked about his father to people. As time went on, he began to feel more assured that his father was not a "bad person," and that the social worker was not going to judge and reject either him or his father. Eventually Malcolm was able to verbalize his feelings about his father.

By their very definition, family secrets are not discussed in public; thus they cause difficulties for social workers who want children to talk about them (Boszormenyi-Nagy & Sparks, 1973; Imber-Black, 1993; Karpel, 1980; Ou & Katz, 1999). Social workers have to "assume a leadership role in uncovering the family taboo and helping the family find 'safe routes' to begin discourse on taboo subjects" (Ou & Katz, 1999, pp. 625-626). In the example of Malcolm, the social worker did indeed assume such a leadership role. The social worker found an opening to begin to talk about incarceration, and slowly began to direct the subject towards Malcolm's father, and ultimately, Malcolm's feelings about both his father and himself.

Because of the stigma, it is important for the children to know that there are others who have experienced the same situations. Group work can be a very effective means of dealing with this issue; however, getting the children involved in a group implies that the participants and their families are open to talking about the incarceration. For many children, group work may be an appropriate goal once they begin to feel comfortable sharing their feelings about their parents in individual sessions. Asking children to draw pictures about family members and to write about themselves and their parents can be helpful in this effort.

It is imperative that social workers remember that although these are children of incarcerated parents, they are also first just children. Despite the serious problems in their families, they want and need to have fun, and to feel good, important, and accepted. Social workers must always be warm, nurturing, and consistent, and willing to empathize with the children's pain and to share their joy.

CURRENT PROGRAMS THAT OFFER SERVICES TO CHILDREN OF INCARCERATED PARENTS

Children of incarcerated parents in urban communities have been an invisible population for quite a long time. However things are beginning to change. In cities throughout the United States, voluntary, often grassroot agencies, are beginning to address the needs of these children. These agencies tend to be small with limited staff and money. Yet they are determined to succeed.

For example, in Harlem, New York, *In Arms Reach* (IAR) was established to work exclusively with children who have an incarcerated parent. Initially IAR provided transportation via van service so that the children could visit their parents. Soon social workers were added to the van trips to deal with the children's feelings both in preparation for the visits as well as after the visits.

Understanding the dynamics of system theory, IAR recognized that parental incarceration affects all aspects of the children's functioning. Consequently, the agency began an after-school tutorial program and a school advocacy program attempting to ensure that the children receive all the educational services to which they are entitled. IAR has teamed up with the recording industry and has used song writing, rapping, and singing to help the children raise their self-esteem while utilizing music as a creative outlet.

In 2005, IAR obtained permission to begin televisiting, whereby children can communicate with their parents in prison via live remote broadcasts. Finally, IAR has entered into a partnership with Big Brothers/Big Sisters of New York to provide mentors to the children to increase their sense of connection, lessen their feelings of isolation, provide positive role models, and expand their understanding of options in their lives (In Arms Reach, 2005).

The importance of mentoring is also reflected in the *Amachi Program*, located in Baltimore and Philadelphia. A West African word, "Amachi" means "who knows what God has brought us through this child." The program is affiliated with churches and synagogues in both cities, which recruit and train adult volunteers, again in partnership with Big Brothers/Big Sisters. The Amachi Program is based on the understanding that the children of incarcerated parents feel alone and different from other children; that they carry a heavy burden and a powerful secret regarding the circumstances of their parents; and that caring, nurturing, and consistent adults can help them expand their possibilities for their future, as well as help them with their daily struggles (Center for Research on Religion and Urban Civil Society, 2003).

In Milwaukee, Wisconsin, the *Family Reunification Program of St. Rose Youth & Family Center* was established to help children deal with the trauma of the arrest and incarceration of their parents. In addition to facilitating visits between children and their incarcerated parents, the program provides age-appropriate support groups after each visit to discuss their feelings and fears. In addition, individual and family therapy with the children and their caregivers are offered on an on-going basis. In the women's prisons of Wisconsin, the *MOMS Program* (Mothers Offering Mutual Support) provides information on parenting from prison, and support groups for incarcerated mothers to discuss their feelings about themselves, as well as to more fully understand the difficulties that are being experienced by their children. Upon the women's release from prison, the program provides aftercare counseling for mothers and their children.

In partnership with the Milwaukee and Racine, Wisconsin, chapters of the Girl Scouts of America, St. Rose's also sponsors a very unique program, *Bonds Beyond Bars*. This program consists of a special Girl Scout troop composed of girls five to 17 years of age who meet with their incarcerated mothers in the Ellsworth Correctional Center and together share scouting activities (St. Rose Center, 2005).

In Austin, Texas, *Family Forwards* provides wraparound services for children with a parent who is incarcerated in an Austin jail. The program provides case management and individual counseling to children and their caregivers. The incarcerated parents are offered a parenting program, which, in addition to providing traditional parenting information, includes a specific component to help them more fully understand the trauma experienced by their children as a result of their incarceration. Both during the incarceration as well as after the release of the parent, the program provides needed referrals to various other community-based services (Family Forward, 2004).

In San Francisco, the *San Francisco Partnership for Incarcerated Parents*, in consultation with Friends Outside, the California Research Bureau, and the Child Welfare League of America, conceived in 2003 "The Children of Incarcerated Parents: A Bill of Rights."

The eight rights are:

1. I have the right to be kept safe and informed at the time of my parent's arrest.
2. I have the right to be heard when decisions are made about me.
3. I have the right to be considered when decisions are made about my parent.
4. I have the right to be well cared for in my parent's absence.
5. I have the right to speak with, see, and touch my parent.
6. I have the right to support as I struggle with my parent's incarceration.
7. I have the right not to be judged, blamed, or labeled because of my parent's incarceration.
8. I have the right to a lifelong relationship with my parent.

(San Francisco Partnership for Incarcerated Parents, 2003).

These rights poignantly encapsulate the trauma, stress, alienation, and loneliness that are often experienced by children with incarcerated parents. The mere idea that there was a heartfelt need to develop these rights speaks to how often the needs of these children have been ignored.

CONCLUSION

With the arrest and incarceration of their parents, children enter an unfamiliar and frightening world. Contact with their parents is highly regulated by complex, frustrating bureaucracies, which value security over the needs of children and families. Children may feel that their negative behavior led to the incarceration of their parents, and feel responsible and guilty because of it. Because of the negative connotations associated with incarcerated people, children often do not feel free or safe to discuss the reality of their families' situations, much less their own feelings. They carry with them a massive burden, with no secure outlet to relieve themselves of their pent-up fears and other emotions and thoughts.

People in low-income urban neighborhoods already feel isolated and alienated from the larger community. Growing up in this environment may lead to a sense of disempowerment and hopelessness (Clark, 1989). These negative feelings become magnified with the incarceration of the parents. Not only are the parents not there to provide and advocate for their children, their incarceration often makes them feel "less than" others. Given the already existing feelings of powerlessness inherent in low-income neighborhoods, these children feel even more marginalized and less able to succeed. Social workers have a responsibility to help these children believe in themselves, and provide hope and opportunity for a better future.

REFERENCES

American Psychiatric Association. (2000). *Diagnostic and statistical manual of mental disorders* (4th ed.). Washington, DC: Author.

bandele, a. (1999). *The prisoner's wife: A memoir.* New York: Washington Square Press.

Barnhill, S. (1996). Three generations at risk: Imprisoned women, their children, and grandmother caregivers. *Generations, 20,* 39-40.

Benko, S., & Oeugh, J. (2005). Estimating drug treatment needs among state prison inmates. *Drug and alcohol dependence, 77,* 269-281.

Bernstein, N. (2005). *All alone in the world: Children of the incarcerated.* New York: The New Press.

Boszormenyi-Nagy, I., & Spark, G. (1973). *Invisible loyalties: Reciprocity in inter-generational family therapy.* New York: Harper & Row.

Biestek, F. (1957). *The casework relationship.* Chicago: Loyola University Press.

Bloom, B., & Steinhart, D. (1993). *Why punish the children? A reappraisal of the children of incarcerated mothers in America.* San Francisco: National Council on Crime and Delinquency.

Center for Research on Religion & Urban Civil Society. (2003). *Amachi: Mentoring children of prisoners in Philadelphia.* www.crrus.org. Accessed June 23, 2005.

Child Welfare League of America. (1997). *Parents in prison: Children in crisis.* Washington, DC: Author.

Clark, K. (1989). *Dark ghetto: Dilemmas of social power.* (2nd ed.) Hanover, NH: Wesleyan University Press.

Fagin, A., & Reid, A. (1991). Moms in jail: Child abuse prevention program at Nassau County (NY) Correctional Facility. *Children Today, 20,* 12–13.

Family Forward. (2004). *Wrap-around services for children of incarcerated parents.* www.familyforward.org. Accessed June 14, 2005.

Gabel, S., & Shindledecker, R. (1993). Characteristics of children whose parents have been incarcerated. *Hospital and Community Psychiatry, 44,* 656–660.

Goldstein, J., Freud, A., & Solnit, J. (1973). *Beyond the best interests of the child.* New York: Free Press.

Hairston, C. F., & Seymour, C. (Eds.). (2000). *Children with parents in prison: Child welfare policy, program, and practice issues.* Somerset, NJ: Transaction.

Hairston, C. F. (1998). The forgotten parent: Understanding the forces that influence incarcerated fathers' relationships with their children. *Child Welfare, 77,* 617–638.

Hairston, C. F.(1996). How correctional policies impact on father-child relationships. *Family and Corrections Network Report, 8,* 3–4.

Hairston, C. F. & Hess, P. (1989). Family ties: Maintaining child-parent bonds is important. *Corrections Today, 51,* 102-106.

Harcourt, B. (2001). *Illusions of order: The false promise of broken window policing.* Boston: Harvard University Press.

In Arms Reach, Inc. (2005). *Parents behind bars: Children in crisis fact sheet.* New York: In Arms Reach Inc.

Imber-Black, E. (1993). *Secrets in families and family therapy.* New York: W.W. Norton.

Irwin, J., & Austin, J. (2001). *It's about time: America's imprisonment binge* (3rd ed.). Belmont, CA: Wadsworth/Thompson.

Johnston, D. (1995). Effects of parental incarceration. In K. Gabel & D. Johnston (Eds.), *Children of incarcerated parents* (pp. 59–88). New York: Lexington Books.

Karpel, M. A. (1980). Family secrets: Conceptual and ethical issues in the relational context. *Family Process, 19,* 295–306.

Mazza, C. (2004). A pound of flesh: The psychological, familial and social consequences of mandatory long-term sentencing laws for drug offenses. *Journal of Social Work Practice in the Addictions, 4,* 65–81.

Mazza, C. (2002). And then the world fell apart: The children of incarcerated fathers. *Families in Society, 83,* 521–529.

Mauer, M. (1999). *The race to incarcerate.* New York: The New Press.

McCloskey, L. A., & Walker, M. (2000). Posttraumatic stress in children exposed to family violence and single-event trauma. *Journal of the American Academy of Child & Adolescent Psychiatry, 39,* 108–115.

Mcguire, K., & Pastore, A. L. (1996). *Bureau of Justice statistics sourcebook of criminal justice statistics-1996.* Albany, New York: The Hindlelang Criminal Justice Research Center, University at Albany.

Myers, B. J., Smarsh, T. M., & Amlund-Hagen, K. (1999). Children of incarcerated mothers. *Journal of Child and Family Studies, 8,* 11–25.

Ou, R., & Katz, D. (1999). Family secrets and the disclosure of distressful information in Chinese families. *Families in Society, 80,* 620–628.

Prisoners' Alliance with Community. (1997). *The non-traditional approach to criminal and social justice.* Unpublished paper.

San Francisco Partnership for Incarcerated Parents. (2002). *Children of incarcerated parents: A bill of rights.* San Francisco: Author.

St. Rose Youth & Family Center. (2005). *Family reunification program.* www.strosecenter.org. Accessed August 7, 2005.

Taylor, R. B., & Taylor R. (2000). Breaking away from broken windows: Baltimore neighborhoods and the nationwide fight against crime, grime, fear and decline. Boulder, CO: Westview Press.

Travis, J. (2002). Invisible punishment: An instrument of social exclusion. In M. Mauer & M. Chesney-Linds (Eds.), *Invisible imprisonment: The collateral consequences of mass imprisonment* (pp. 15–36). New York: Free Press.

U.S. Department of Justice. (2000). *Report on minor children who have a mother or father in prison.* Washington, DC: U.S. Department of Justice, Bureau of Justice Statistics.

Weissman, M., & LaRue, C. M. (2001). Earning trust from youths with none to spare. In C. Seymour & C. F. Hairston (Eds.), *Children with parents in prison* (pp 111–125). Piscataway, NJ: Transaction.

Wilson, J. Q., & Kelling, G. L. (1982). Broken windows. *The Atlantic Monthly, 249,* 29-38.

Women's Prison Association. (2003). *WPA focus on women and justice: Barriers to Reenter.* New York: Women's Prison Association.

Chapter 10

URBAN TEEN PARENTS

Martha G. Roditti

Single parenthood has become part of American culture, found in every socioeconomic group. However, unlike other single parents, unwed adolescent parents often face additional challenges, such as limited educational attainment, poverty, and unemployment. Unlike the teenage parents of previous decades, many of the urban women under 20 who are having babies today are poor to begin with, and remain poor as single parents. Poverty has been found to supersede age, race, and illegitimacy as the predominant factor influencing the quality of life of both teen parents and their children (Hardy & Zabin, 1991). In addition, the lives of many teen mothers in urban communities today are complicated by their history of physical and sexual abuse, as well as by the powerful influences of a hyper-sexualized society.

This chapter will discuss the phenomenon of teen parenting in its historical context, and as it relates to sexual activity, fathering, the stages of adolescent development, poverty, and public policy. It concludes with a description of effective intervention programs and practice issues.

HISTORICAL PERSPECTIVE ON UNMARRIED PARENTS AND THEIR CHILDREN

Public perception of children born out of wedlock and of their unmarried parents has shifted over time. Prior to the 1600s, European and Colonial American children born out of wedlock were not stig-

216

matized or viewed with great shame; they were often taken into the father's home and raised with their half-siblings without disgrace to themselves or their parents. Changes in religious beliefs, combined with the worsening economic conditions of the 1500s and 1600s, brought changes in attitudes towards children born outside of marriage. As poor children became more of an economic burden for society, the circumstances of the child's birth were targeted and became more shameful. By the 1600s, Puritan Americans dealt with out-of-wedlock "bastards" with a moral belligerence that was meant to scare the "extra-marital fornicators" (Kadushin & Martin, 1988). The offenders, mostly white women and men, were publicly shamed by their communities and their children were stigmatized (Abramovitz, 1988). The illegitimate child was considered the "son of no one" (filius nullius) or "son of the people" (filius populi), without a name and without a right to support (Kadushin & Martin, 1988; Trattner, 1999).

Despite the prevailing religious morals, premarital sex and illegitimacy have persisted throughout American history. During the Revolutionary era (1776-1780s), between one-third to one-half of first-born children were born outside of marriage (Trattner, 1999). During the eighteenth, nineteenth, and most of the twentieth century, single unwed mothers continued to be viewed as "ruined" or "fallen" and their children were stigmatized as "illegitimate." Only during the second half of the twentieth century was there a shift towards greater acceptance of women who bear children outside of marriage and decreased stigmatization of their children.

The history of abortion in this country parallels society's attitudes towards illegitimacy and towards women. Throughout the early years of American history, abortion was commonly accepted and was used as a form of birth control. However, by the end of the Civil War, as the U.S. population of men was significantly reduced, a greater value was placed on childbirth. The use of contraceptives was considered immoral, and, during the latter part of the nineteenth century, states passed various laws outlawing abortion and contraception. This culminated in the passage of the Federal Comstock Act in 1873, which outlawed both contraception and abortion (Day, 2003). The newly formed, almost exclusively male, American Medical Association joined in the lobbying efforts against abortion and its practice by female midwives.

In response to these developments, hundreds of maternity homes for unwed mothers were established in urban areas throughout the

U.S. to help young pregnant girls have their children safely and secretly. These "refuge" homes were first established in the late nineteenth century by white, middle-class, evangelical Protestant women—often members of the Women's Christian Temperance Union, teachers, or missionaries—in a dual effort to redeem what they saw as desperate, powerless female victims of urbanization and industrialization, and to assert their own female moral authority (Kunzel, 1993). Florence Crittenton Homes, Salvation Army Homes for Unwed Mothers, and various other religiously-based institutions helped and sheltered wealthy as well as poor young women (Kadushin & Martin, 1988). Many of these institutions also aimed to save girls who were involved in prostitution. For example, during the early 1900s, Donatella Cameron House in San Francisco was noted for rescuing Chinese "slave" girls from street prostitution.

Historically, although some unmarried white teen mothers kept their children and raised them with the help of their mothers and perhaps older sisters, most were encouraged to place their children for adoption. From the 1930s to the 1960s, adoption services were an essential component of maternity homes and were also offered by child welfare agencies. Social workers provided extensive casework services to birth mothers and to potential adoptive couples. According to Mayden (1994), during the 1950s, the shame of unwed pregnancy caused nearly 98 percent of all girls living in the Florence Crittenton Homes to give their children up for adoption. By the 1990s, with changing societal views towards single parenthood, few of these homes were left. Rather, present-day homes tend to serve pregnant teens who are victims of physical and sexual abuse, or those who are emotionally disturbed, substance abusers, or homeless.

The familial dynamics, as well as the economic and social environment in which teen parents and their children live, have changed dramatically over time. Prior to the 1960s, a pregnant young woman was likely to get married and have a husband who had a job. Moreover, the couple was likely to have parents, grandparents, or other extended family members who could help support them and maybe even help raise the baby. Today, however, pregnant teens tend to be single and lack the familial and economic supports common in previous generations (McDonald & Armstrong, 2001; Simons, Finlay, & Yang, 1991).

DEMOGRAPHICS: TEEN CHILDBIRTH

Over the past 25 years, there has been a significant drop in the rates of pregnancy and parenting through the developing world. While the rate of birth to teenagers in the United States declined by nearly a third during the 1990s, the rate of births to unmarried teens in the U.S. continues to be among the highest in the Western world (Child Trends, 2004).

Since 1960, an average of one-half million children have been born to adolescents in the U.S. each year, varying from an all-time high of 656,460 births in 1960 to a record low of 421,626 in 2003. During the past half century, the rate of child-bearing to teen mothers ages 15 to 19 decreased significantly, from 96 births per 1,000 women in 1957 to 41.7 births per 1000 women in 2003. This downward trend is found in adolescents of all races and ages, with the rates for unmarried African-American young women falling most steeply—decreasing by half since 1991 for those aged between 15 to 17 years (from 79.9 to 39.9 per 1,000), and by 29 percent among the 18 to 20 year olds. Among unmarried white teenagers, the rates have also declined steeply, by 36 percent for those aged 15 to 17 years, and by 14 percent for 18- to 19-year-olds. The birth rate for Native-American teens fell 33 percent, while the lowest decrease, 20 percent, was for Hispanic teens aged 15 to 19 (Facts at a Glance, 2005; Martin et al., 2003).

Table 10-1 shows the number of children born to young women in the U.S. since 1960:

Table 10-1
Number of Births to Females Under Age 20: 1960 - 2003

Ages:	1960	1970	1980	1986	1990	1991	1995	2000	2002	2003
Under 15	6,780	11,752	10,169	10,176	11,657	12,014	12,242	8,519	7,315	6,665
15-17	182,408	223,590	198,222	168,572	183,327	188,226	192,508	157,209	138,731	134,617
18-19	404,558	421,118	353,939	293,333	338,499	331,351	307,365	311,781	286,762	280,344
Total Under 20	593,746	656,460	562,330	472,081	533,591	531,591	512,115	477,509	432,808	421,626

Source: Child Trends, March 2005.

As indicated in Table 10-2, between 1960 and 2003, the majority of teen births were to women between 18 and 19 years of age. While there was a slight increase in births among high school-age girls in 1995, these data refute the common myth of an "epidemic" of child-birth among teenage girls. It is worth noting, however, that while the absolute numbers have gone down, the proportion of births among the youngest girls, those under 15, has increased since 1960 (Child Trends, 2005).

Table 10-2
Changes in Percentages of Child Births by Age: 1960-2003

Ages:	1960	%	1995	%	2003	%
Under 15	6,780	1%	12,242	2%	6,665	2%
15-17	182,408	31%	192,508	38%	134,617	32%
18-19	404,558	68%	307,365	60%	280,344	66%
Total Under 20	593,746	100%	512,115	100%	421,626	100%

Adapted from Child Trends, March 2005.

Marital Status

Over the past half-century, there has been a dramatic shift in the marital status of teen mothers: the proportion of teen births to unmarried mothers has increased from 13 percent of all teen births during 1950 to 79 percent of teen births during 2000. This may reflect the overall rise in age of marriage for all women and men, as well as the decreased stigma of unmarried motherhood (Facts at a Glance, 2005; Guttmacher Institute, Report on Public Policy, 2002).

Early Sexual Activity and Sexually Transmitted Diseases

In comparison to teenagers in other developed countries, such as Canada, Great Britain, France, and Sweden, teenagers in the U.S. are more likely to begin to be sexually active earlier–before age 15. They are also more likely to have shorter and more sporadic sexual relationships, and to have more than one partner in a given year. In addition, they have higher rates of sexually transmitted diseases (STDs) than teenagers in other countries, possibly because of lower condom use, as well as having a greater number of sexual partners. Also problematic is the 20 percent increase in the rate of the STD chlamydia among young girls in the U.S. between 1997 and 2001. Chlamydia increases the risk for infections and other STDs, and may impact on the health of their babies (Facts in Brief, 2002; Guttmacher, 2002).

PUBLIC POLICIES AFFECTING TEEN PARENTS

Teen parents were of particular interest during the 1996 welfare debate, which culminated in welfare reform legislation in the form of Temporary Assistance for Needy Families (TANF). At that time, almost one-half of all welfare recipients were single women who either were, or had been, teen mothers. About half of this group had begun to receive public assistance within five years of becoming a parent; most received assistance for two years. These findings contributed to stricter eligibility requirements for teen parents under TANF. To be eligible for assistance, minor mothers need to participate in school or job training and live in an approved housing arrangement. For teen parents who cannot live in their own home, TANF included a provision for housing in "Second Chance Homes." These homes are designed to provide supervised and supportive living arrangements in which the teens are required to learn parenting skills, child development, family budgeting, health, and nutrition, as well as skills to promote their long-term economic independence. The majority of existing Second Chance Homes are residential in nature, accommodating small numbers of teenage mothers and their children—approximately six or eight teen mothers at a time (U.S. Department of Housing and Urban Development, 2000).

TANF has targeted the fathers of the babies as well as teen mothers. Under the current law, when a custodial parent applies for benefits from TANF, a child support case is also required to be opened. The state then locates the noncustodial parent, establishes paternity, and orders a support award. The order is enforced by TANF's Family Support Division and modified as the father's circumstances change. After a support order is established, noncustodial fathers are required to pay a certain amount; they are not given credit for past or current in-kind support, such as clothes, toys, or school supplies. At the same time, Congress mandated that the states provide work activities for non-custodial fathers who are unemployed, and provided funding for demonstration projects aimed at helping low-income, noncustodial fathers pay child support and become engaged in their children's lives (Sorensen, 1999).

Despite the federal requirements, many states do not have sufficient services to meet the needs of these young families, such as alternative living arrangements or education programs, meaningful employment programs or training, services for the learning disabled, substance abuse treatment, mental health services, or child-care programs. For example, the availability of subsidized child-care for teens varies from one area of the country to another, depending on the state's initiative and use of federal funds. Depending on the state, subsidized childcare is available through TANF, through Head Start, and through some state subsidized child care programs. The federal At-Risk Child-Care Programs also provide limited funding for childcare, and allows states to target their populations depending on how they define the "at-risk" population. In general, teen parents need help with care for their infants, and publicly-funded center based infant-care services are very limited (Sipe & Batten, 1994).

While the intention of TANF ostensibly was that the requirements will improve long-term outcomes for both teen parents and their children, there is little evidence to date that these policies have improved the well-being of these vulnerable families. In fact, there is evidence to the contrary (DeParle, 2004; Ozawa & Yoon, 2005). In addition, there are no new data suggesting that teen parents today have any less need for welfare than in the past (Center for Law and Social Policy, 2002).

ADOLESCENT DEVELOPMENT

In order to understand the forces leading to teen parenthood, it is important to differentiate between puberty and adolescence. Puberty is a biological process of maturation "which involves hormonal transformation resulting in higher levels of androgens, estrogens, and testosterone" (Prover, 1991, p. 20); it is not dependent on the life experience of the individual. Historically, it was not stigma or efforts at social control that kept young girls from becoming pregnant during their early teen years; it was because they did not become sexually mature until they were 15 or 16 years old (Vinovskis, 1988). In contrast, by the 1990s, the mean age of the onset of menstruation in the U.S. was 12.6 years, a drop of almost four years since the late 1800s. Perhaps due to changes in nutrition, some girls begin menstruation as early as nine years of age, while the average age for the onset of puberty for boys is 13 years (Children's Defense Fund, 1993). Adult levels of hormones are generally reached by age 16, which is the average age for sexual intercourse for both sexes (Prover, 1991).

Young girls seem to have different attitudes towards the onset of puberty and different subjective experiences than young boys. Whereas, young boys tend to welcome the emotional and physical changes in their bodies, such as facial hair and voice changes, and feel greater confidence in their emerging adulthood and sexuality, girls, on the other hand, tend to be ill at ease with the changes in their bodies during puberty. They tend to become acutely aware of their bodies, are fearful of the changes, lose self-esteem, and become painfully self-conscious and critical of themselves (Martin, 1996).

Adolescence, as differentiated from puberty, is a developmental process that, though it interacts with biological changes, is subject to psychological, social, and cultural forces. Erikson's (1963) work on adolescence, and the work of the theorists who followed him, identified the two major tasks of adolescence as (1) moving from the dependency of childhood to the relative independence of adulthood, and (2) establishing a personal identity. The pull toward conformity and group identity can conflict with the equally important development of individuality, which includes exploring and establishing a vocational identity; pursuing creative interests such as music, art, drama, or writing; and building on values absorbed from parents to develop a personal philosophy of life (Prover, 1991).

DYNAMICS OF ADOLESCENT PARENTHOOD

The issue of why very young women become mothers can be broken down into several questions:

1. Why do young women become sexually active?
2. How do they decide to use or not use contraceptives?
3. Why do they choose to have or not have an abortion?
4. Why do they keep the child rather than give the child up for adoption?

Why Do Young Women Become Sexually Active?

The underlying causes of sexual activity have received minimal attention. There are many reasons why very young women become sexually active, including developmental stage, physical maturation, impulsivity and risk taking, peer pressure, educational attainment, substance abuse, sexuality in their environment, family turbulence, and lack of powerful, positive role models. Poverty and nonvoluntary sex are also factors (Manlove et al., 2001).

Peer pressure and perceived peer behavior profoundly affect adolescents. Perceptions of sexual activity among peers tend to be wildly exaggerated, particularly among the youngest teens. According to Males (1994), twelve-year-old sexually active girls thought that 80 percent of the girls their age were having sex, while actually only five percent were sexually active. Boys' perceptions were less exaggerated, but still higher than reality. Boys in particular feel pressure to have sex because of a belief that "everyone is doing it" and that it's a way of "proving your manhood" (The National Campaign to Prevent Teen Pregnancy, October 2003).

Researchers have documented a relationship between early sexual activity, early childbearing, and substance abuse. For example, Boyer and Fine (1992) identified the relationship between the use of drugs and alcohol, and pregnancy among young girls. For many adolescents, their first sexual experience occurs when either or both partners are intoxicated. Among those who were 14 years of age and drinking at their first intercourse, 27 percent became pregnant within a year; for heavy drug users, the rate was 56 percent. However, this correlation was not apparent with girls who started to have sex at age 16 (Brindes & Jeremy, 1988). Although many victims of sexual abuse report the use of drugs and alcohol as effective means of numbing themselves from the adverse feelings that surface as a result of the trauma (Nelson-Zlupko, Kauffman, & Dore, 1995), the interrelationship among substance abuse, sexual abuse, and adolescent pregnancy has yet to be fully explored.

Current research has concluded that the quality of parents' relationships with their teenage children plays a role in the decisions their children make about having sex at a young age. Factors impacting their decisions include the extent of shared activities with parents, parental presence in the home to supervise and monitor behavior, parental social support, and communication of love and caring. Further, research shows that parents who are clear about their attitudes that sexual activity and pregnancy should be delayed, appear to have children who delay having sex at an early age and who do not have unprotected sex (Albert, 2005; Liebowitz, Castellano & Cuellar, 1999).

The Decision to Use or Not Use Contraceptives

According to the Guttmacher Report on U.S. Teenage Pregnancy Statistics (2002), the primary reason why U.S. teenagers have the highest rates of pregnancy, child-bearing, and abortion among the developed countries is due to their lower use of contraceptives. In general, American teens are poorly educated about contraceptives. Moreover, contraceptives are expensive, are difficult to obtain, and require considerable motivation to use. The use of contraceptives also represents a conscious decision to engage in sex, which some adolescent girls may not feel ready to acknowledge. In addition, some girls may find it difficult to stand up to their boyfriends who do not want them to use contraceptives and/or who refuse to use condoms themselves.

Despite the reluctance of many U.S. teens to use contraceptives, the use of contraceptives during their first sexual experience has increased, possibly in response to education about the spread of HIV/AIDS. Between 1988 and 2002, the proportion of never-married teens who used any method of contraception at first sex increased from 67 percent to 75 percent for females and from 71 percent to 82 percent for males, a likely factor contributing to the decrease in the birth rate (Facts at a Glance, 2004).

The Decision to Abort

Between 1985 and 1996, the last year for which comprehensive abortion incidence data were collected, the rate of abortions by young women decreased by more than one-third–from 46 to 29 per 1,000 teen women. Despite this sharp decline, the U.S. adolescent abortion rate still remains one of the highest among developed countries (Facts in Brief, January, 2002). The decision of adolescent girls to have abortions depends on such factors as their level of knowledge regarding abortion, the availability and affordability of abortion services, and family and peer pressures (Musick, 1993).

Fewer women currently are able to afford family planning programs due to a lack of health insurance. Consequently, for many women, family planning and the risks of early child-bearing, such as premature birth, low birth weight, and medical risks to the young mother, are not discussed with a medical practitioner. Moreover, abortion has also become an increasingly highly charged political issue. Due to the current political and social climate, occasional but highly-publicized attacks on doctors at locations where abortions are performed, teens, as other women, may feel harassed and that they take their lives in their hands when they enter a clinic to have an abortion (Finer & Henshaw, 2003). As a result, some teens may feel that they have no choice but to continue with their pregnancy.

Adoption vs. the Decision to Keep the Child

As social pressures against illegitimacy lessened and pressures to keep a child have increased , fewer mothers in the U.S. have chosen adoption for their children (DellaCava, Phillips, & Engel, 2004). Since the mid-1970s, the number of children relinquished for adoption has declined from almost 9 percent to a low of 1 percent for never married women. Child relinquishments rates for children of black women dropped from 1.5 percent to nearly 0 percent, while the rates for white women declined from nearly 20 percent to less than 2 percent (National Adoption Information Clearinghouse, 2005). Some of the pressures contributing to the decision to relinquish a baby for adoption are culturally and economically based. A middle class white girl whose sexual experimentation results in pregnancy will be more likely to have an abortion or give her child up for adoption than her more financially disadvantaged counterpart (Musick, 1993). On the other hand, young women from African-American and Latino families have traditionally been less likely to give a child up for adoption outside the family, and are more likely to have their children raised by other family members (Gordon, Chase-Lansdale, & Brooks-Gunn, 2004).

Some unmarried women hear about the adoption option and are encouraged to give up their children for adoption, although many receive little or no information about the process or its implications. The ethics of informed consent required in the program guidelines for Title X of the 1970 Public Health Service Act dictate that when a woman at a Title X clinic faces an unintended pregnancy and requests information about her options, she must receive information about all her options in a nonjudgmental manner, using "nondirective counseling" to arrive at a decision that reflects the woman's own self interest. Adoption counseling, however, belongs to the purview of adoption agencies (Dailard, 1999).

While more than half of the states require parental involvement before allowing a minor to have an abortion, these same states consider an adolescent parent to be fully competent to make a decision on their own regarding adoption of her child. Nonetheless, since all adoptions, regardless of the mother's age, have to be approved by a court, some adoption agencies and judges may require that a young woman's parents be involved in the adoption decision (Boonstra & Nash, 2000).

OTHER PSYCHO-SOCIAL FACTORS INFLUENCING TEENS TO BECOME MOTHERS

Various psychological and socioeconomical reasons influence a teen girl's decision to become a mother: the need to have someone to love, and to dress up and look nice; the belief that they will have someone who will love them unconditionally; the desire to feel like an adult; the wish to escape from the parental home and be independent; to make up for their low self-esteem; and to win attention. For some young women, motherhood is the only possible role that they perceive as possible for themselves. This is particularly true for young women who live in chaotic households with young, sexually active mothers and their partners (Manlove et al., 2001).

Studies show a strong association between sexual abuse and first intercourse at a young age, multiple sexual partners, lower contraceptive use, and teenage pregnancy (Manlove et al., 2001). Boyer and

Fine (1992) found that 66 percent of a sample of 535 pregnant and parenting teens in Washington State had been sexually victimized. On average, the respondents were 9.7 years old at first molestation, with 24 percent reporting a first molestation at age five or younger. About 44 percent of the sample had a history of being raped; the average age at first rape was 13.3 years old. The average age of the perpetrator was 22.6. Similar results were found in a study of 445 pregnant and parenting teens done by the Ounce of Prevention Fund in its programs in Illinois (Musick, 1993). Moreover, researchers have found that teen parents who had been sexually abused were less likely to use contraceptives than sexually active adolescents in general (Boyer & Fine, 1992).

Cultural dynamics also play an important role in teen parenting (Davis et al., 2004). "Onset of sexual activity is a significant turning point in the lives of adolescents and is an experience shaped by the social and cultural environments in which they live. Ethnic group variation and gender differences in sexual behaviors reflect, in part, differences in these environments and their associated norms, cultural values, and opportunity structures" (Upchurch, Aneshensel, McNeely, & Mudgal, 2001, p. 1158). Indeed, cultural variations in beliefs about the age at maternity may be a factor that explains teenage parenting and the different views that teenagers hold about motherhood, responses to the mothering role, and the type of support they receive (Dalla & Gamble, 2000; Musick, 1993).

POVERTY AND TEEN PREGNANCY

Poverty is a critical factor in teen pregnancy (South & Baumer, 2001; Manlove et al., 2001; Hardy & Zabin, 1991; Wilson, 1987). "Regardless of race, a child in a female-headed family is five times more likely to be poor than a child in a male-headed or two parent family. . . . The lower the level of a mother's education and income, the more likely her children are to initiate early sexual activity. This may be related to the young people not seeing any other options for their own lives. Higher rates of teenage sexual activities are found in communities with higher rates of divorce, poverty and crime" (Brindes & Jeremy, 1988, pp. 66-67). Additional research indicates that "57 percent of teen girls from high risk environments (lower class, poor inner-city neighborhood residence, female-headed family, five or more siblings, a sister who is a teenage mother, and loose parental supervision of dating) will become pregnant by age 18 as compared to only 9 percent of girls from low risk social backgrounds" (Wilson, 1987, p. 75).

Pregnancy also has been linked to school drop-out rates for young women. According to research studies, the younger a teen is when she has her first child, the less likely she is to complete high school and to have a good-paying and satisfying job (Brindes & Jeremy, 1988). Also contributing to their poverty is the lack of support from the fathers of their children. According to government data, during 1997, only 10 percent of mothers between the ages 15 to 17 received any child support payments (U.S. Census Bureau, 2000).

ADOLESCENT MOTHERHOOD AT DIFFERENT STAGES OF DEVELOPMENTAL

Young mothers, like teenagers in general, are not a homogeneous group. Adolescence spans a whole decade, and the individual's life experiences, as well as physical, cognitive, and psychological development change quickly; therefore, it is important to consider the stage of adolescence of a particular teen mother. For example, the twelve-year-old, seventh grade mother is a quantum leap from the nineteen-year-old mother who graduated from high school.

Researchers categorize teenagers as falling into four stages: preadolescence (ages 10 to 12); early adolescence (13 to 14); middle adolescence (15 to 17); and late adolescence (18 to 19); each age group deals with its own unique stage of development.

Motherhood During Early Adolescence (Under Age 15)

As indicated previously, during 2003, adolescent girls under age 15 gave birth to 6,665 babies (Child Trends, March 2005). While this represents only 2 percent of all births, these junior high school age girls are the most vulnerable and least able to provide proper parenting. Although they are developing the primary and secondary sex characteristics of puberty and may look like young women, they still are children physically, psychologically, and socially, and are unprepared for motherhood. Emotionally they are still dependent on their families or other adults. Their behavior is inconsistent and confusing to adults, as one day they may act like independent teenagers and the next day they act like young children (Prover, 1991). They struggle over the values of their families and the tantalizing prospects of an oversexualized society. The attention they attract from men confuses them, and they are especially vulnerable to sexually predatory adult males (Hardy & Zabin, 1991; Musick, 1993).

Motherhood in Middle Adolescence (15 to 17)

Teenage mothers of high school age (10th, 11th, and 12th graders who are 15 to 17 years old) had 32 percent of all births to young women under age 20 during 2003. For middle-adolescents, while peers can continue to play an important role, individual relationships become more meaningful and dating can consume much of their lives (Prover, 1991). Experimentation with heterosexual and homosexual relationships is common and may be transient or develop into a sexual identity. Emotionally, high school age teens have the capacity to become self-reliant and act more independently. They are capable of developing their own sense of morality and a system of ethical thought that is separate from their peer group or family. By this age, most adolescents can think abstractly, reason, and understand complex issues (Piaget, 1965).

With adequate support, middle-adolescent mothers and fathers may be capable of parenting a child. They have the capacity to plan and make decisions for their lives and some capacity for empathy and insight. School-based programs, such as sex education, parenting classes, child development, and family services have been shown to be effective for this age group (Manlove, Franzetta, McKinney, Papillo, & Terry-Humen, 2004b). Middle-adolescents are responsive to help when provided by peers and trusted adults, and are open to education and change. It should be noted, however, that during 2001, 22 to 30 percent of teen mothers under 18 had their second child within 24 months of the birth of their first child (National Campaign to Prevent Teen Pregnancy, 2004).

Motherhood in Late Adolescence (18 to 19)

During 2003, late adolescent women gave birth to 66 percent of all births to women under age 20. While this group is included in the statistics of teen pregnancy, their life experiences are much different from young teens (Musick, 1993). Typically, women in this age group have graduated from high school and either started a career or continued with their education. A teen parent who has had her first child in high school and never completed school or used supportive services has a high probability of having a second child before she is 20. Consequently, many opportunities for educational and vocational advancement remain out of her reach, sometimes forever.

ROLE OF MEN IN TEEN PARENTING

The abdication of parental responsibility by men in this country crosses class and race, and has a special impact on the social and emotional development of girls:

> The absence of appropriate male figures in fathering (or grandfathering) roles along with its other growth thwarting effects appears to foster a kind of learned helplessness in relationship with males. For example, a girl's father gives her the feeling of protection in a violent, scary urban world where friends may be meaninglessly killed. A functioning, mature man can give a girl a mirror to her own femininity, rather than a sense of herself as a sex object. There is solid research demonstrating that fathers who are present in their families are a protective factor against early sexual behavior, pregnancy and births. This can have serious and wide reaching consequences for the girl's choice of partners, her sexual behavior, and her later capacity to protect her own children from similar experience. Such vulnerability to males often extends beyond the purely interpersonal domain and affects attitudes and actions in school and work. (Musick, 1993, p. 75)

While the extent to which a girl suffers from the abandonment or death of a father needs much more research, particularly as it affects the development of poor young women, studies show that fathers who leave when their daughters are under 13 are a contributing risk factor for troubling sexual behavior in their daughters (Ellis et al., 2003).

In addition to having been abandoned by their own fathers, many teen mothers are also abondoned by the fathers of their children. For example, a Hardy and Zabin (1991) study of 398 fathers of babies born to girls under 20 showed that although more than 95 percent of the fathers were informed about the birth of their child, due to limited education and income, they did not provide financial support to the mother. Moreover, a follow-up study 18 months after the child was born revealed that most of the fathers still lived with their own parents, usually a single mother, and that contact between father and child substantially diminished over time.

Male Partners of Adolescent Girls

Women of all age groups tend to be younger than their partners. Half of all pregnancies among 15- to 17-year-old young women occur with partners who are more than two years older than themselves (Saul, 1999). The younger the mother, the greater the age gap; for girls under age 15, about six times more babies are fathered by men over age 20 than by those their own age (Males, 2004).

The adverse effects of partner age difference may lessen as females mature. Research suggests that the "wantedness" of sexual involvement is inversely related to the age difference between a young woman and her partner; that is, the greater the age difference, the less likely the sex to be mutually desirable. This sexual involvement may be related to the very young girl's limited sense of control over the situation and to her lack of ability to communicate her wishes. Furthermore, females who had had first sexual intercourse at ages 11 to 12 and who had a partner five or more years their senior, had an elevated risk of attempted suicide, substance abuse, lack of use of condoms, and pregnancy. In contrast, females who had had first intercourse between the ages of 13 and 15, having older partners was associated only with truancy, and among females whose age at first intercourse was 16 to 18, having older partners was not linked to any of these negative outcomes (Kaestle, Morisky, & Wiley, 2002).

In order to deter sexual relationships between young women and older men, there has been a growing interest in better enforcement of statutory rape laws. While the legal definition of statutory rape is set by each state, statutory rape has been defined as sexual activity among teens aged 15 or younger with a sexual partner three or more years older (Child Trends, 2005). Studies indicate that of females aged 13 or younger, 65 percent experienced statutory rape at first sex, compared to 41 percent of females aged 15. The incidence of statutory rape is higher among teens who do not live with both biological parents, whose parents have lower educational attainment, and whose mothers gave birth in their teen years. Moreover, statutory rape is linked to other risky behaviors, including lower use of contraception at first sex, lower likelihood for being tested for HIV, and greater likelihood of pregnancy (Child Trends, 2005).

CHILD MALTREATMENT AND TEEN PARENTS

Sexual abuse is a major factor in the decision to remove a girl from home and place her in the child welfare system (Saewy, Magee, & Pettingell, 2004); it also appears to be to be a risk factor for early pregnancy (Fiscella, Kitzman, Cole, Sidora, & Olds, 1998). Studies have found that girls in out-of-home-care such as foster care, kinship care, and group homes or institutions are twice as likely to become pregnant during adolescence than their peers who live at home. Many of those with a history of out-of-home care struggle with poverty, health problems, poor educational attainment, housing problems, substance abuse, criminal behavior, and problems parenting their children. They tend to begin sexual activity earlier and are less knowledgeable about reproduction, contraception, and sexually transmitted diseases than their peers (Brindes & Jeremy, 1988; Fiscella et al., 1998). Further, living away from related adults is one of the major risk factors associated with child maltreatment by teen parents (Flanagan, Coll, Andreozzi, & Riggs, 1995).

INTERVENTION PROGRAMS AND PRACTICE ISSUES

Nowhere is the need for an ecological perspective more important than when working with teen parents. Successful programs for young parents need to involve the young mother, her family, the father and his family, and all of the social and cultural systems surrounding them: school, work, substance abuse programs, public welfare, social service programs, mental health, recreation, churches, and community programs.

Since under federal law, schools cannot expel young women because they are pregnant, many urban schools offer options, such as attending regular classes, attending special classes in special schools, enrolling in classes on parenting and child care, or participating in specialized programs for pregnant teens and teen parents. While it would seem reasonable that high schools and middle schools should have child care on site, many administrators and policy-makers resist such programs, claiming that infant care may not be good for infants, or that infant care on high school campuses may sanction and promote teen pregnancy. However, studies have shown that school-based, quality early childhood centers for infants and children of teen parents are effective in increasing school attendance, increasing the likelihood of graduating from high school, and decreasing the likelihood of welfare dependency (Crean, 2001; Starnes, 1990). Moreover, teen mothers and their babies benefited from the mentoring provided by well-trained child care providers, a positive environment, and nurturing parenting programs (Sipe & Batten, 1994). Unfortunately, such programs serve only a small portion of those needing them.

For the most part, successful programs "focus on specific behavioral goals . . . deliver clear messages about sexual activity and/or contraceptive use, provide basic information about risks associated with teen sexual activities and STDs, address social pressures towards having sex, provide activities to practice communication and refusal skills, incorporate multiple teaching methods and personalized information to individual needs, are tailored to participants' age level, culture, and level of sexual experience. . ." (Manlow, Franzetta, McKinney, Papillo, & Terry-Humen, 2004a, p. 6). Flexibility and sensitivity to teen parents' needs are essential.

One example of a comprehensive program based on the ecological perspective is the San Francisco Family Service Agency's Teenage Pregnancy and Parenting Project (TAPP), a city-wide comprehensive case management program for pregnant and parenting teens. TAPP utilizes a systems-oriented approach that involves the teen father and mother as well as grandparents and relatives on both sides, close friends, and the schools. Focusing on objectives including the reduction in second births to teenage parents, reduction of welfare dependency, academic enrollment and retention of pregnant and parenting teenagers, reduction of low birth-weight babies, and reduction in risk behaviors, TAPP also provides a myriad of support services, including child development and parenting education, childcare support services, nutrition and health education, job readiness, mental health programs, relationship violence prevention, and academic counseling. These support services are provided at TAPP as "one-stop" shopping or are facilitated through longstanding partnerships with other youth-serving agencies (Family Service Agency, Teenage Pregnancy and Parenting Project, 2005). TAPP case managers help ensure that pregnant and parenting adolescents have access to all available health, education, and social services for which they are eligible, regardless of whether or not they are in school. Continuous, comprehensive case management is provided by well-trained social workers who follow the young person for up to six years, from the prenatal and postnatal period through the needed adjustments to the infant, family, and school. It is not unusual that the case manager is the only stable person in the young woman's life. The Hilltop Developmental Center provides child-development education and center-based developmental childcare services for the babies of TAPP participants. It also provides a breastfeeding clinic, along with nutrition and nursing services in the schools. The Teen Life-Skills Program offers life-skills support groups for pregnant and parenting teenagers and their siblings, providing educational and recreational group activities to promote positive and healthy lifestyles. Numerous programs throughout the country have variations on the TAPP model and also offer other approaches for reaching teens (Hardy & Zabin, 1991; Sipe & Batten, 1994).

Existing programs for teen parents need to be expanded and additional supportive and clinical services made available to reduce the detrimental impacts of sexual abuse and sexual experimentation of teen mothers. Practitioners who uncover a history of abuse need the skills and added clinical supports to effectively help the young women. Workers who visit homes of their most troubled teens often find no family members available to help. Mothers and grandmothers of the teen parent often are as needy and helpless as the youth. Generally, the best way to help a young teen parent is to work as intensely as possible with her family to promote supportive behaviors and to keep them from sabotaging her progress. Group work with adolescents is also a useful tool when dealing with these issues.

Practitioners who work with teen parents need to have a clear sense of self and of personal boundaries. The turbulence of adolescence is heightened by the crisis of birth and parenting, and any person who chooses to work in this field must have resolved his or her own issues regarding adolescence and teen pregnancy (Manlow et al., 2004a).

PREVENTION PROGRAMS

In an effort to support adolescents transitioning out of foster care, the federal government passed the Foster Care Independence Act of 1999, also known as the John H. Chafee Foster Care Independence Program. Using a youth development perspective, this Act provides funds to help youth, including pregnant and parenting teens, make the transition from foster care to self-sufficiency. Its intention is to offer them the education and vocational and employment training necessary to obtain employment and/or prepare for post-secondary education; to offer training in daily living skills, substance abuse prevention, pregnancy prevention, and health activities; and to promote connections to dedicated adults.

The model of positive youth development (Catalano, Berglund, Ryan, Lonczak, & Hawkins, 1998) has replaced the previously predominant preventative approach to working with youth. The traditional approach focused on "fixing" an identified problem and on the assumption that a naturally occurring developmental process would result in long-term change. However, research and evaluation of prevention programs demonstrated that many of these programs were not successful in preventing problem behavior such as teen pregnancy and substance abuse. Consequently, in the 1990s a conceptual shift occurred in programming for prevention services. The concepts of positive youth development are grounded in developmental theory and include strategies to promote bonding; foster resiliency; promote social, emotional, cognitive, behavioral, and moral competence; foster self-determination, spirituality, clear and positive identity, and belief in the future; provide recognition for positive behavior and opportunities for pro-social involvement; and foster pro-social norms (Catalano et al., 1998). Such strategies have proven to be effective interventions for adolescents at risk for antisocial behavior.

Resiliency and Teen Parents

Despite risky behaviors, many teen parents are able to overcome numerous obstacles in their lives. Studies of school-age children who have been able to succeed despite conditions of chronic poverty and violence have exhibited the following common resiliency traits:

1. They were well liked by peers and adults;
2. Their dominant cognitive style was reflective rather than impulsive;
3. They demonstrated an internal locus of control and a belief that they were capable of influencing their environment positively; and
4. They were able to use flexible coping strategies in overcoming adversity, including a sense of humor (Bernard, 1992; Garbarino, Dubrow, Kostelny, & Pardo, 1992; Werner, 1990).

Understanding and focusing on resiliency is crucial in working with teen mothers. It is essential to build on the "strengths" of young people instead of focusing on the "risk" factors. While the home life and environment of many children may be stressful, good clinical practice can enhance and build upon these strengths. Some of the teens call this "respect" (Siqueira & Diaz, 2004).

POLICY RECOMMENDATIONS

Advocacy by helping professionals is vital in order to promote federal, state, and local policies that optimize opportunities for teenage parents. We have the evidence that informing teenagers about sexuality, sexually transmitted diseases, and contraceptives can reduce unintended pregnancies (Boonstra, 2001). Yet, while other industrialized countries have managed to develop public policies to educate their children concerning contraception and abortion, why is this not done in the U.S.?

More children are raised by single mothers with inadequate or total lack of emotional or financial support from the fathers. Poor quality of education, lack of employment, incarceration, and the substance abuse epidemic have been given as explanations for the disappearance of fathers. However, these reasons do not fully explain such a pervasive and serious phenomenon. Our nation's history is full of times of great stress without the type of male abdication of responsibility seen in today's families. More research is required to better understand this dynamic and comprehensive policies need to be developed that address solutions to this problem.

Some education and prevention programs have been developed and targeted at children, particularly in their middle school years. Accessible and affordable child-care for teen parents could be part of school programs, as these have been seen to be effective in keeping parents in school.

Over the past decade, many public and private efforts aimed at pregnancy prevention have focused on abstinence. The few programs evaluated do not show any effect on reproductive health outcomes. However, studies show that, however controversial and poorly funded they are, family planning programs, sex education programs, early childhood literacy, youth development, community volunteering, nurse home visiting, and teenage pregnancy prevention programs do work and should be maintained (Manlove et al., 2001).

Support for diminishing prevention and intervention programs could be provided through collaborative use of a variety of federal, state, local, and foundation monies. Since urban communities are so diverse, strategies to develop and fund programs must take into account the needs of each urban area with its unique population and culture. The following recommendations are based on those suggested by the Center for Law and Social Policy (2002) and existing literature in the field:

- *Improve recruitment of teen parents in need of services.* Develop a model for identifying and tracking the neediest pregnant teens using the public assistance, education, social service, and medical systems.
- *Improve services to teen parents.* Provide teens with intensive, comprehensive services. Serve younger teen parents, especially those of school age, differently than the older parents.
- *Support fathering programs.* Provide additional funding to programs that have demonstrated a capacity to creatively and effectively manage the delivery of services to young fathers. Involve the fathers in the development and ownership of the services.

• *Improve the organization of services to teen parents.* Support community alliances or networks focusing on the effective use of community resources and programs that have a stable and continued presence in the teen's life. Support the provision of child-care assistance for young parents and the maintenance of educational alternatives for completing high school. Investigate possibilities for transitional housing arrangements.

CONCLUSION

Teens are some of the most creative people in this country today. They have the energy and competence to take on the world, and many of them do. They succeed despite the most overwhelming odds. Teens who have children cut short their childhood and enter a world of commitment that traditionally has been reserved for adults. They can make good or poor choices depending on the resources available to them and the presence of caring human beings to mentor them through hard times. We do our teens a great disservice by pathologizing and stigmatizing them; by discounting their abilities and concentrating on their "mistakes." By only looking at unmarried teen parents as problems, we overlook them as human beings with their own individual histories and with their unique potentials for the future.

REFERENCES

Abramovitz, M. (1988). *Regulating the lives of women.* Boston: South End Press.

Albert, B. (2004). *Science says: Parental influence and teen pregnancy. The National Campaign to Prevent Teen Pregnancy,* 8, 1–4.

Bernard, B. (1991). *Fostering resiliency in kids: Protective factors in the family, school and community.* San Francisco: Western Regional Center for Drug-Free Schools and Communities.

Boonstra, H., & Nash, E. (2000). Minors and the right to consent to health care. *The Guttmacher Report on Public Policy,* Allen Guttmacher Institute. Agi-usa.org. Accessed November 29, 2004.

Boonstra, H. (2002). Teen pregnancy: Trends and lessons learned. *The Guttmacher Report on Public Policy.* Allen Guttmacher Institute. Agi-usa.org. Accessed November 29, 2004.

Boyer, D., & Fine, D. (1992). Sexual abuse as a factor in adolescent pregnancy and child maltreatment. *Family Planning Perspectives, 24*(1), 4–12.

Brindes, C. D., & Jeremy, R. J. (1988). *Adolescent pregnancy and parenting in California: A strategic plan for action.* San Francisco: University of California, Center for Population and Reproductive Health Policy, Institute for Health Policy Studies.

Catalano, R. R, Berglund, M. L, Ryan, J. A. M., Lonczak, H. S., & Hawkins, J. D. (1998, November 13). *Positive youth development in the United States: Research findings on evaluations of positive youth development programs.* Seattle: WA: Social Development Research, University of Washington School of Social Work. http://aspe.hhs.gov/ hsp/PositiveYouthDev99/. Accessed December 18, 2004.

Center for Law and Social Policy. (2002). *Add it up, teen parents and welfare: Undercounted, oversanctioned, underserved.* Washington: DC. Center for Law and Social Policy.

Child Trends Data Bank. (2004). Teen births. *Child Trends Data Bank.* 12/16/04. http://www.childtrendsdatabank.org/indicators/13TeenBirth.cfm. Accessed December 18, 2004.

Child Trends. (March 2005). *A demographic portrait of statutory rape* (2005). http://www.childtrends.org/Files/Statutory_Rape_Handout.pdf. Accessed June 17, 2005.

Children's Defense Fund. (1993). *Progress and peril: Back children in America: A fact book and action primer.* Washington, DC: Children's Defense Fund.

Crean, H. (2001). School-based child care for children of teen parents: Evaluation of an urban program designed to keep young mothers in school. *Evaluation and Program Planning,* v/3, 267–75.

Dailard, C. (1999). Family planning and adoption promotion: New proposals, long-standing issues. *The Guttmacher Report on Public Policy: Issues and Implications, 2* (5).

Dalla, R. L., & Gamble, W. C. (2000). Mother, daughter, teenager–Who am I? Perceptions of adolescent maternity in a Navajo reservation community. *Journal of Family Issues, 21*/2, 225-245.

Davies, S. L., Di Clemente, R. J., Wingood, G. M., Person, S. D., Crosby, R. A., Harringon, K. F., & Dix, E. S. (2004). Relationship characteristics and sexual practices of African American adolescent girls who desire pregnancy. *Health Education & Behavior, 31*/4, 85-96.

DellaCava, F. A., Phillips, N. K., & Engel, M. H. (2004). Adoption in the U.S.: The emergence of a social movement. *Journal of Sociology and Social Welfare, 31,* 141-160.

DeParle, J. (2004). *American dream: Three women, ten kids, and a nation's drive to end welfare.* New York: Viking Books.

Day, P. J. (2003). *A new history of social welfare* (4th ed.). Boston, MA: Allyn and Bacon.

Ellis, B. J., Bates, J. E., Dodge, K. A., Fergusson, D. M., Horwood, L. J., Pettit, G. S., & Woodward, L. (2003). Does father absence place daughters at special risk for early sexual activity and teenage pregnancy? *Child Development, 74*/3, 801-821.

Erikson, E. (1963). *Childhood and society* (2nd ed.). New York: W. W. Norton.

Facts At A Glance. (2005). *Annual Newsletter on Teen Pregnancy.* Washington, DC: Child Trends.

Family Service Agency, Teenage Pregnancy and Parenting Project (TAPP), http://www.fsasf.org/programs/children_youth_family.html?PHPSESSID=5f1877a809 a3f500ab98c1a2d493ba48. Accessed September 1, 2005.

Finer, L. B., & Henshaw, S. K. (2003). Abortion incidence and services in the United States in 2000. *Perspectives on Sexual and Reproductive Health, 35* (1), 6–15.

Fiscella, F, Kitzman, H. J., Cole, R. E., Sidora, K. J., & Olds, D. (1998). Does child abuse predict adolescent pregnancy? *Pediatrics, 101* (4), 620–624.

Flanagan, P., Coll, C. G., Andreozzi, L., & Riggs, S. (1995). Predicting maltreatment of children of teen mothers. *Pediatrics & Adolescent Medicine, 149/4,* 451-455.

Garbarino, J., Dubrow, N., Kostelny, K., & Pardo, C. (1992). *Children in danger: Coping with the consequences of community violence.* San Francisco: Jossey-Bass.

Gordon, R. A., Chase-Lansdale, P. L., & Brooks-Gunn, J. (2004). Extended households and the life course of young mothers: Understanding the association using a sample of mothers with premature, low birth weight babies. *Child Development, 75* (4), 1013–1038.

Guttmacher Institute. (1994). *Sex and America's teenagers.* New York: Guttmacher Institute.

Guttmacher Institute. (2002). *Facts in brief. Teenager's sexual and reproductive health.* Washington, DC: Guttmacher Institute.

Guttmacher Institute. (2002, February). *Guttmacher report on public policy: Divergent trends.* New York: Guttmacher Institute.

Hardy, J. B., & Zabin, L. S. (1991). *Adolescent pregnancy in an urban environment.* Washington, DC: Urban Institute Press.

Kadushin, A., & Martin, J. A. (1988). *Child welfare services* (4th ed.). New York: Macmillan.

Kaestle, C. E., Morisky, D. E., & Wiley, D. J. (2002). Sexual intercourse and the age difference between adolescent females and their romantic partners. *Perspectives on Sexual and Reproductive Health,* 34/6, November/December 2002.

Kunzel, R. (1993). *Fallen women, problem girls: Unmarried mothers and the professionalization of social work 1890-1945.* New Haven: Yale University Press.

Liebowitz, S. W., Castellano, D. C., & Cuellar, I. (1999). Factors that predict sexual behaviors among young Mexican-American adolescents: An exploratory study. *Hispanic Journal of Behavior Sciences, 21/4,* 470–479.

Males, M. (1994). Adult men: The unspoken factor in teen pregnancy and disease, *Family Life Matters,* 23, 7.

Males, M. (2004). Teens and Older Partners. ETR's Resource Center for Adolescent Pregnancy. http://www.etr.org/recapp/research/index.htm. Accessed February 17, 2005.

Manlove, J., Franzetta, K., McKinney, K., Papillo, A. R., & Terry-Humen, E. (January 2004a). *A good time: After-school programs to reduce teen pregnancy.* Child Trends and Campaign to Prevent Teen Pregnancy. Teenpregnancy.org. Accessed January 15, 2005.

Manlove, J., Franzetta, K., McKinney, K., Papillo, A. R., & Terry-Humen, E. (2004b). *No time to waste: Programs to reduce teen pregnancy among middle school-aged youth.* National Campaign to Prevent Teen Pregnancy. Teenpregnancy.org. Accessed February 17, 2005.

Martin, J. A., Hamilton, B. E., Sutton, P. D., Ventura, S. J., Menacker, F., & Munson, M. L. (2003). *Births: Final data for 2002–National Vital Statistics Reports, 52/*10.

Hyattsville, Maryland: U.S. Department of Health and Human Services, National Center for Health Statistics.

Martin, K. A. (1996). *Puberty, sexuality and the self: Girls and boys at adolescence.* New York: Routledge.

Mayden, B. (1994). Florence Crittenton Homes: The 20th century. *Children's Voices 4,* 12–13.

McDonald, K. B., & Armstrong, E. M. (2001). Re-romanticizing black intergenerational support: The questionable expectations of welfare reform. *Journal of Marriage and Family, 63,* 213–223.

Musick, J. S. (1993). *Young, poor and pregnant: The psychology of teenage motherhood.* New Haven, CT: Yale University Press.

National Adoption Information Clearinghouse. (2005). Voluntary relinquishment for adoption: Numbers and trends. Author. http://naic.acf.hhs.gov/pubs/s_place. cfm. Accessed December 2, 2005.

National Campaign to Prevent Teen Pregnancy. (2003). Science says: *The sexual attitudes and behavior of male teens. Putting what works to work.* National Campaign to Prevent Teen Pregnancy. www.teenpregnancy.org. Accessed March 10, 2004.

National Campaign to Prevent Teen Pregnancy. (2004). Science says: *Another chance— preventing additional births to teen parents.* Putting what works to work. National Campaign to Prevent Teen Pregnancy. www.teenpregnancy.org. Accessed January 20, 2005.

Nelson-Zlupko, L., Kauffman, E., & Dore, M. M. (1995). Gender differences in drug addiction and treatment: Implications for social work intervention with substance-abusing women. *Social Work, 40,* 45–54.

Ozawa, M., & Yoon, H. S. (2005). "Leavers" from TANF and AFDC: How do they fare economically? *Social Work, 50,* 3, 239–249

Piaget, J. (1965). *The moral judgment of children.* New York: Free Press.

Prover, J. (1991). *Latency and adolescence.* Los Angeles: University of California at Los Angeles, Inter-University Consortium, Department of Children's Services Training Project.

Saewy, E. M., Magee, L. L., & Pettingell, S. E. (2004). Teenage pregnancy and associated risk behaviors among sexually abused adolescents. *Perspectives on Sexual and Reproductive Health, 36*/3 98–106.

Santelli, J. S., Ameba, J., Ventura, S., Lindberg, L., Morrow, B., Anderson, J. E., Lyses, S., & Hamilton, B. E. (2004). Can changes in sexual behavior among high school students explain the decline in teen pregnancy rates in the 1990's? *Journal of Adolescent Health, 35*/2, 80–90.

Saul, R. (1999). Using and misusing data on age differences between minors and their sexual partners. *The Guttmacher Report on Public Policy*, August, 1999.

Simmons, J. M., Finlay, B., & Yang, A. (1991). *The adolescent and young adult fact book.* Washington, DC: Children's Defense Fund.

Sipe, C. L., & Batten, S. T., with Stephens, S. A., & Wolf, W. C. (1994). *School-based program for adolescent parents and their young children: Overcoming barriers and challenges to implementing comprehensive school based services.* Baal Cindy, PA: Center for Assessment and Policy Development.

Siqueira, L. M., & Diaz, A. (2004). Fostering resilience in adolescent females. *The Mount Sinai Journal of Medicine, 71*/3, 148–154.

Sorensen, E. (1999, March). *Obligating dads: Helping low-income non-custodial fathers do more for their children.* Washington, DC: Urban Institute.

South, S. J., & Baumer, E. (2001). Community effects on the resolution of adolescent premarital pregnancy. *Journal of Family Issues, 22* (8), 1025–1043.

Starnes, L. (1990). *Child care facilities in public schools benefit students, schools, communities and children.* Nashville, TN: Vanderbilt University.

Trattner, W. I. (1994). *From Poor Law to welfare state: A history of social welfare in America* (5th ed.). New York: Free Press.

U.S. Census Bureau (2000). *Child support 1997.* www.census.gov/hhes/www/child-support/97tables/tab4s.html. Accessed June 18, 2004.

U.S. Department of Health and Human Services, Administration on Children, Youth and Families. (2005). *Child maltreatment 2003.* Washington, DC: U.S. Government Printing Office.

U.S. Department of Housing and Urban Development. (2000). *Second chance homes: Providing services for teenage parents and their children.* www.hud.gov/offices/pih/other/sch/sch-paper3.cfm. Accessed June 18, 2004.

Upchurch, D. M., Aneshensel, C. S., & McNeely, C. S. & Mudgal, J. (2001). Sociocultural contexts of time to first sex among Hispanic adolescents. *Journal of Marriage and Family, 63*/4, 1158–1165.

Vinovskis, M. A. (1988). *An "epidemic" of adolescent pregnancy.* New York: Oxford University Press.

Werner, E. E. (1990). Protective factors and individual resilience. In S. J. Meisel & J. P. Shonkoff (Eds.), *Handbook of early childhood intervention.* New York: Cambridge University Press.

Wilson, W. J. (1987). *The truly disadvantaged: The inner city, the underclass, and public policy.* Chicago: University of Chicago Press.

Chapter 11

URBAN STREET YOUTH:
SEX, DRUGS AND HIV

ADELE WEINER AND DANIEL POLLACK

Concern about urban street children as a social problem dates back to pre-Colonial times. In fact, the problem of parentless and/or homeless youth was addressed by the English Poor Law of 1601 (Bremner, 1970). Following this model, as with other social welfare policies, the care of "orphaned, abandoned, and incorrigible runaways in early America was assigned to municipal authorities" (D'Angelo, 1987, p. 513). Today much remains the same; most communities fail to exert control over transient youth. Such individuals may lead productive, stable lives, while others may engage in illicit activities or function at a subsistence level of survival. Runaway youth often migrate to urban areas either because of a desire to evade attempts to locate them and/or their belief that opportunities for survival may be more numerous in cities. The most needy street youth, "those living in abandoned buildings, on roofs and under freeways and surviving any way they can" (Pennbridge, Freese, & MacKenzie, 1992, p. 24), come to the attention of law enforcement and social service agencies. This chapter will explore the needs of urban street youth, and discuss various policies, programs, and skills needed to meet those needs.

GOVERNMENTAL ROLE

In the early 1970s Congress held hearings on the how to help homeless and runaway youth resulting in the passage of the Runaway and

Homeless Youth Act of 1973. The original principals have been reaffirmed, expanded upon and reauthorized as the Runaway, Homeless and Missing Children Protection Act of 2003. As amended, this legislation outlines the federal government's role and responsibility in addressing runaways and homeless youth. Congress made ten critical findings in assessing these issues that remain as continuing concerns:

1. Juvenile runaways are at risk of incurring serious health problems.
2. The exact nature of the problem is unknown because reliable national statistics do not exist.
3. Runaways are in need of temporary shelter and counseling services.
4. Local police departments and juvenile justice agencies should not be saddled with this problem.
5. There is a need for federal government intervention.
6. Runaways have inadequate access to health care and intensive aftercare services.
7. There is a need for runaways to further their high school education and obtain employment.
8. The federal government is responsible for creating a national reporting system.
9. Early intervention services are needed to discourage runaway youth.
10. Street-based services are needed to reach out to runaways where they are presently found (42 U.S.C. §5701).

In 1992, the National Clearinghouse on Runaways and Homeless Youth was established to provide a centralized source for collection and dissemination of information related to programs and services for homeless youth. In the same year, a management information system was developed to collect information across three family and youth services programs, which are currently funded by the U.S. Department of Health and Human Services, Administration for Children and Families, Family and Youth Service Bureau: the Runaway and Homeless Youth Basic Center Program is designed to "address the immediate needs (e.g., outreach, temporary shelter, food, clothing, counseling, and aftercare services) of runaway and homeless youth and their families"; the Drug Abuse Education and Prevention Program, designed to "improve and expand drug prevention, education and information services"; and the Transitional Living Program for Homeless Youth, designed to "support projects in local communities that provide long-term shelter, skills training and support services to homeless youth; to assist homeless youth in making smooth transitions to self-sufficiency; and to prevent long-term dependency on social services" (USDHHS, ACF, 1994, p. 24772).

The 2005 reauthorization of the Runaway and Homeless Youth Act has expanded the Basic Center and the Transitional Living Programs (National Alliance to End Homelessness, 2005). Street Outreach Programs are authorized to try to identify and contact vulnerable youth and to provide alternatives to homelessness. Maternity Group Homes have been added as an allowable use of transitional housing funds. The Runaway and Homeless Youth Act also provides funding for support programs such as the National Runaway Switchboard, which is a communications system developed to link runaways or their families with crisis counseling and support programs (http://www.nrscrisline.org).

This series of legislation was very important in redirecting the responsibility for identification, prevention, and rehabilitation of runaway youth from the juvenile justice system to the social service system. The police is generally the first governmental organization to identify a minor runaway. In most states, parental notification is mandatory if a youth is arrested or detained; yet, the age at which this is required differs by state. This is complicated by "fake IDs" that presents the minor's age as over 18, or by the lack of any identification since some children who do not wish to return home may lie about their age and/or name. Depending on the age of the runaway, and the age of emancipation in a given state (age at which a youth is considered to be an adult), he/she may be remanded to juvenile authorities. Younger runaways may be placed in foster care or group homes. Older runaways may complete a process by which they can be declared legally emancipated from their parents or caretakers.

Licensed social workers who work with runaways need to comply with professional ethical behavior as well as the legal requirements. For example, while a social worker might want to help the runaway to contact his/her parent(s), confidentiality and a client's right to self-determination suggest adolescents have the right to refuse contact. Agencies and programs may have different policies for dealing with these circumstances. Some may require the youth to notify his/her parents and others may simply require that the worker discuss the parental notification process with the youth with a goal of eventually making contact. It is important to note that notifying parents of the youth's whereabouts is not equivalent to requiring them to return home. In some cases, while parents may be notified, they may not care, or the youth may refuse to return home. Of course, if the adolescent indicates that there is any abuse or neglect, social workers are required to follow individual state reporting guidelines.

Current legislation recognizes that there is a pressing need to identify runaway youth, ascertain where they were while they were away, determine why they ran away in the first place, make assessments of the individual situation, plan and implement suitable housing/treatment plans, and identify those people who entice runaways into illegal activities such as drug dealing and prostitution.

THE PROBLEM OF DEFINITION

Trying to determine who are "true" runaways in need of interventive services is a complicated problem. One issue is determining the age at which individuals are considered adults. Some reporting agencies or service programs concern themselves with adolescents under the age of 16, some with youth younger than age 18, and some provide intervention up to the age of 21. This inconsistency is discussed by Finkelhor, Hotaling, and Sedlak (1990), who note in a federal report that "if children were already away and refused to return home, they were also counted as Runaways, depending on their age and the amount of time away: 2 nights away if they were 15 or older, and 1 night if they were 14 or younger" (p. 11).

Some minors may lie about their age when requesting services. For example, in an outreach program serving over 2600 New York City streetwalking prostitutes, only 34 clients identified themselves as under age 21 (Weiner & Wallace, 1994). It is likely that many more were, in fact, younger, but lied about their ages due to fear of being referred to the juvenile authorities. Therefore, estimates of the number of runaways are frequently inconsistent and inaccurate.

In addition, while there appears to be some consensus about what is meant by runaways or street youth, definitions are not operationally standardized. As in the early English Poor Laws, the various categories of youth who were not living in traditional family arrangements are grouped together, as if the factors causing their circumstances and the means with which to cope are the same. Various terms are used to refer to a variety of adolescents who are living in non-familial arrangements, including transient youth, runaways, thrownaways, street youth, "in-and-outers," and homeless youth. These inconsistently used terms are neither clearly defined nor mutually exclusive. Kufeldt, Durieux, Nimmo, and McDonald (1992) provide a basic definition: "Running away is defined as staying away from the family home for 24 hours or more, without parental knowledge or against their will" (p. 385). This definition is reflected by the federal government which defines runaway and homeless youth as "a person under 18 years of age who absents himself from home or place of legal residence without the permission of his or her family" (45 CFR§1351.1, 1993). This definition seems overly broad, and Kufeldt and Nimmo (1987) attempt to distinguish between the sporadic runners and true runaways/homeless.

> The former are those who absent themselves frequently from home, staying away for short periods, whereas the runaways leave and stay away. The in and outs run an average of two times per year, staying away from home for approximately two weeks. The runaways/homeless are more likely to have left home during the past year and to have been away from home from one month to three years. (p. 57)

This distinction presents a picture of two different types of runaways: those who leave for short periods of time, several times a year, but eventually return home, and those who, for all intents and purposes run away from home and remain away without intending to return. While many do return within 48 hours, in 1999, the majority of runaways/thrownaways remained away from home for 24 hours to up to a week; fewer than 1 percent never return home (Hammer, Finkelhor, & Sedlak, 2002).

Many with a history of periodic running may never be reported as runaways by their parents, under the assumption that they would eventually return. Hammer et al. (2002) found only 21 percent of runaways were reported to the authorities for the purpose of locating them. It may be that many caretakers do not wish to involve the police in the lives of their children/families, police intervention is not seen as helpful, the parents have information about the child's location, and/or the caretakers may not wish to locate the child. Hammer, Finkelhor, Sedlak, and Porcellini (2004) suggest that caretakers may be giving adolescents greater independence and/or may have become less able to establish limits on youth behaviors, including staying away from home. They also propose that the increased use of cell phones and other modes of communication may allow adolescents to leave messages or negotiate arrangements that preclude caretakers being alarmed. Thus, there appears to be a sizeable number of youth who spend multiple, short periods of time on the street, without the supervision of adults.

Long-term runaways may or may not make permanent lives for themselves; many never come to the attention of social service or law enforcement agencies. Some find suitable living arrangements and jobs, and develop relationships with significant others. It is not unreasonable to assume that some number of adolescent runaway girls may "elope" with older boyfriends and develop stable relationships. Some runaways have traditionally used the military as a means of leaving their homes. Such individuals may or may not show up in statistics as runaways, but in fact, have left home without their parents' consent. Unfortunately, in some cases, children have been abducted but are mistakenly reported as runaways.

Not all runaways are truly runaways; many are "thrownaways"– children who are more or less pushed out of their families. Finkelhor et al. (1990) indicate that children are thrownaways as opposed to runaways if one of the following four circumstances is met:

1. the child had been directly told to leave the household;
2. the child had been away from home, and a caretaker refused to allow the child back;
3. the child had run away, but the caretaker made no effort to recover the child or did not care whether or not the child returned; or
4. the child had been abandoned or deserted (p. 14).

These authors estimated that approximately 22 percent of runaways were, in fact, thrownaways. Hier, Korboot, and Schweitzer (1990) found significantly lower levels of hostility and antisocial behavior for those who left of their own volition (runaways) compared with those who were forced to leave (thrownaways), suggesting that thrownaway children may not have been functioning "ideally," and thus are forced to leave by their parents. An alternative explanation suggests that the parents and/or family, as a whole, is not functioning adequately and copes with problems using expulsion of the perceived problem member.

The distinction between runaways/thrownaways may not always be clear. Such individuals may be living in abusive relationships or are not having their needs met by their familial living arrangements (which may include foster care). Assessment might show that the running behavior in such circumstances is both appropriate and functional. Of those youth who called the National Runaway Switchboard in 2004, only 5 percent self-identified as "thrownaway" (National Runaway Switchboard, 2005a), indicating that these youth might feel more comfortable identifying themselves as runaways who have taken control of their lives, rather than admitting to rejection by their families. Evidence exists that gay male youth may be at high risk for being forced out of their homes because of their sexual orientation (Kruks, 1991).

In addition to the traditional notion of street children as runaways or orphans, there are youth who are members of homeless families. Due to the regulation of homeless shelters or other housing programs, some youth may live alone on the streets or request help from programs designated for runaway youth. Such individuals are not truly runaways but, for the purpose of expediency, access services from agencies designed for runaways and thus may show up in these statistics.

A last category of adolescents are generically termed "street kids." While not meeting the actual definition of being away from home without parental consent, these youth, most commonly seen in urban settings, may be truant from school, spend days or nights unsupervised, and are not integrated into the lives of their families. Such individuals may be involved with gangs, drugs, prostitution and other illicit activities, and may be absent from home for short periods of time. While not officially runaways, these youngsters engage in behaviors that are indistinguishable from those who are truly runaways and may intermingle with runaways in a variety of programs. These youth may also represent potential runaways or thrownaways.

DEMOGRAPHICS OF RUNAWAYS

Studies of the population receiving services provide a skewed picture of the actual runaway population. "Runaways and homeless young people will generally not seek help for themselves unless they are in the middle of a severe personal crisis" (Yates, Pennbridge, Swofford, & Mackenzie, 1991, p. 557). Thus, studies reporting on the issues and problems facing youth who reside in shelters for runaways and/or use programs targeted for such youth, represent only one subgroup of this population.

Despite these problems with documenting the numbers of runaway youth, the Basic Center and Transitional Living Programs recorded that 83,359 youth had received services during 1997 (GAO, 1999). The National Runaway Switchboard estimates that one in seven youths between the ages of 10 and 18 will run away, 1.3 million children are on the street every day, and 75 percent of runaways are female (National Runaway Switchboard, 2005b).

The National Incidence Study of Missing, Abducted, Runaway and Thrownaway Children (Hammer et al., 2002) estimated that 1,682,900 youth had a runaway/thrownaway episode in 1999. Seventy-one percent could have been endangered during their runaway/thrownaway episode due to drug use, sexual or physical abuse, presence in a location where criminal activity was taking place, or because of their young age (13 years old or younger); 67,000 of these runaways/thrownaways were between the ages of 7 and 11. Runaways/thrownaways make up the largest proportion of missing children reported to authorities (45 percent).

In comparing data from 1988 and 1999, Hammer et al. (2004) indicated that the rates of runaway youth have decreased from 7.09 per 1,000 children in 1988 to 5.28 in 1999. They suggest this might not reflect a true decrease in the rates, but a redefinition of youth as away from home without permission rather than as runaways. They also propose that the attention that has been paid to this social problem, and the development of programs to meet the needs of this population, may also account for the reduced rates. The authors caution, however, that large numbers of youth are still in critical or vulnerable circumstances.

RISKS FOR RUNNING

Several studies have attempted to understand some of the factors that create a risk for running away. D'Angelo's (1987) extensive review of the literature indicates that more runaways come from single parent families, experience intense family conflict, and spend less time in family activities than do nonrunaways. Usually it is a combination of factors that contribute to running away.

> Many homeless youth have a constellation of other problems, such as sub-stance abuse, histories of physical and/or sexual abuse, low self-esteem, depression, suicidal behaviors, sexual identity formation problems and mistrust of adults. (Goulart & Madover, 1991, p. 573)

They are also unsuccessful in school, displaying a higher incidence of low grades, missed classes, truancy, suspension, and dropping out more often than their peers (D'Angelo, 1987). They tend to avoid organized social activities and relationships with youth who are engaging in socially acceptable behavior. D'Angelo suggests that repeated frustration in family and school settings leads to social ineptness. Riley, Grief, Caplan, and MacAulay (2004) identified common themes among families whose children have runaway from home. Broadly, these include (1) children's poor school performance and the parent's inability to address their needs, (2) children's personal problems and the parents' inability to cope, and (3) cultural differences between parents born outside the United States and their children.

Estimates indicate that as many as 25 percent of youth on the streets may be gay/lesbian/bisexual (National Runaway Switchboard, 2004). Cochran, Steward, Ginzler, and Cauce (2002) found that gay/lesbian/bisexual youth left home more often than their heterosexual counterparts. Whitbeck, Chen, Hoyt, Tyler, and Johnson (2004) suggest that these youth are at double jeopardy due to society's negative views of their sexual identity and exposure to more stressors at home and school. As a result, they participate in more risky behaviors than heterosexual youth. They were more likely to report having been kicked out of their homes because of conflicts over their sexual identity, had higher rates of major depressive episodes, posttraumatic stress, and substance abuse than their heterosexual counterparts.

Abuse and Sexual Behavior of Runaways

Numerous studies have documented the high incidence of physical and sexual abuse in the lives of runaways (Kurtz, Jarvis, & Kurtz, 1991; Powers, Eckenrode, & Jacklitsch, 1990). Thrownaway youth appear to experience more violence and conflict within their families than runaways (Finkelhor et al., 1990). Runaways report more sexual and physical abuse than nonrunaways (Kurtz et al., 1991). Hammer et al. (2002) identified 17 features of endangerment experienced by runaway/thrownaway youth. Physical or sexual abuse at home or fear of abuse upon return were the most common, as reported by 21 percent of the respondents.

In one sample of runaways who had been sexually abused, more than one-third indicated that the sexual abuse was extremely violent; this rate was higher for females than males (Tyler, Whitbeck, & Cauce, 2001). Whitbeck et al. (2004) found that lesbian runaways were more likely than heterosexual females to have been sexually abused by their caretakers, and gay/lesbian/bisexual youth were more likely to have been sexually and physically victimized while on the streets.

Psychosocial Problems

Given their histories and social support systems, it is not unexpected that runaways display a variety of psychosocial difficulties including depression, substance abuse, suicidal behaviors, and sexual acting out. The stress of being homeless creates a "heightened sense of vulnerability, hypervigilance, anxiety and fear that may be adaptive to street life" (Whitbeck et al., 2004, p. 329). Thus some of the psychological problems may have contributed to the act of running away and also may have been exacerbated by the stress of life on the street. Rotheram-Borus (1993) found 37 percent of the runaways in her sample had attempted suicide prior to seeking services in a runaway program, many within one month of entering a shelter. She noted that these findings are much higher than the national rate of 6 to 13 percent for high school samples. Females also reported significantly more suicide attempts. A study of adolescents interviewed by street outreach workers in 1995-1996, found 23 percent of males and 39 percent of females had high levels of clinical depression. These rates were much higher than those found among high school students in general

(Whitbeck, Hoyt, & Bao, 2000). In this sample, affiliation with deviant peers was also found to be associated with risky sexual behaviors, alcohol and drug use, and street victimization. Tyler, Whitbeck, Hoyt, and Johnson (2003) found that rates of self-mutilation were high (69 percent) among homeless youth. Older and gay/lesbian/bisexual youth reported the greatest number of self-injury incidents.

Substance abuse is also a common component of runaways' lives and at higher levels than among nonrunaways. Fors and Dean (1991) determined that illicit drug use was between two and seven times higher for street youth. The drug use patterns varied for different geographic regions and there appeared to be a high level of poly-drug use. In a summary of three National Institute on Drug Abuse (NIDA) funded studies, Wyman (1997) found that for almost every drug surveyed, youths living on the streets had higher rates of drug abuse and were involved in more serious drug use when compared to youth in shelters or at home. More street youths used heroin and other injection drugs, methamphetamines, and crack cocaine. Seventy-five percent of street youths were using marijuana; approximately one-third were using hallucinogens, stimulants, and analgesics; and 25 percent were using crack, other forms of cocaine, inhalants, and sedatives. Cochran et al. (2002) found that gay/lesbian/bisexual homeless youth reported using 11 of 12 substances (the exception being marijuana) more frequently than heterosexual homeless youth.

Drug use among runaways has multiple ramifications. It introduces youth to the criminal subculture, including drug dealing or other serious crimes (prostitution, stealing, mugging) in order to support their drug habits. Such activities may bring them to the attention of the criminal justice system and/or social service agencies. In addition, runaways may become involved in exchanging sex for drugs, money, food, or housing. Pennbridge et al. (1992) have termed such sex "survival sex" in comparison to "recreational sex." Half of the males and one-third of the females engaged in survival sex (Anderson, Freese, & Pennbridge, 1994). Green, Ennett, and Ringwalt (1999) interviewed a sample of adolescents in shelters and on the streets. As might be expected, street youth (27.5 percent) were much more likely to have engaged in survival sex than those in shelters (9.5 percent). Pregnancy and/or having a sexually transmitted disease (STD) were found to be associated with survival sex, indicating that those engaging in such behaviors might not be practicing "safer sex" by using condoms.

When engaging in survival sex, the runaways were likely to be high on drugs or alcohol (Pennbridge et al., 1992). This is the foundation of the pattern of drugs, sex, and HIV.

PATTERNS OF RISK FOR HIV

The AIDS epidemic has forced professionals to look at the patterns of sexual behaviors and drug use among both adults and adolescents. As already noted, runaways have higher levels of depression and suicide attempts, drug use and sexual experiences, and fewer social supports than teenagers in the general population. The Centers for Disease Control (CDC, 1998) recognized that continuing efforts need to be made to address "the needs of adolescents who are most vulnerable to HIV infection, such as homeless or runaway youth, juvenile offenders, or school drop-outs" (p. 1). Runaway youth had much higher levels of sexual risk behavior than general adolescent populations, used condoms inconsistently during their most recent intercourse, and had high rates of drug use including sharing syringes (Greenberg & Neuman, 1998). The increased risk of HIV infection forces researchers to look at the interaction of these social variables for this vulnerable population.

Several studies have raised concern that the use of drugs and the sexual patterns among street youth place them at higher risk for contracting HIV than nonrunaway adolescent populations (Pennbridge et al., 1992; Rotheram-Borus, Meyer-Bahlberg, Cheryl, Haignere, Exner, Matthieu, Henderson, & Gruen, 1992; Kooperman, Rosario, & Rotheram-Borus, 1994; Anderson et al., 1994). Pennbridge et al. (1992) reported that the HIV infection rates among adolescent runaways ranged from 2.1 percent in Houston, 5.3 percent in New York City, to 12.0 percent in San Francisco. Gould (1993) found that, "In major cities, like New York, Washington and Miami, infection in teenage runaways is close to 10 percent" (p. 36), compared to a national average of 3.26 percent among adults and adolescents over the age of 13.

Alcohol has been demonstrated as a factor in HIV transmission among adolescents in general. Many more runaways (71 percent) use alcohol than adolescents in general (48 percent) (Kooperman, Rosario,

& Rotheram-Borus, 1994). The excessive use of alcohol in this population impairs judgment, resulting in unprotected sexual activity with
individuals who are casual acquaintances and/or whose sexual histories may not be known. The use of most recreational drugs impairs the
judgment of users, posing "an indirect risk by disinhibiting sexual risk
behavior" (Kooperman et al., 1994, p. 96). The researchers (1994) also
suggest that

> Alcohol and drug use may increase the risk for HIV infection by bringing run-
> aways into the social networks of substances abusers, partially because shelters
> are typically available in those settings where there are many alcoholics and
> IDUs [injection drug users]. (p. 96)

The use of injection drugs (heroin, injectable cocaine, etc.) and
smokable crack/cocaine increases the direct transmission of the HIV
virus. Injection drug users are infected by sharing drug-injecting
equipment. The IV-drug subculture fosters the mystique of sharing
drug injecting equipment, and adolescents may share needles deliber-
ately to show trust or be one of the group.

Crack/cocaine has been shown to be a factor in the transmission of
HIV for individuals who exchange sex for drugs (Wallace, Weiner, &
Steinberg, 1992). Crack/cocaine creates a short intense high requiring
users have to exchange sex for drugs frequently to maintain their high.
One of the effects of the drug is hypersexuality which also increases
the frequency of engaging in sexual behaviors. In addition, the use of
crack pipes burns the lips and mouth while the direct application of
the drug to the mouth and nasal passages results in the breakdown of
the mucus membrane of the mouth. Thus, the practice of oral sex,
without a condom, increases the transmission risk of the HIV virus
through sores in the oral cavities. Among streetwalking prostitutes, fellatio is the primary activity (Wallace et al., 1992). We might expect that
this activity is also common among both male and female runaways
who are exchanging sex for drugs, money, or other necessities.

Researchers have established the higher risk of HIV involved in
"survival sex" (Pennbridge et al., 1992). Among the small sample of
New York City adolescent prostitutes, 22.6 percent tested positive for
HIV (Wallace & Weiner, 1994). Individuals are more likely to use
drugs to cope with the situation of necessary sex, and while high, less
likely to practice "safer sex." While under the influence of drugs or

alcohol, street youth are unable to negotiate the proper use of protective devices with their sexual partners. This is further complicated by the willingness of certain individuals to pay more for intercourse or other sexual activities without a condom. Many men purchase street sex to do precisely the kinds of activities they might not do with their wives or girlfriends, including sex with a male. Gay male sex is openly purchased in many urban settings and youth who do not consider themselves to be gay may engage in such activities for survival. Since they do not consider themselves to be gay, they may not practice "safer sex" or they may use drugs to deal with activities they find distasteful.

Runaways may know about safer sex practices and needle cleaning but fail to do either in a consistent manner. Pennbridge et al. (1992) found 34 percent of individuals who had used injection drugs within the last 30 days had shared needles. Although Rotheram-Borus and Kooperman (1991) found that runaways had relatively high levels of knowledge and positive attitudes toward AIDS prevention, condom use was relatively inconsistent. Only 16.2 percent of the males and 19.4 percent of the females indicated that they always used a condom. During the previous three-month period, males had an average of 4.7 sexual partners while females had 2.0. The rate of condom use may have increased somewhat. In a more recent study, sexually active youth in New York reported always using a condom 30 percent of the time (Kooperman et al., 1994).

Despite their high risk for HIV, runaways are unlikely to be tested for it. Sharing needles for injection drugs or having a drug-using sexual partner were the predominant reasons for considering being tested. When asked to speculate what they would do if they find out they were HIV positive, 29 percent of the runaways anticipated self-destructive behaviors, 37 percent suggested health enhancing behaviors, and only 8 percent would tell a new sex partner (Kooperman, Rotheram-Borus, Dobbs, Gwadz, & Brown, 1992). Thus, it appears runaways are at high risk of HIV infection and of spreading it to others. Moreover, they "may try to survive with little or no contact with medical professionals, the result being that their health problems may go untreated and worsen" (DHHS, ACF, 1994).

A MODEL FOR INTERVENTION

According to Riley et al. (2004), runaway youth should be defined as troubled youth from dysfunctional homes, instead of defining them by their delinquent behavior. Progressive policies have resulted in distinguishing runaway youth from youth who are considered delinquent, and in moving them from the juvenile justice to the social service systems. Such a shift in conceptualization and policies requires a multifaceted three-pronged approach to intervention in order to address the problem of runaway youth in urban communities:

- Prevention
- Outreach and Crisis Intervention
- Rehabilitationand Permanency Planning

Prevention

Prevention focuses on policies, programs, and interventions designed to avert the circumstances that cause youth to become runaways. In a reauthorization of the Runaway and Homeless Youth Act, Congress continues to recognize the importance of preventive interventions as "early intervention services (such as home-based services) are needed to prevent runaway and homeless youth from becoming involved in the juvenile justice system and other law enforcement systems" (42 U.S.C. §5701, 2000, p. 2). Whitbeck and Hoyt (1999) suggest that runaway youth are "running from something or drifting out of disorganized families rather than running to something" (p. 6); this has serious implications for the development of prevention and reunification programs.

Since it appears that runaways often run because of stresses in their lives, intervention needs to begin with recognition of familial, interpersonal, school, and drug problems. As we have seen, many of these children come from minimally functioning or dysfunctional families and often send out many distress signals before they run, such as truancy, suicide attempts, drug use, and sexual acting out. Professionals who work with adolescents (social workers, school personnel, recreation staff) need to be trained to recognize danger signals in order to make appropriate preventive interventions. Social service and criminal justice agencies need to be better trained to recognize sexual and physical abuse of adolescents and to intervene appropriately with the perpetrators, while simultaneously offering protection and other forms of help to the adolescent and his or her family.

Since many adolescents feel alienated from adults, and in fact have been mistreated by them, the training of peer counselors may be a useful approach. This approach has already proven to be successful in both drug prevention and HIV/AIDS counseling programs. In a peer counseling model, adolescents are trained to identify individuals who might be at risk for running away, provide counseling and/or information, and assist in making referrals and linkages to appropriate professional services. The peer counselor serves as a positive role model who may have dealt with similar problems. Many adolescents feel more comfortable talking to their peers and are more likely to approach a service agency or professional using this referral process. The peer counselor serves as a bridge between the world of the at-risk adolescent and the professionals.

The development of programs to address the special needs of gay and lesbian youth is critical. Studies have shown these adolescents are at high risk of being thrown out of their homes; have high rates of substance abuse, self-injury, and suicide attempts; and may engage in sexual behaviors that place them at risk for contracting HIV. They are also more likely to be the victims of abuse and violence from their schoolmates and others. Internalized homophobia may increase their levels of self-destructive behaviors. Such adolescents need positive gay/lesbian role models and opportunities to interact with adults who are accepting of them. The Hettrick-Martin Institute in New York City is one of the agencies that has developed a spectrum of services available to such youth, which includes a school, street-outreach, recreation, substance abuse and HIV positive support groups, and counseling.

Outreach and Crisis Intervention

Crisis intervention should be offered during the period of time when adolescents are living on the street, using drugs, and engaging in the sale of sex to meet their basic needs. Traditional outreach work, from storefront agencies, mobile van units, and walking in the neighborhoods and streets, may be the first contact with very vulnerable and needy adolescents. Outreach workers identify individuals who are experiencing difficulties or those at risk. Thus, a social worker might make a contact with a member of a street group and "hang out with them." A nationally known program, Covenant House in New York City, has outreach workers in Times Square, the Port Authority Bus Terminal, and train stations to identify runaways as they arrive in the city, before they have an opportunity to become involved with illicit activities or entrenched in dangerous street life. Peer counselors, former runaways or street kids, might work in a team with a professional and help the crisis intervention worker identify runaways and provide introductions and entree into the urban street subculture. This approach has been used to develop relationships with street walking prostitutes (Wallace, Weiner, & Steinberg, 1992), and historically to do outreach to street gangs.

Generally, adolescents are not trusting of adults, and runaways are especially wary of them. Thus, working with such a population, one must be genuine and empathic. Adolescents, more than any other population, are constantly testing and may make themselves as "unlikeable" as possible to see if the worker really cares. They are easily disillusioned if they believe the worker is not being totally honest with them. Since runaway youth are likely to engage in self-destructive and/or illegal activities, it strains the worker to maintain a nonjudgmental attitude. Once the social worker develops a reputation of being trustworthy, other runaways may approach on their own. "Meeting the clients where they are at" is one of the basic underpinnings of social work. Beginning interactions may start with listening and the provision of basic needs, such as food, clothing, or cigarettes:

> An outreach worker who is not a cigarette smoker and dislikes the idea of being a nicotine "pusher," often carries a pack a cigarettes and some matches when doing outreach work. The social act of asking for a "smoke" and offering one can often be the first request and response in these relationships. In the scheme of things, this drug is much less harmful than some of the alternatives and may lead to the development of a trusting relationship. This worker also finds it helpful to carry a supply of snack foods and candies. At times, the worker offers to share a sandwich, which was supposedly his "lunch." This is all done as if it is natural for the worker to be carrying these items. Another strategy involves the worker suggesting that he would like a soda, a cup of coffee, or an ice cream cone and offering one to the adolescent.

Of course, if the circumstances of the runaway are extreme or present a clear danger, the relationship may have to move quickly to the provision of such needed services as food, housing, medical care, or drug detoxification. As with all clients, it is extremely important that the social worker in such circumstances make every attempt to include the adolescent in the decision-making process. Sometimes it is necessary to allow the adolescent to "refuse treatment." For example, the runaway may be given a meal but allowed to refuse to come into a shelter. Under such circumstances, it might be appropriate to have a check-back system—offering the worker's business card and asking the runaway to call or stop by to let the social worker know how he or she is doing. Workers need to have a nonjudgmental attitude and maintain a relationship so that eventually the runaway may make the decision to enter the shelter or seek needed medical care. Since many of these youth have experienced nontrusting or abusive relationships with adults, the professional must continue to show concern without preaching. Despite statements to the contrary, most adolescents want caring from an adult and may eventually accept help. If they do not get the help when they ask for it, many of these youths are likely to engage in self-destructive behavior.

The crisis intervention stage assumes that there are services available for access when the client asks for them. Such programs should meet the needs of adolescents/runaways and not mingle them with a general adult population that may be dysfunctional or may represent the population that has victimized them. Thus, there need to be *adolescent-only* runaway shelters, drop-in centers, detoxification programs, medical clinics, and psychiatric services. Staff dealing with this client population must receive support and competent, ongoing supervision from their agencies.

Another option may be the development of programs that offer alternatives to escaping to the streets. Staller (2004) suggests that the development of good adolescent shelter programs might result in adolescents leaving homes and going directly to shelters instead of living on the street. Consequently, they would avoid unsupervised, potentially dangerous periods of times on the street. Such programs would differ dramatically from the current foster care system. Runaways in such shelters would be allowed to participate in the decision-making process and retain their freedom to leave. Staff could involve families as appropriate in assessment and intervention for long-term planning.

Opponents might argue that such a shelter system might increase the size of the runaway population since adolescents might perceive these as better living arrangements than living at home. Such a shelter system would serve as a safety net for the most difficult situations. Finally, such shelters might offer the last opportunity to reach such youth and provide services to safely transition them into adulthood.

Rehabilitation and Permanency Planning

Once the life of the runaway is stabilized and his/her basic needs are being met, it is possible to begin to plan for the future, including arrangements for a permanent residence, returning to a school, or job training. While in some circumstances it might be possible for the adolescent to attempt family reconciliation, a study by Yates et al. (1991) found that only 20 percent of runaways who seek help in shelters were good candidates for immediate family reunification and 35 percent could not return home. Other studies found that while 50 percent of the runaways returned home, 33 percent needed alternative, safe, long-term living arrangements (DHHS, ACF, 1994).

Family reconciliation does not always include returning home. It may include meeting selected family members in treatment groups or family therapy, although in some circumstances this is clearly impossible and would be detrimental to the runaway. Adolescents should have the prerogative to refuse to see their parents or to refuse to return home. Interventions may involve helping the runaway to decide whether to remain in a shelter/group home, live with a different relative, enter foster care, or become an emancipated minor, in which case they may need help in learning skill of independent living. Discussions might focus on such activities as appropriate behavior in the workplace, stress management, money management and budgeting, communication skills, and negotiating "safer sex." Arrangements for transitional living, drug and alcohol support groups, and HIV services should be made as needed.

In New York City, the above model is incorporated into a program called "Enter," which is designed to provide independent living training for runaway and homeless youth. Under the supervision of case managers, participants live in pairs in agency owned apartment buildings. They must have a job or be in school, and be responsible for maintaining their apartments, meal planning, and shopping. Various group activities are provided to help them develop the skills they will need in the community. Since most of the costs are funded under the federal Transitional Living Program for Homeless Youth, participants are required to open a bank account and set aside a portion of their salary so that they will be able to secure an apartment after completion of the program.

CONCLUSION

There is a sizeable group of adolescent runaways who are at high risk for suicide, drug use, prostitution, illegal activities, and HIV infection. Social workers and other professionals need to develop additional services for prevention, outreach interevention, and rehabilitation services that meet the needs of these vulnerable youth. While some programs and policies do exist, policy changes are required to provide sufficient funding so that specialized services for adolescents can be made available.

The schools, already overburdened with the social needs of students, do have mechanisms for identifying child abuse, substance abuse, and other destructive behaviors, and for reaching out to adolescents in need—before they run. Linkages between schools and community services for youth need to be strengthened. There are models that appear to work runaways and those at risk for running away—peer counselors, outreach and drop-in centers, and transitional living programs. Such programs need to be targeted for funding, strengthening, and expansion.

Being a runaway does not just mean not having a place to sleep. It is also about not having a personal place, a place to keep reminders of the past; most poignantly it is about not having a connection with one's family. It is important for professionals to remember these losses when reaching out to help such youth and offer help in ways that affirm their dignity and self-worth.

REFERENCES

42 USC § 5701 (2000, August 30). Administration for Children and Families, Department of Health and Human Services, Family and Youth Services Bureau; Runaway and Homeless Youth Act. http://www.acf.dhhs.gov/programs/fysb/Missing.pdf. Retrieved 8/8/05.

45 CRF § 1351.1 (1993). Administration for Children and Families, Department of Health and Human Services (1994, May 12). Runaway and homeless youth program. Federal Register, p. 24772-24810.

Anderson, J. E., Freese, T. E., & Pennbridge, J. N. (1994). Sexual risk behavior and condom use among street youth in Hollywood. *Family Planning Perspectives, 26*(1), 22–25.

Bremner, R. H. (1970). *Children and youth in America: A documentary history.* Cambridge, MA: Harvard University Press.

Cochran, B., Steward, A., Ginzler, J., & Cauce, A. (2002). Challenges faced by homeless sexual minorities: Comparison of gay, lesbian, bisexual and transgender homeless adolescents with their heterosexual counterparts. *American Journal of Public Health, 92*(5), 773–777.

D'Angelo, R. (1987). Runaways. In *Encyclopedia of social work* (pp. 513–521). Silver Spring, MD: National Association of Social Work.

Department of Health and Human Services, Administration for Children and Families. (1994, May 12). Runaway and homeless youth program. *Federal Register,* pp. 24772–24810.

Finkelhor, D., Hotaling, G., & Sedlak, A. (1990). *Missing, abducted, runaway and thrownaway children in America,* First Report. Washington, DC: U.S. Department of Justice, Office of Juvenile Justice and Delinquency Prevention.

Fors, S. W., & Dean, G. R. (1991). A comparison of drug involvement between runaways and school youth. *Journal of Drug Education, 21*(1), 13–25.

General Accounting Office. (1999). *Homelessness: Coordination and evaluation of programs are essential.* Reports to Congressional Committees. GAO/RCED 99-49.Washington, DC: U.S. Government Printing Office.

Goulart, M., & Madover, S. (1991). An AIDS prevention program for homeless youth. *Journal of Adolescent Health, 12*(7), 573–575.

Gould, P. (1993). *The slow plague: A geography of the AIDS pandemic.* Cambridge, MA: Blackwell.

Greenberg, J. B., & Neuman, M. S. (Eds.). (1998). *What we have learned from the AIDS evaluation of street outreach projects: A summary document.* Atlanta, GA: Centers for Disease Control and Prevention.

Greene. J. M., Ennett, S. T., & Ringwalt, C. L. (1999). Prevalence and correlates of survival sex among runaway and homeless youth. *American Journal of Public Health, 89*(9), 1406–1409.

Hammer, H., Finkelhor, D., & Sedlak, A. J. (2002). Runaway/thrownaway children: National estimates and characteristics. *National Incidence Studies of Missing, Abducted, Runaway and Thrownaway Children,* Washington, DC: U.S. Department of Justice.

Hammer, H., Finkelhor, D., Sedlak, A. J., & Porcellini, L. E. (2004). National estimates of missing children: Selected trends, 1988-1999. *National incidence studies of
missing, abducted, runaway and thrownaway children,* Washington, DC: U.S.
Department of Justice.

Hier, S. J., Korboot, P. J., & Schweitzer, R. D. (1990). Social adjustment and symp-
tomatology in two types of homeless adolescents: Runaways and throwaways.
Adolescence, 25(100), 761–771.

Kooperman, C., Rosario, M., & Rotheram-Borus, M. J. (1994). Alcohol and drug use
and sexual behaviors placing runaways at risk for HIV infection. *Addictive
Behaviors, 19*(1), 95–103.

Kooperman, C., Rotheram-Borus, M. J., Dobbs, L., Gwadz, M., & Brown, J. (1992).
Beliefs and behavioral intentions regarding human immunodeficiency virus testing among New York City runaways. *Journal of Adolescent Health, 13*(7), 576–581.

Kruks, G. (1991). Gay and lesbian homeless/street youth: Special issues and concerns. *Journal of Adolescent Health, 12*(7), 515–518.

Kufeldt, K., Durieux, M., Nimmo, M., & McDonald, M. (1992). Providing shelter for
street youth: Are we reaching those in need? *Child Abuse and Neglect, 16*(2),
187–199.

Kurtz, P. D., Jarvis, S. V., & Kurtz, G. L. (1991). Problems of homeless youths:
Empirical findings and human services issues. *Social Work, 36*(4), 311–314.

National Alliance to End Homelessness. (2003). Issue Brief, The Runaway
and Homeless Youth Act. http://www.endhomelessness.org/pol/papers/
RHYAUpdate10-03.pdf. Accessed May 23, 2005.

National Runaway Switchboard. (2005a). 2004 Statistics. http://www.nrscrisisline.
org/2004stat.asp. Accessed June 2, 2005.

National Runaway Switchboard. (2005b). News and Research. http://www.nrscrisis-
line.org/news.asp. Accessed June 2, 2005.

National Runaway Switchboard. (2004) Being out, coming home: Helping GLBTQ
youth in crisis. http://www.nrscrisisline.org/lit_services2.asp. Accessed February
17, 2005.

Pennbridge, J. N., Freese, T. E., & MacKenzie, R. G. (1992). High-risk behaviors
among male street youth in Hollywood, California. *AIDS Education and Prevention,
Supplement,* 24–33.

Powers, J. L., Eckenrode, J., & Jacklitsch, B. (1990). Maltreatment among runaway
and homeless youth. *Child Abuse and Neglect, 14*(1), 87–98.

Riley, D. B., Greif, G. L., Caplan, D. A., & MacAulay, H. K. (2004). Common
themes and treatment approaches in working with families of runaway youth. *The
American Journal of Family Therapy, 32,* 139–153.

Rotheram-Borus, M. J., & Kooperman, C. (1991). Sexual risk behaviors, AIDS
knowledge, and beliefs about AIDS among runaways. *American Journal of Public
Health, 81*(2), 208–210.

Rotheram-Borus, M. J., Meyer-Bahlberg, H. F. L., Cheryl, K., Haignere, C. S.,
Exner, T. M., Matthieu, M., Henderson, R., & Gruen, R. S. (1992). Lifetime sexual behaviors among predominantly minority male runaways and gay/bisexual
adolescents in New York City. *AIDS Education and Prevention Supplement,* 34–42.

Rotheram-Borus, M. J. (1993). Suicidal behavior and risk factors among runaway youths. *American Journal of Psychiatry, 150*(1), 103–107.

Staller, K. M. (2004). Runaway youth system dynamics: A theoretical framework for analyzing runaway and homeless youth policy. *Families in Society, 85*(3), 379–390.

Tyler, K. A., Hoyt, D. R, Whitbeck, L. B., & Cauce, A. M. (2001). The impact of child sexual abuse on later sexual victimization among runaway youth. *Journal of Research on Adolescence, 11*(2), 151–176.

Tyler, K. A., Whitbeck, L. B., Hoyt, D. R., & Johnson, K. D. (2003). Self-mutilation and homeless youth: The role of family abuse, street experiences and mental disorders. *Journal of Research on Adolescence, 13*(4), 457–474.

Wallace, J. I., Weiner, A., & Steinberg, A. (1992). Patterns of condom use, crack use and fellatio as risk behaviors for HIV infection among prostitutes. *American Public Health Association Annual Meeting*, Washington, DC.

Weiner, A., & Wallace, J. I. (1994). Foundation For Research on Sexually Transmitted Diseases, Inc., New York: unpublished data.

Whitbeck, L. B., Chen, X., Hoyt, D. R., Tyler, K. A., & Johnson, K. D. (2004). Mental disorder, subsistence strategies and victimization among gay, lesbian, and bisexual homeless and runaway adolescents. *The Journal of Sex Research, 41*(4), 329–342.

Whitbeck, L. B., Hoyt, D. R., & Boa, W. N. (2000). Depressive symptoms and co-occurring depressive symptoms, substance abuse, and conduct problems among runaway and homeless adolescents. *Child Development, 71*(3), 721–732.

Whitbeck, L. B., & Hoyt, D. R. (1999). *Nowhere to grow*. Hawthorne, N.Y.: Aldine de Gruyter.

Wyman, J. R. (1997). Drug abuse among runaway and homeless youths calls for focused outreach solutions. *National Institute on Drug Abuse–NIDA NOTES*, 12(3).

Yates, G. L., Pennbridge, J., Swofford, A., & Mackenzie, R. G. (1991). The Los Angeles system of care for runaway/homeless youth. *Journal of Adolescent Health, 12*(7), 555–560.

Epilogue

THE ROLE OF THE COMMUNITY

Chapter 12

IT TAKES A VILLAGE: MOBILIZING URBAN COMMUNITIES FOR IMPROVED CHILD WELFARE SERVICES

Hilda Rivera and Stephen Burghardt

Ensuring that all children grow up in a loving and safe environment is everyone's responsibility. However, while know that "it takes a village to raise a child," little has been written about how to mobilize communities to become more responsive to the many challenges that urban children face in today's society. The reality is that in today's fast-paced urban communities, although attention is often paid to individual, family, and group interventions, community involvement for the purpose of meeting the multiple needs of children is neglected.

This chapter will discuss the meaning of community as its relates to child welfare policy and practice and provide recommendations for how social workers can mobilize urban communities and promote their involvement in achieving family stability and permanency planning. The use of coalitions as an example of community approaches to child welfare services will be discussed.

COMMUNITY INVOLVEMENT IN HISTORICAL PERSPECTIVE

The importance of communities for the development and well-being of children cannot be overemphasized; children do not grow up in isolation, but in communities. When we think about some of the ways that an urban community can affect children, we think about the quality of its schools; its parks, fields, and other sport facilities; its commitment to ensure public protection and safety; its access to health services, as well as social and economic opportunities; its appreciation of cultural values and arts programming; and its availability of positive role models, among others.

Children living in distressed urban communities plagued by tremendous socio-economic problems face multiple challenges. Poverty, school failure, family disruption, drugs, social isolation, discrimination, and violence are just some of the problems that affect the daily lives of many urban children and their families. For children who do not live in their own home because of parental neglect or abuse, child welfare agencies have the responsibility for assessing the safety of the family environment and either returning the child or, if that is not possible, planning a permanent new home for the child. Achieving family stability and permanency planning is an important goal for all children, but especially for the African-American and Latino children who represent the vast majority of children served by the child welfare system (Martin, 2000). To accomplish this, child welfare agencies must change from working in isolation to working collaboratively with the communities in which these children live (Downs, Moore, McFadden, & Costin, 2000; Omang & Bonk, 1999; Power & Eheart, 2001; Wynn, Merry, & Berg, 1995).

The social work profession has a long history of recognizing the important connection between the social environment and the lives of children and their families (Trattner, 1999). Working to improve community conditions that affect the well-being of children and their families has been an important part of the profession since the start of the Settlement House Movement at the end of the nineteenth century (Addams, 1910). From its beginning, the Settlement House Movement focused on increasing community cohesion and on the participation of community members in efforts to marshal resources, organize advocacy efforts, and promote social justice for children and their families.

Today, there is renewed interest in developing comprehensive child and family welfare services that would transform the existing fragmented system into one that actively mobilizes communities to work on behalf of their children and families. This trend offers opportunities for social workers to look at communities as sources of assets rather than deficits (Kretzman & McKnight, 1993; Naparstek & Dooley, 1997; Poertner, McDonald & Murray, 2000; Rosenthal & Cairns, 1994).

CHILD WELFARE POLICY AND PRACTICE:
A CALL FOR COMMUNITY INVOLVEMENT

Recent changes in child welfare policies reflect the understanding that programs are more effective when they work in collaboration with communities. The approach of connecting child welfare services more closely to communities is finding support in federal, state, and local policies. At the federal level, the 1997 passage of the Adoption and Safe Families Act (ASFA), Public Law 105-89, has called for communities and child welfare agencies to come together and work collaboratively to achieve timely family stability and permanency planning for children who have experienced neglect, abuse, or abandonment. Reform-based work in states such as Illinois, Kentucky, and Ohio have all included an emphasis on building collaborative community initiatives. These initiatives are considered key components in the prevention of child abuse and neglect and in permanency planning services. The importance of the neighborhood has also been recognized in efforts to achieve family stability. For example, Kentucky has gone as far as to rename its preventive service programs "Community Services," and to locate services directly within the neighborhoods where their families live.

The potential benefits of developing child welfare services that are community based, comprehensive, accessible, and committed to work collaboratively with community members have been discussed in the literature, as noted below. Among these potential benefits are:

1. Increased community commitment to engaging in activities that promote safety and protection for all children (Mulroy & Shay, 1997; Rosenthal & Cairns, 1994);
2. Better understanding and support at the community level of the child welfare agency's mission, policies, and services (Omang & Bonk, 1999);
3. Improved ability of staff to recruit, retain, train, and support culturally diverse foster parents and preadoptive families (Onyskiw, Harrison, & Spady, 1999);
4. Greater ability to foster formal and informal community networks and support systems (Power & Eheart, 2000); and
5. Stronger community interest in participating in child welfare advocacy and lobbying efforts (Wynn, Merry, & Berg, 1995).

One model community effort, which has taken place in New York City, is exemplified in the groundbreaking work of Geoffrey Canada in the Harlem Children's Zone (Severson, 2005). This program focuses on a targeted neighborhood where data reveal that children have the poorest test scores, high rates of entry into the child welfare system, and high indicators of other poverty-related conditions, such as obesity and diabetes. Canada and his team of educators, social workers, and community organizers are working to influence schools, mobilize and train parents, create meaningful after-school programs, and establish job training programs for youth and their adult family members. The efforts of this organization are focused "not just on education, social service and recreation, but on rebuilding the very fabric of community life" (Harlem Children's Zone). This emphasis on integrating neighborhood-based services within one large targeted community has required that the various agencies and their staff be out in the streets and involved with each other's programs. By building such a network of services to maximize the safety and well-being of children, the Harlem Children's Zone has highlighted the creation of social capital as part of its long-term strategy (Putnam, 2000).

Another highly effective community-based approach has been undertaken by Casey Family Services in New England, a research and advocacy arm of the Annie E. Casey Foundation. In this innovative program, a voluntary agency has joined with state providers to design a community-based approach to post-adoption services (Greenblatt & Dobbyn, 2005).

CHALLENGES TO COMMUNITY INVOLVEMENT

In spite of the benefits of community involvement in child welfare services, this approach also brings with it many challenges. These include agency constraints, community reactions and mistrust, and negative media coverage.

Agency Constraints

The currently fragmented child welfare services draw their authority from separate bureaucracies. Often, for example, public child welfare programs are part of larger social service departments facing competition from various bureaucracies for valuable resources. This has been identified as a significant problem in states such as Florida and New Jersey (Livio, 2003; Wilson, 2002). Such tensions have been the basis for creating the "stand-alone" child welfare agencies in New York City and Illinois (Macdonald, 1994; Weinberger, 1998).

In addition, the lack of staff training and support prevent many social workers in the child welfare field from developing a more community-oriented practice. For example, most professional social workers are trained for case and group approaches to intervention and clients are expected to attend their sessions, either voluntarily or involuntarily. In community practice, on the other hand, social workers must be trained for outreach and community engagement, requiring very different techniques and expertise (Rosenthal & Cairns, 1994). Further, many workers lack opportunities to learn new skills about community-building and empowerment approaches focusing on strengths rather than weaknesses of communities (Kretzmann & McKnight, 1993; Naparstek & Dooley, 1997; Power & Eheart, 2000).

Child welfare agencies attempting to establish collaborative relationships with the communities where children and their families live have to take a close and critical look at how they conduct community outreach, program planning, and the delivery of services (Rivera, 2002). It is important for agencies to begin by conducting an assessment in the community to evaluate what organizational and administrative areas need to be changed or further enhanced. Such an assessment may identify that there is a need for hiring bilingual personnel or for changing the hours of operation.

In addition to addressing the agency's constraints, it is important to identify the agency's assets. Often, social workers at child welfare agencies are not accustomed to fostering collaborative efforts and think that they do not have anything to offer to the community they are trying to serve, or that it is too late or too difficult to initiate working relationships with community members or organizations. However, child welfare agencies with a strong and sincere commitment to work with the community need to help their staff identify their role in working with community members and organizations, and to appreciate that it is never too late to start establishing a relationship.

Community Reactions and Mistrust: Not in My Backyard

New programs are often met with initial community resistance through fears of what has become known as the "not in my back yard" dynamic, sometimes referred to as NIMBY. Such responses of neighborhoods are due to fears that social service programs will result in additional social problems for the community, and that they will also drive down property values. This is complicated by the fact that many community members do not understand the services provided by child welfare agencies (Martin, 2000). Only by maintaining a consistent and open presence in the neighborhood, where staff and clients are seen as vital members of the community at large, can negative perceptions and tensions be diminished. It is important to appreciate that building a trustworthy and collaborative relationship not only takes time, but also requires a great deal of energy and commitment from everyone involved.

Impact of the Media

The stigma and community mistrust of the child welfare system may be intensified by media coverage, which tends to spotlight the failures while ignoring the successes of the system. In recent years, for example, *The Miami Herald* in Florida and the *Newark Star-Ledger* in New Jersey published on-going series of articles about the failures of their state child welfare systems following the reporting of sensational cases of child abuse. While such adverse publicity can help to stoke the political flames for additional funding (successful in New Jersey, far less so in Florida), it has also resulted in defensiveness and insularity within the child welfare systems, thereby reinforcing the distance between the child welfare system and the community.

RECOMMENDATIONS FOR MOBILIZING
URBAN COMMUNITIES

Support of social work staff by agency administration is essential before the staff can reach out into the community. This support must include the willingness to take risks and to change the "old ways of doing business." It is a process that takes time to develop and requires patience before the outcomes can be observed. Social workers have to start by taking small steps and spending more of their time building rapport in the community rather than sitting in their offices.

Following are recommendations aimed at helping social workers begin the process of mobilizing urban communities in the interest of improving child welfare services:

First, social workers should *get to know the community where services are being offered.* This includes gathering information about the community's history, cultural traditions, resources, and needs. It is important to recognize the diversity that exist within communities, and to and take into account that communities can be defined in a variety of ways, including common geographic location, or interest, or identity.

There are different ways for gathering community information, ranging from conducting a formal community assessment, using qualitative and quantitative instruments, to spending some time walking around the neighborhood and talking with the residents. Information gathered from different people in the community is invaluable for planning services that are responsive to the community's needs. The community assessment process itself provides a great opportunity for learning about the many resources and assets that already exist in the community.

Second, social workers should *make themselves known in the community.* It is important that social workers raise public awareness about their resources and goals, such as the prevention of child abuse, and their efforts to ensure children's safety and protection. On-going community outreach and networking are vital for addressing negative perceptions and concerns that are sometimes spread about child welfare agencies (Rivera, 2002). It is also essential to educate the community about available child welfare services and about new opportunities for collaboration. For example, an open house at an agency makes it possible for community members and other organization representatives to get to know the agency's staff and learn about its programs. Social workers should make a point to attend community board meetings or other community events in order to network and build relationships.

Third, social workers should be *clear about how the community is defined and plan activities that promote community involvement.* They must recognize the unique expertise of members of a particular community and engage them in appropriate collaborative work that can make a difference in the well-being of children and their families.

There are different strategies for inviting community members to take an active role in child welfare agencies. For example, the development of a community advisory board could be instrumental for creating a plan to recruit culturally diverse foster parents and prospective adoptive families. In addition, it is important to establish communication mechanisms that allow community members to express their concerns, ideas, and opinions. For example, community focus groups could be useful for getting feedback on new programs. Likewise, it is essential to create systems to review the feedback received from community respondents and to address any questions and concerns in a respectful and timely manner. Also, expressions of appreciation such as follow-up letters and thank you notes are important.

Lastly, *child welfare agencies need to join together to build coalitions.* Such coalitions can bring previously separate child welfare agencies, community groups, and organizations into a collaborative structure that allows for sharing of expertise, as well as the opportunity to develop, maximize, and sustain funds and resources while working towards a common goal (Mattessich & Monsey, 1992; Roberts-DeGennaro, 1997). Successful coalitions are characterized by their commitment to common goals and issues, effective leadership, shared responsibility and accountability, and well-established communication mechanisms (Mizrahi & Rosenthal, 2001). Given the challenges that child welfare agencies confront in building and maintaining trust within neighborhoods, such efforts seem more than worthwhile.

Coalitions of child welfare organizations have been known to be highly effective. For example, in Indianapolis, the Annie E. Casey Foundation has helped sponsor the Family Strengthening Coalition, a city-wide coalition of traditional partners such as the United Way and grass roots groups located in low-income neighborhoods of the city. In addition to jointly sponsoring activities, such as block parties, health fairs, and other forms of social capital creation that extend beyond traditional child welfare services (Putnam, 2000), coalition member services are strengthened through better information and referral. Members get to know each others' programs and how their own work complements and enhances the efforts of other members. The long-term goals of greater safety and social and economic stability for families—both hallmarks of child welfare reform—become the benchmarks by which this group measures and celebrates its success.

CONCLUSION

Moving beyond traditional child welfare services, establishing neighborhood-based child welfare coalitions, and engaging with various members of the community offer much promise for the future enhancement of child welfare services in urban areas. Some of the lessons that emerge from this work need to be reiterated for all ongoing collaboratives engaged in enhancing the lives of children. Key lessons are:

- Professionals must learn to be proactive in approaching and developing relations within the community. People do not come to you, as occurs under most child welfare interventions, school settings, or mental health clinics. Learning the skills of community engagement traditional to organizing is important work that professionals must undertake.
- Professionals in collaboratives must learn the skills of negotiation where their authority does not guarantee immediate results. In community work, one's authority emerges in great part from the work, not the position one holds. While the degree of control one has over resources (especially financial) obviously affects decision-making, long-term credibility is deepened and kept through the integrity of on-going effort in the coalition's work, not the talk at the table.
- Cultural competency issues are very important, and issues related to race, ethnicity, and social class need to be considered. Being comfortable with and being able to note the abilities and interests of community members are critical to both building trust and to increasing one's credibility to get things done. There are a lot of smart, capable people out there who can be helpful to the process. Cultural competency and engagement skills are essential to work with the mix of people critical to long-term effectiveness.

Training in community organizing strategy and tactics and knowledge of how to implement an action plan within a realistic time frame are necessary for professionals involved in community work. These skills exceed traditional "generic practice" models. The writings of Fisher (2004), Rothman et al. (2005), and Smock (2003) can be useful for skill development.

The depletion of resources caused by the long-term conservative attack on welfare state spending increases the emphasis on community-based collaborations for the foreseeable future. Using the lessons throughout this book can hopefully increase the progressive response to the risks children and families face in the early twenty-first century.

REFERENCES

Addams, J. (1910). *Twenty years at Hull House*. New York: Macmillan.

Downs, S. W., Moore, E., McFadden, E. J., & Costin, L. B., (2000). *Child welfare and family services: Policies and practices*. Boston: Allyn and Bacon.

Fisher, R. (2004). *Let the people decide*. Boston: Twayne.

Greenblatt, S., & Dobbyn, B. (2005). ACF and the Casey Center collaborate with New England Adoption Program managers to enhance systems change. In *Common Ground*. Boston: New England Association of Child Welfare Commissioners and Directors.

Harlem Children's Zone. www.hcz.org. Accessed September 5, 2005.

Kretzmann, J. P., & McKnight, J. L., (1993). *Building communities from the inside out: A path toward finding and mobilizing a community's assets*. Evanston, IL: Northwestern University, Center for Urban Affairs and Policy Research.

Livio, S. (2003). Child abuse scandal widens. *Newark-Star Ledger*, June 3, p A-1.

Martin, J. A. (2000). Diversity issues in foster care practice. In J. A. Martin (Ed.), *Foster family care: Theory and practice* (pp. 198–206). Boston: Allyn and Bacon.

Mattessich, P. W., & Monsey, B. R. (1992). *Collaboration: What makes it work*. St. Paul, MN: Amherst H. Wilder Foundation.

Mizrahi, T., & Rosenthal, B. B. (2001). Complexities of coalition building: Leaders' successes, strategies, struggles, and solutions. *Social Work, 46*(1): 63–78.

Mulroy, E. A., & Shay, S. (1997). Nonprofit organizations and innovation: A model of neighborhood-based collaborations to prevent child maltreatment. *Social Work, 42*(5): 515–524.

Naparstek, A. J., & Dooley, D. (1997). Countering urban disinvestments through community-building initiatives. *Social Work, 42*(5): 506–514.

Omang, J., & Bonk, K. (1999). Family to family: Building bridges for child welfare system with families, neighborhoods, and communities. *Policy and Practice 57*(4), 15–21.

Onyskiw, J. E., Harrison, M., & Spady, D., (1999). Formative evaluation of collaborative community-based abuse prevention project. *Child Abuse and Neglect, 23*(11), 1069–1081.

Poertner, J., McDonald, T. P., & Murray, C., (2000). Child welfare outcomes revisited. *Children and Youth Services Review, 22*(9/11): 789–810.

Power, M. B., & Eheart, B. K. (2001). Crisis in a foster home: The need for a caring community. *Children and Youth Services Review, 23*(9/10): 719–742.

Power, M. B., & Eheart, B. K. (2000). From foster care to fostering care: The need for community. *Sociological Quarterly, 41*(1), 85–102.

Putnam, R. (2000). *Bowling alone.* New York: Simon & Schuster.

Rivera, H. P. (2002). Developing collaborations between child welfare agencies and Latino communities. *Child Welfare, 81*(2), 371–384.

Roberts-DeGennaro, M. (1997). Conceptual framework of coalitions in an organizational context. *Journal of Community Practice, 4*(1): 91–107.

Rosenthal, S. J., & Cairns, J. M. (1994). Child abuse prevention: The community as co-worker. *Journal of Community Practice, 1*(4): 45–61.

Rothman, J., Erlich, J., Cox F., and Tropman, J., (2005). *Strategies for community organization and development.* Itasca, IL: Peacock Press.

Severson, K. (2005). Harlem school introduces children to Swiss chard. *New York Times,* Sept. 9, p. B-5.

Smock, K. (2003). *Democracy in action.* New York: Columbia University Press.

Trattner, W. (1999). *From poor law to welfare state.* New York: Simon & Schuster.

Wilson, C. (2002). Panel blames DCF workers, caretakers for deception. *Miami Herald,* May 27, p. B-1.

Wynn, J. R., Merry, S. M., & Berg, P. G. (1995). *Children, families, and communities: Early lessons from a new approach to social services.* Washington, DC: American Youth Policy Forum.

INDEX

9/11 (*see* September 11, 2001)

A

Abortion, 86, 217, 225–226
Abuse
  and adolescent parents, 233
  and runaways, 253
  and trauma, 104–105
Addams, Jane, 11, 100
Adolescents
  development, 222–223
  health issues, 76, 85–86
  pregnancy/parenthood, 85–86
    and abortion, 86, 225–226
    and adoption, 226–227
    under age 17, 229–230
    child maltreatment, 233
    demographics, 219–221
    influencing factors, 227–228
    policies, 221–222
    and poverty, 228–229
    prevention, 236–237
    role of fathers, 230–233
  puberty, 222–223
  and substance abuse, 183–184
Adoption, 226–227
Adoption and Safe Families Act (ASFA, 1996), 152, 156, 178, 197, 204, 271
Adoption Assistance and Child Welfare Act (1980), 151
Aid to Dependent Children (ADC), 14, 32
Aid to Families with Dependent Children (AFDC), 14, 20, 32
AIDS (*see* HIV/AIDS)
Air quality, 76
Al-Anon, 183
Alateen, 183

Alcohol, 177
  and HIV/AIDS, 255–256
  and mental health, 107
  see also Substance abuse
Alliance for Concerned Black Men (Washington, DC), 133
Amachi Program, 211
In Arms Reach (IAR, New York, NY), 210
Asperger's disorder, 99
Asthma, 79–81
At-Risk Child Care Programs, 222
Attention deficit hyperactive disorder (ADHD), 98–99, 106–107
Autism, 98

B

Barrio (*see* Gangs)
"The Battered Child Syndrome" (JAMA, 1962), 149
Beethoven Project (Chicago, IL), 131
Bergh, Henry, 148–149
Beyond the Best Interests of the Child (1974), 151
Big Brothers/Big Sisters, 111, 210–211
Birtwell, Charles, 147
Bonds Beyond Bars (Wisconsin), 211
Boys and Girls Clubs of America, 132
Brace, Charles Loring, 146–147
Brown v. Board of Education (1954), 16
Bush, George W., 22, 53

C

Canada, Geoffrey, 272
Cannon, Ida M., 86
Carstens, C. C., 147
Casey Family Services, 272
Center for Mental Health Services, 101

281

Center for Substance Abuse Prevention, 187
Chicago Area Project, 131
Chicago HIV Prevention and Adolescent
    Mental Health Project (CHAMP), 112
Child Abuse Prevention and Treatment Act
    (CAPTA, 1974), 149–150
Child and Adolescent Service System
    Program (CASSP), 101
Child development
    adolescence, 222–223
    and poverty, 35–37
Child labor, 11
Child Protective Services (CPS), 145
    history, 148–150
    reform, 152–153
Children in Need of Parents (1959), 148
Children of Alcoholics Screening Test
    (CAST), 183
Children's Aid Society, 10, 147
Children's Health Insurance Program
    (CHIP), 78, 91
Chlamydia, 221
    see also Sexually transmitted diseases
Citizenship and Immigration Services (CIS),
    53
Civil Rights Act (1964), 16–17
Civilian Conservation Corps (CCC), 14
Community Mental Health Act (1963), 101
Community Outreach Program (St. Paul,
    MN), 131
Conduct disorder, 98–99, 111
Connolly, Mary and Francis, 148–149
Contraception (*see* Sexual activity)
Counseling, 88
    see also Intervention
Covenant House (New York, NY), 260
Crack cocaine, 98, 152–153
    "crack babies," 182
    and HIV/AIDS, 256
Criminal justice system (*see* Incarceration)

D

Day care, 6
Depression, 98, 106–107
antidepressants, 109
Desegregation, 16–17
*Diagnostic and Statistical Manual of Mental
    Disorders* (DSM-IV, 2000), 170

Disruptive/delinquent behavior, 106–108
    see also Mental health issues
Donatella Cameron House (San Francisco,
    CA), 218
Drug Abuse Education and Prevention
    Program, 245–246
Drug courts and diversion programs,
    184–185
Drug-Free Communities Act (1997), 185
Drugs (*see* Substance abuse)

E

Earned Income Tax Credit, 22
Ecological Systems model, 71
    see also Intervention
Education
    during the Great Depression, 13
    of immigrants, 58–60
    and mental health, 99–100
    Mexico's system, 59
    and poverty, 34–35
    school programs, 7
Education for All Handicapped Children's
    Act (1978), 178
Emergency Assistance Program, 20
Empowerment Zone, 131
English Poor Laws (1601), 244, 248
Enter (New York, NY), 262–263
Enterprise Communities, 131
Environment (*see* Urban environment)
Equal Opportunity Commission, 17
Escuela secondaria (*see* Education)

F

Families
    and incarceration, 196–203
    kinship (foster) care, 161–165
    linking to services and benefits, 44–45
    and poverty, 38
    and substance abuse, 169–187
Family Educational Rights and Privacy Act
    (FERPA, 1974), 112
Family Forwards (Austin, TX), 211–212
Family Intervention Project, 133
Family Reunification Program of St. Rose
    Youth and Family Center (Milwaukee, WI),
    211

Family Strengthening Coalition (Indianapolis, IN), 276
Fetal alcohol syndrome, 107, 173
Five Points Mission (New York, NY), 147
Florence Crittenton Homes, 218
Folks, Homer, 147
Foster care (*see* Placement, out-of-home)
Foster Care Independence Act (1999), 158, 236

G

Gangs
  and the *barrio* (Latinos), 135–138
  definitions, 123
  media/public perception, 125
  nature of, 128–129
  and protection, 129–130, 136–137
  reducing involvement, 130–134
  risk factors, 129–130, 135–136
  theoretical perspectives, 125–129
  and violence, 124
Gangs of New York (2002), 147
Gerry, Elbridge, 148
Girl Scouts of America, 211
Giuliani, Rudy, 193
Globalization, 51–52
Great Depression (*see* History)

H

Harlem Children's Zone (New York, NY), 272
Head Start, 18, 222
HEADSS Assessment Framework, 86
Health Insurance Portability and Accountability Act (HIPAA, 1996), 112
Health issues
  and adolescents, 85–86
  assessment, 86–87
  case study, 89–93
  intervention, 87–88
  lack of health care, 77
  policies, 77–78
  and poverty, 75–76
  role of social worker, 86–89
  and urban environments, 76
  see also individual conditions; Medicaid; Mental health issues

Heroin, 16
Hettrick-Martin Institute (New York, NY), 259
Hilltop Developmental Center, 235
History
  1960s, 16–18
  1970s to 1990s, 18–20
  2000s, 21–22
  Child Protective Services (CPS), 148–150
  foster care, 146–148
  Great Depression, 12–14
  mental health services, 100–102
  nineteenth century, 9–10
  post-WWII, 15–16
  substance abuse policy, 176–179
  unmarried parents, 216–218
  welfare services, 269–270
HIV/AIDS, 244–263
  and adolescents, 85
  and contraceptive use, 225
  risk factors, 255–257
Homelessness
  families, 250
  and health issues, 76
  and mental health, 107
  see also Street youth
Homosexual activity, 252–253, 257
Hoover, Herbert, 12
HOPE VI, 22
Hopkins, Harry, 13
  see also WPA
House of Umoja (Philadelphia, PA), 131
Housing, subsidized, 22
  "Second Chance Homes," 221
How the Other Half Lives (1890), 147
HUD (*see* U.S. Department of Housing and Urban Development)
Hughes Act (1970), 178, 180
Hull House (Chicago, IL), 11
Human immunodeficiency virus (*see* HIV/AIDS)

I

Illegitimacy (*see* Adolescents)
Immigrants, 50–73
  demographics, 55–67
  education, 58–60
  employment opportunities, 60–61, 60–61

global trends, 51–55, 64–66
  impact of 9/11, 52–55
history, 9
hostility toward, 54–55
income, 61–62
language, 62–63
legal status, 66–67
origins (national), 56–57
race, 63–64
regulation, 53–55
treatment of, 67–70
Immigration and Naturalization Service
  (INS), 53
  see also Citizenship and Immigration
  Services
Immunization, 77
Incarceration
  "broken window" theory, 192–193
  impact of parental arrest, 196–197
  "invisible" punishments, 195
  issues for children
    communication, 200–202
    emotional, 202–203
    visitation, 198–200
  prison industry (US), 193–195
  transitioning out, 203–207
  working with children, 207–210
Independent living (*see* Placement, out-of-
  home)
Independent Living Initiative (1985), 158
Individuals with Disabilities Education Act
  (IDEA, 1991), 178
Intellectual disabilities, 108
Intervention
  and adolescent parents, 233–236
  and gangs, 132–133
  health issues, 87–88
  and immigrants, 70–72
  and mental health, 115–116
  and poverty, 42–46
  street youth, 258–263
  wraparound approach, 115

J

Job Corps, 18
Job Opportunity and Basic Skills Training
  Program, 20
John H. Chafee Foster Care Independence
  Program (*see* Foster Care Independence
  Act)

Johnson, Lyndon, 32
Juvenile Accountability Block Grants
  (JABG), 134

K

Katrina, Hurricane (2005), ix, 21

L

Latinos (*see* Gangs)
Lead poisoning, 81–82
  and mental health, 98
Life Cycle model, 71
  see also Intervention
Life Skills Training Program, 111
Litargirio (*see* Lead poisoning)

M

Manchild in the Promised Land (1965), 15
Media/public perception
  of gangs, 125
  and welfare services, 274
Medicaid, 18, 32, 77–78
Medication, psychotropic, 109–110
  see also Health issues; Mental health issues
Mental health issues
  case study, 115–116
  clinical services, 114–115
  demographics, 98–99
  disabilities (intellectual), 108
  disruptive/delinquent behavior, 106–108
  and educational system, 99–100
  history (of services), 100–102
  interactive systems, 97–98
  and runaways, 253–255
  and trauma, 102–106
  see also Health issues; Therapy; Trauma
Mental Hygiene Movement, 100
Mental retardation (*see* Intellectual disabilities)
Mentoring programs, 111
Migration strategies, 64–66
  see also Immigrants
Minuteman Project, 55
Mobilization for Youth (MFY), 17, 137
Models Cities Program, 17
Mothers Offering Mutual Support (MOMS,
  Wisconsin), 211

N

National Association of Black Social Workers (NABSW), 30–31
National Association of Social Workers (NASW), 30
National Child Labor Committee, 11
National Clearinghouse on Runaways and Homeless Youth, 245
National Institute of Mental Health (NIMH), 101
National Institute on Alcohol Abuse and Alcoholism (NIAAA), 178
National Institute on Drug Abuse (NIDA), 178
National Mental Health Act (1946), 101
National Youth Administration, 13
National Youth Anti-Drug Media Campaign, 185–186
Neighborhood Youth Corps, 18
Neutral Zone (Washington State), 130
New Deal, 13–14
New Orleans (*see* Katrina, Hurricane)
No Child Left Behind, 112
"No-Parent Family," 21–22

O

Obesity, 82–85
Obstacles, 5–23
Operation Positive Change, 112
Oppositional defiant disorder, 99, 111
Oregon Project, 150–151
Ounce of Prevention Fund (Illinois), 228
Out-of-home placement (*see* Placement, out-of-home)

P

Parents
incarcerated, 195–210
loss of (death, separation, incarceration), 107–108
"psychological parent," 151
teenage, 216–239
    see also Adolescents
unmarried (history), 216–218
    see also Placement, out-of-home
Permanency planning (see Placement, out-of-home)

Personal Responsibility and Work Reconciliation Act (PRWORA, 1996), 14–15, 20, 32, 195
Pervasive developmental disorders, 98–99
Placement, out-of-home, 145–166
    case study, 153–165
    history, 146–148
    independent living, 157–161
    kinship care, 161–165
    permanency planning, 150–152
        case study, 153–157
        reform, 152–153
    and street youth, 262–263
Policy, social, 11–12
    and adolescent parents, 237–239
        teen pregnancy, 221–222
    children of incarcerated parents, 210–212
    federal, 16–18
    and gangs, 134–135
    and health issues, 77–78
    impact, 31–33
    and mental health, 110–116
    public/private partnerships, 113–114
    and substance abuse
        current, 179–187
        historical, 176–179
    welfare services, 271–272
Pollutants, environmental, 76, 80, 98–99
Positive Attitudes toward Learning in School (PALS), 112
Positive Behavioral Interventions and Supports, 112
Post-traumatic stress disorder (PTSD), 98
Poverty, 21–22, 29–47
    assessment, 37–38
    case study, 39–46
    and child development, 35–37
    and education, 34–35
    and health issues, 75–76
    income of immigrants, 61–62
    and race, 33–34
    statistics (US), 18–21, 31
    and teen pregnancy, 228–229
Pregnancy, teen (*see* Adolescents)
Presbyterian Children's Home, 113–114
Prison (*see* Incarceration)
Problem-Solving Skills Training, 111
Promoting Alternative Thinking Strategies, 111

Psychotropic medication (*see* Medication, psychotropic)
Public Health Service Act (1970), 227
Public Works Administration, 14

R

Raising Healthy Children, 111
In Re Gault (1967), 151
Reactive attachment disorder, 99
REAL ID Act (2005), 53–54
Research and Training Center on Family Support and Children's Mental Health, 101
Riis, Jacob, 9–10, 147–149
Roosevelt, Franklin D., 13
Rumination disorder, 99
Runaway and Homeless Youth Act (1973), 244–246, 258
Runaway and Homeless Youth Basic Center Program, 245–246, 251
Runaway, Homeless and Missing Children Protection Act (2003), 244–245, 258
Runaways (*see* Street youth)

S

Salvation Army, 10
    Homes for Unwed Mothers, 218
San Francisco Partnership for Incarcerated Parents, 212
September 11, 2001, ix, 50
    impact of, 52–55
Settlement movement, 11–12, 270
Sexual activity
    contraception, 225
    and HIV/AIDS, 244–263
    motivation of women, 224–228
    and runaways, 252–255
    "survival sex," 254–257
    and teen pregnancy, 220–221
Sexually transmitted diseases (STD)
    and adolescents, 85
    and mental health, 97–98
    and teen pregnancy, 220–221
    see also HIV/AIDS
Sickle cell disease, 82–83
Social agencies, 10, 14–15
    see also Welfare services
Social Security Act (1935), 14–15, 20, 31–32

Social work, 30–31
    advocacy, 89
    and gangs, 137–138
    principles, 43–44
    role of social worker, 86–89
Society for the Prevention of Cruelty to Children (SPCC), 10, 149
Southern Christian Leadership Conference, 16
"Stage-of-migration" framework, 71
    see also Intervention
Street gangs (*see* Gangs)
Street Outreach Programs, 246
Street youth
    definitions, 247–250
    demographics, 251
    governmental role, 244–247
    outreach, 259–262
    prevention, 258–259
    psychosocial problems, 253–255
    rehabilitation, 262–263
    risk factors, 252–255
    "thrownaways," 249–250
Subsidized housing (*see* Housing, subsidized)
Substance abuse
    biological factors, 173–174
    by children, 175–176
        adolescents, 183–184
    drug gangs, 124
    enforcement/punishment, 179–180
    helping families, 181–183
    history, 15, 176–179
        crack epidemic, 152–153
        scope of problem, 171–173
    and HIV/AIDS, 244–263
    maternal (during pregnancy), 173–174, 181–182
    and mental health, 98
    prevention, 185–187
    psychological/social factors, 174–175
    and runaways, 254–255
    tobacco, 80
    treatment, 180–185
    see also Alcohol; *individual substances*
Suicide, 108
"Survival sex," 254–257
Syphilis, 97–98
    see also Mental health issues; Sexually transmitted diseases

T

Teen Life-Skills Program, 235
Teen pregnancy (*see* Adolescents)
Teenage Pregnancy and Parenting Project
    (TAPP, San Francisco, CA), 234–235
Temporary Assistance to Needy Families
    (TANF), 20–21, 32, 78, 221
Therapy, multisystemic, 114–115
    see also Mental health issues
There Are No Children Here (1992), 36
"Thrownaways," 249–250
    see also Street youth
Title X (*see* Public Health Service Act)
Transitional Living Program for Homeless
    Youth, 246, 251, 263
Trauma
    and the brain, 105–106
    common events, 103–105
    of immigrants, 69–70
    see also Mental health issues
Truman, Harry S., 16

U

United States Children's Bureau, 11, 13
Upward Bound, 18
Urban environment
    growth of neighborhoods, 7–8
    and health issues, 76
    and poverty, 38–41
    understanding, 7–8
    see also History
UrbanWorld, 160

U.S. Children's Bureau, 100
U.S. Department of Housing and Urban
    Development (HUD), 131
U.S. Public Health Service, 100

V

Violence
    and gangs, 124
    and health issues, 79
    and trauma, 103–105

W

War on Poverty, 17–18, 32
Welfare services
    challenges and constraints, 272–274
    creation, 14–15
    improving, 269–278
    recommendations, 274–276
    reform (1996), ix, 20, 32
    see also Social agencies
Wheeler, Etta, 148
Wilson, Mary Ellen, 148–149
Works Progress Administration (WPA), 13
Wraparound approach, 115

Y

Youth gangs (*see* Gangs)

Z

"Zoloft Trial" (2005), 109

- Brooke, Stephanie L.—**THE USE OF THE CREATIVE THERAPIES WITH CHEMICAL DEPENDENCY ISSUES.** '09, 300 pp. (7 x 10), 33 il., 3 tables.

- Luginbuehl-Oelhafen, Ruth R.—**ART THERAPY WITH CHRONIC PHYSICALLY ILL ADOLESCENTS: Exploring the Effectiveness of Medical Art Therapy as a Complementary Treatment.** '09, 216 pp. (7 x 10), 67 il., (12 in color), paper.

- Thompson, Richard H.—**THE HANDBOOK OF CHILD LIFE: A Guide for Pediatric Psychosocial Care.** '08, 378 pp. (7 x 10), 5 il., 15 tables, $79.95, hard, $55.95, paper.

- Wilkes, Jane K.—**THE ROLE OF COMPANION ANIMALS IN COUNSELING AND PSYCHOTHERAPY: Discovering Their Use in the Therapeutic Process.** '09, 172 pp. (7 x 10), 2 tables, paper.

NOW AVAILABLE!

- Blomquist, Barbara Taylor—**INSIGHT INTO ADOPTION: Uncovering and Understanding the Heart of Adoption. (2nd Ed.)** '09, 212 pp. (6 x 9), $27.95, paper.

- Bakken, Jeffrey P. & Festus E. Obiakor—**TRANSITION PLANNING FOR STUDENTS WITH DISABILITIES: What Educators and Service Providers Can Do.** '08, 214 pp. (7 x 10), 4 il., 25 tables, $51.95, hard, $31.95, paper.

- Coulacoglou, Carina—**EXPLORING THE CHILD'S PERSONALITY: Developmental, Clinical and Cross-Cultural Applications of the Fairy Tale Test.** '08, 364 pp. (8 x 10), 22 il., 41 tables, $78.95, hard, $53.95, paper.

- Geldard, Kathryn & David Geldard—**PERSONAL COUNSELING SKILLS: An Integrative Approach.** '08, 316 pp. (7 x 10), 20 il., 3 tables, $49.95, paper.

- Junge, Maxine Borowsky—**MOURNING, MEMORY AND LIFE ITSELF: Essays by an Art Therapist.** '08, 292 pp. (7 x 10), 38 il, $61.95, hard, $41.95, paper.

- Kendler, Howard H.—**AMORAL THOUGHTS ABOUT MORALITY: The Intersection of Science, Psychology, and Ethics. (2nd Ed.)** '08, 270 pp. (7 x 10), $59.95, hard, $39.95, paper.

- Plach, Tom—**INVESTIGATING ALLEGATIONS OF CHILD AND ADOLESCENT SEXUAL ABUSE: An Overview for Professionals.** '08, 192 pp. (7 x 10), $49.95, hard, $29.95, paper.

- Smith, Sheri, Rosalind Ekman Ladd & Lynn Pasquerella—**ETHICAL ISSUES IN HOME HEALTH CARE. (2nd Ed.)** '08, 258 pp. (7 x 10), $56.95, hard, $36.95, paper.

- Wedman-St. Louis, Betty—**LIVING GLUTEN-FREE: Meal Plans, Recipes, and Consumer Tips.** '08, 186 pp. (6 x 9), $28.95, spiral (paper).

- Wiseman, Dennis G.—**THE AMERICAN FAMILY: Understanding its Changing Dynamics and Place in Society.** '08, 172 pp. (7 x 10), 4 tables, $31.95, paper.

- Arrington, Doris Banowsky—**ART, ANGST, AND TRAUMA: Right Brain Interventions with Developmental Issues.** '07, 278 pp. (7 x 10), 123 il., $63.95, hard, $43.95, paper.

- Cowden, Jo E. & Carol C. Torrey—**MOTOR DEVELOPMENT AND MOVEMENT ACTIVITIES FOR PRESCHOOLERS AND INFANTS WITH DELAYS: A Multisensory Approach for Professionals and Families. (2nd Ed.)** '07, 348 pp. (7 x 10), 195 il., 13 tables, $73.95, hard, $53.95, paper.

- Crandell, John M. Jr. & Lee W. Robinson—**LIVING WITH LOW VISION AND BLINDNESS: Guidelines That Help Professionals and Individuals Understand Vision Impairments.** '07, 220 pp. (7 x 10), 14 il., $49.95, hard, $34.95, paper.

- Malouff, John M. & Nicola S. Schutte—**ACTIVITIES TO ENHANCE SOCIAL, EMOTIONAL, AND PROBLEM-SOLVING SKILLS: Seventy-six Activities That Teach Children, Adolescents, and Adults Skills Crucial to Success in Life. (2nd Ed.)** '07, 248 pp. (8 1/2 x 11), 3 il., $44.95, spiral (paper).

- Soby, Jeanette M.—**PRENATAL EXPOSURE TO DRUGS/ALCOHOL: Characteristics and Educational Implications of Fetal Alcohol Syndrome and Cocaine/Polydrug Effects. (2nd Ed.)** '06, 188 pp. (7 x 10), 7 il., 21 tables, $44.95, hard, $28.95, paper.

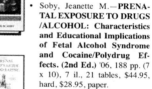

- Curtis, Judith A.—**THE RENAL PATIENT'S GUIDE TO GOOD EATING: A Cookbook for Patients by a Patient. (2nd Ed.)** '03, 226 pp. (7 x 10), 30 il., $36.95, (spiral) paper.

- Salmon, Margaret B.—**FOOD FACTS FOR TEENAGERS: A Guide to Good Nutrition for Teens and Preteens. (2nd Ed.)** '03, 138 pp. (7 x 10), 33 il., 13 tables, $24.95, paper.

- Laban, Richard J.—**CHEMICAL DEPENDENCY TREATMENT PLANNING HANDBOOK.** '97, 174 pp. (8 1/2 x 11), $35.95, spiral (paper).
